World–
Famous
Mistresses

World-Famous Mistresses

C. E. Maine

Odhams Books

First Published: 1970

Published for Odhams Books by
The Hamlyn Publishing Group Limited
Hamlyn House, 42 The Centre,
Feltham, Middlesex

SBN 600 72652 5

Printed in Great Britain by C. Tinling & Co. Ltd.
London & Prescot

Contents

Illustrations

Introduction

According to one dictionary a mistress is a "woman illicitly occupying place of wife". It is a definition with which the majority of wives would no doubt agree, but in its wider context the mistress has always enjoyed (if that is the word) an important and often influential place in human society all over the world, varying in significance from the slave-like concubines and odalisques of the east to the cossetted and protected female powers-behind-the-throne so characteristic of European royalty over the last few centuries.

Mistresses are usually associated with men of power and wealth – they have to be "afforded" and kept in proper style. They are usually more than just playthings. Their composite image is difficult to define, for while they lack the formal approval of respectable orthodox society, they nevertheless possess the enviable cachet of being desired and possessed for themselves as beloved women – a situation in which approval or disapproval matters little to the principals concerned.

Too often a mistress has not only been a "woman illicitly occupying place of wife", but also "illicitly occupying place of Queen", for mistresses throughout history have been very much the sport of kings – although even the humblest proletarian male may have a mistress rather than a prostitute. It is not really a question of money so much as the indefinables of infatuation and emotion, but even so there is invariably some kind of reward for services rendered.

Mistresses in the higher echelons of power and government always seem to possess a certain glamour, whether they merit it or not. From Cleopatra to Christine Keeler they exert a hypnotic fascination on a world largely indoctrinated in the virtues of an ecclesiastically based moral

9

philosophy of monogamy. In the east morality is more liberal, but within more rigid terms of reference. All over the world men from the lowest to the highest have ruined their careers and their lives for the sake of their mistresses, and they have willingly sacrificed their reputations for a cherished woman who only too often has been motivated by avarice and a lust for power.

The coveted appointment of King's favourite was by no means an easy one to maintain, for the competition was intense. Not only did the royal mistress have to be on her guard against enemies jealous of her power and influence – not to mention female rivals anxious to step into her shoes (or rather climb into the King's bed) – but she had also to be at all times beautiful, charming and agreeable, and always ready to respond to the slightest whim of the man on whom her status and security depended. True, the royal mistress had little else to do all day – or night – but it was nevertheless a full-time and exacting occupation.

Some of the famous mistresses of history were able to wield considerable power for good or evil. Some exercised influence only over their paramour in a personal sense; others were able to change the affairs of a nation. While Louis XIV of France, for example, managed to keep his mistresses under strict control, his successor allowed the Pompadour to meddle disastrously in matters of state.

In this volume many famous mistresses have necessarily been omitted – to write about them all in any detail would require a score of such volumes – but the chosen women are those who on the whole left their mark upon history in one way or another, either politically or culturally. The author has attempted to avoid undue emphasis on the nineteenth century, which was perhaps the "hotbed" period of immorality throughout Europe, and has tried to cast the mistress-trapping net widely throughout time and space. What perhaps emerges from this study is that men and women have behaved in much the same way since the dawn of time, and that frequently it is the woman who dominates the relationship – the man is caught in the tender trap!

Even so, the nineteenth century has not been overlooked.

Introduction

It was an age when society placed women who occupied "irregular" positions into certain well-defined categories. At the bottom of the ladder were the common street-walkers, and somewhat higher in status were the prostitutes of the brothels some of which possessed an exclusive and aristocratic clientele. Next came the demi-mondaines who usually occupied their own houses or apartments and survived on gifts from a variety of lovers. At the top of the ladder was the kept mistress, loyal to one man, whose status was virtually respectable, who often moved in the best social circles, and who was frequently of good birth and well educated.

These women were so widely accepted (and often cultivated, for their influence on their male partner) that their liaisons were openly acknowledged. In many cases the mistress carried more social influence than the unfortunate wife. And it was an age when letter writing and diary keeping were regarded as an art so that, happily, a great deal of lively comment on the social mores of the time have come down to us.

Balzac, Liszt, Kafka, Lewes (whose mistress was George Eliot), Byron, Keats and Burns all had their mistresses. They are not included in this volume, for the list is endless. But the permissive society of the day accepted them almost without criticism. While some of the liaisons were more or less permanent, in others men sped butterfly-like from woman to woman, leaving a trail of misery behind them.

While a few of the world-famous mistresses became famous in their own right – George Sand and George Eliot, for example – the vast majority merely reflected the glory of their lovers and played a subordinate role. Even so, they are invariably fascinating personalities. The fact that today they are dead and buried and their beauty has vanished for ever is a saddening thought in a contemporary society which is becoming equally permissive but far less flamboyant.

Chapter 1 The Hamilton Ménage-à-trois

When you are very poor and also very pretty there is little incentive to remain respectable unless you wish to stay poor – and this was particularly true in the London of 1779. That was the year when 14-year-old Emily Hart (born Amy Lyon) first came to London with her mother to take a job as nursemaid in the home of a well known surgeon. She was not without experience, for she had already been trained as a nursemaid by a friendly doctor and his wife in the village of Hawarden where she had been brought up by her widowed mother and grandmother. On her own admission she was a wild and thoughtless little girl, and the new job, which hardly suited her restless and vivacious personality, was not destined to last for long.

The bustle of the big city and the sight of the comings and goings of the smart rich folk gave young Emily visions of a life more exciting by far than that of a mere nursemaid. Precisely what she did in the greater part of 1780 and 1781 is not clear, for she was always reticent about that period of her life, but there is little doubt that she soon made up her young mind to exchange respectable poverty for a more luxurious, if less honourable, style of living.

At that time there was in London a "Temple of Aesculapius" – a dubious kind of "health club" with erotic overtones, run by a quack doctor. The temple was filled with strange apparatus in an ambience of music, paintings and stained glass. The "doctor", who was nothing if not a showman, gave long and often suggestive lectures against a background of staged tableaux in which lightly clad young ladies posed as goddesses. For a while Emily was almost certainly one of those thinly veiled young ladies, and it is likely that there she met her first protector, Sir Harry Featherstonehaugh.

Sir Harry, a sporting baronet of about 26 years of age, took Emily to his country seat at Up Park, near Portsmouth. His friends were a rumbustious, hard-drinking and hard-riding set whose company she thoroughly enjoyed, for she could be as high-spirited and boisterous as anyone. Among them, however, was a young man of more serious demeanour, the Honourable Charles Greville, 32-year-old second son of the Earl of Warwick. He, attracted by her physical charms, also sought to educate her mind and restrain her lively temperament, and so it was to him, and his more responsible and kindly nature, that she turned when she found herself in trouble – for at the age of 16 she found herself pregnant. There was apparently some doubt as to who was the father, and he could have been any one of the guests at Up Park. For this reason, perhaps, and because he was sure it was not himself, Sir Harry cast her out.

Emily fled to her grandmother's home in Hawarden. From there she wrote to Charles Greville, and his sympathetic reply encouraged her to write again. Careless of her spelling, she wrote such a heart-rending letter so hopeful of practical aid that it was almost impossible to resist. "What shall I dow?" she wrote. "Good God, what shall I dow? ... O how your letter affected me when you wished me happiness. O.G. that I was in your posesion or in Sir H what a happy girl would I have been! ... O for God's sake tell me what is to become on me."

Greville's response to this appeal was kindly but cautious. She should, he advised, live quietly until the birth of the child, after which, provided she could assure him that she was "clear of every connexion", she could come to London and he would then be free to "dry up the tears of my lovely Emily and give her comfort". He also sent her some money, but warned her to be careful of it.

Greville himself was not very well off. On an income of £600 a year he was trying to cut a dash in town, and had acquired a large house in Portman Square which was now proving a financial embarrassment. In the nick of time, however, he was offered a post in the Board of Admiralty which carried with it free lodgings in King's Mews (near today's Trafalgar Square). Although he could not really afford a mistress, he leased for Emily a small but pleasant house near the village of Paddington Green, close to what was then known as Edgware Row. There he installed her and (at his own suggestion) her mother, and allowed her £50 a year for herself and £150 a year for household expenses.

Emily lived in this house from 1782 to 1786, and it was during this interlude that she changed her name again, adopting the more fashionable "Emma". She was well aware of her good fortune, and did all she could to please her protector – indeed, she soon fell genuinely in love with him. She even tried to curb her high spirits and volatile temper because they tended to embarrass and annoy the sober and reflective Greville. He in turn coached her in the social graces and had her taught singing. Her portrait was painted several times by Romney.

Greville was evidently pleased with his fair acquisition, for he liked to bring his friends along to meet Emma. Among them was Sir William Hamilton, his uncle, who was at that time the British Ambassador in Naples. Sir William, a widower, was a genial and amiable character who was quite taken by the beauty and charm of the girl whom he called "the fair tea-maker of Edgware Row". He came to know

Emma well, for in 1784, while in England, he spent a great deal of time with Greville and at Edgware Row.

The unwanted child, "little Emma", remained with the grandmother in Hawarden, although Emma occasionally took her for a visit to the seaside. She regarded her daughter more with compassion than affection, and seemed to take very little real interest in her welfare. Greville was nobly providing for the child, too – an additional drain on his meagre purse.

As time went on his financial worries became more and more severe. It had always been his aim to marry a rich wife, and it seemed to him that his money problems and his political ambitions made it necessary to pursue this goal without further delay – but he would have to divest himself of Emma. This he proceeded to do, but in a way that could only benefit her and improve her status. He wrote to his uncle in Naples, explaining the situation quite openly, and suggested that Sir William might like to take Emma off his hands. A pecuniary advantage of such an arrangement would be that Sir William could hardly marry someone like Emma and was therefore more likely to remain childless, so that Greville might ultimately inherit his estate.

For nine months Greville's letters to his uncle extolled Emma's charms and acclaimed her virtues. "She likes admiration," he wrote, "but merely that she may be valued and not to profit by raising her price. She has good natural sense and quick observation and perfectly to be depended on." Greville claimed that he had "weaned her from disipation by giving a stimulus to her pride and made her conduct suitable to my retired stile . . ." He also told his uncle that "she is the only woman I ever slept with without having had any of my senses offended, and a cleanlier sweeter bedfellow does not exist".

Impressed, and indeed transported, by such excellent references, Sir William amiably agreed to help his nephew by taking delectable Emma under his own wing. In December 1785 Greville told Emma that during the following summer he would be away for several months; she would not be able to accompany him, but if she wished she could stay with his uncle in Naples. Emma accepted the suggestion, and wrote to Sir William saying she would enjoy a short stay with him and promising to keep well out of the way when he was engaged on official business. In fact, it is unlikely that she was deceived by the subterfuge, for later she discussed with Greville the possibility of a permanent parting, and hinted that if he neglected her she might listen favourably to any offers Sir William should choose to make.

It was the end of a chapter and the beginning of another. Emma arrived in Naples on 26 April, 1786 – her 21st birthday. Sir William, who had been looking forward to her arrival with much impatience, made a tremendous fuss of her. If Emma because of her lack of education was not much impressed by the cultural and historical sights of Italy, she was certainly greatly impressed by her new way of life. Her youthful beauty and gay personality created a stir in staid embassy circles, rich and grand people were effusively kind to her, and she was accepted without hesitation into Neapolitan society. Her letters to Greville were full of tributes to Sir William's generous guardianship and extravagant accounts of her social successes – but she continued to protest her love and to scold Greville for not writing to her more often.

By the following January, however, Emma had transferred her warm affections from the nephew to the uncle. Sir William was exceedingly fond of Emma and proved to be a less critical taskmaster than Greville. She was allowed to act as hostess at the Embassy – to Greville's disapproval – but she performed the job well and toned down her natural ebullience to match the occasion, perhaps because she was awed by the high social standing of the people she had to entertain. Sir William encouraged her to continue her singing lessons, and eulogized her good behaviour and social popularity in his letters to Greville.

Within three years Emma had so consolidated her position that, in the interests of attaining proper status, she decided to persuade Sir William to marry her. At first he rejected the idea, but with subtle persistence spread over two years she gradually wore him down. By March 1791,

Greville's suspicions that his former mistress was about to become his aunt were confirmed by a letter from a friend visiting Naples who wrote that Emma's influence over Sir William exceeded all belief, while his attachment was perfect dotage.

Emma was, in fact, telling everybody that Sir William was going to England to obtain the King's consent to marry her – and this turned out to be perfectly true. In May the two of them, accompanied by Emma's mother, travelled to London where they were granted permission by George III. In September 1791 they were quietly married in Marylebone.

During that summer Emma enjoyed the gaieties of London society which she frequently entertained with her famous "attitudes". These extraordinary exhibitions appear to have been a novel attraction of the day and created some impact. Dressed in a simple white tunic with her hair streaming down her back, she would provide herself with two large cashmere shawls and a few props, such as an urn, a scent box or a tambourine; then she would take up her position in the middle of the room, covered entirely with one of the shawls. Thus concealed, she would arrange the other shawl and the props according to the "attitude" which she wished to strike, and finally cast off the outer shawl to reveal herself in the pose of a statue of classical design – as Medea, Niobe, Diana and so on. After the wedding Horace Walpole, with his waspish wit, commented: "Sir William Hamilton has actually married his gallery of statues."

Sir William and Lady Hamilton returned to Naples via Paris where Emma was received by Marie Antoinette, who gave her a letter to deliver to her sister Maria Carolina, Queen of Naples. Emma was delighted and enchanted by this summit of social climbing – and if she was at all aware that the French monarchy was already threatened by the shadow of the Terror that was to bring about their deaths at the guillotine less than two years later she was probably quite uninterested.

As for Sir William, he continued to be besotted by his Emma. A year after the marriage he told a friend that Emma had "gained the hearts of all, even of the Ladies, by her humility and proper behaviour, and we shall, I dare say, go on well". But others who met her were not quite so blind to her faults. Lady Elizabeth Foster, who saw her give a performance of her "attitudes", said she was "handsome, but coarse and vulgar". Her singing, she thought, was praiseworthy for the expression and vivacity of her countenance, but although her voice was strong, it had "a forced expression and neither softness nor tenderness". She was pretty, admittedly, but her conversation was dull and her pronunciation "very vulgar". Before her marriage Lord Bristol said: "Take her as anything but Mistress Hart and she is a superior being – as herself she is always vulgar." The Comtesse de Boigne went so far as to call Emma a "bad woman", who had a "low mind within a magnificent form".

Nevertheless, Emma was received into the best society and soon became a favourite at the Court of Naples – and a confidante of the Queen. Such privileged acceptance exercised her mind continually, and she would boast about it in her letters to Greville and others, relating with relish how she had spent an evening with the Queen *"en famille"*. Her interests hardly spread beyond parties, clothes and illustrious people, but finally even Emma began to notice that the political situation had become alarming. By February 1793 England was at war with France, and in September a man-of-war, H.M.S. *Agamemnon,* sailed into Naples with despatches for Sir William requesting troops to reinforce the garrison at the port of Toulon.

The captain of the *Agamemnon* was a young man, aged 34, named Horatio Nelson. Sir William must have had a good eye for character for he remarked to Emma that Nelson was "a little man who can't boast of being very handsome but will, I believe, one day astonish the world". Nelson was ashore for four days and spent a great deal of time at the Embassy where, inevitably, he met Emma.

There was no question of love at first sight – indeed, Emma probably gave Nelson little thought at that time. She was then 28 years old and, in the fashion of beauties of her style, was already full-blown. Only three years later an acquaintance commented to his wife that Lady Hamilton was

19

beginning to lose her figure, while in the four years before they were to meet again Nelson lost his right arm and the sight of his right eye in naval engagements. He had interests elsewhere, of course, and was known to have a mistress in Leghorn. His relationship with Emma at that first encounter was formal, if sociable, and mainly concerned with Admiralty business.

Nelson, hitherto a little known officer, was beginning to emerge from obscurity and being given a chance to display his naval genius. Although Naples, officially neutral, was trying to maintain an uneasy peace with France, now led by a warlike little man named Napoleon, Emma was able to use her influence with the Queen of the Two Sicilies to allow Nelson to obtain supplies in Syracuse. Without those supplies it is possible that he might not have gone on to win the great victory over the French in the battle of the Nile on 1 August, 1798 – a much needed victory for the English.

The news reached Naples a month later in a letter from Nelson himself to Sir William, and everyone went mad with joy – except the French element who lay low. Emma, her spelling not much improved, wrote Nelson an ecstatic letter in which she declared: "My dear, dear Sir – God, what a victory! I wou'd not like to die till I see and embrace the Victor of the Nile. Oh, brave Nelson – Savour of Itali. Oh that my swolen heart cou'd now tell him personally what we owe to him!"

When she learned that Nelson was sailing into Naples, Emma dressed herself from head to foot in navy blue with gold anchors stitched all over the garment. On the arrival of her hero – as Nelson rather tactlessly informed his wife in a letter – Emma fell into his arms, more dead than alive, exclaiming "Oh God, is it possible?" Nelson's wife, Fanny, was to read much in praise of Lady Hamilton's kindness and charm in future letters from her husband.

For nearly a month Nelson stayed in Naples while Emma assiduously nursed him for an eye wound he had received during the battle. But political events were about to uproot the Hamiltons and bring about the circumstances that were to lead to the famous and controversial ménage-à-trois. What happened was that the Queen of Naples, partly out of revenge for the execution of her sister Marie Antoinette, persuaded King Ferdinand to march against Napoleon in an attempt to free the Papal States from French domination. The expedition was a disastrous failure. The French in turn marched on Naples. The King and Queen and most of the royal family decided to flee to Sicily. With the active assistance of the Hamiltons they were smuggled on to Nelson's ship, H.M.S. *Vanguard.* During the stormy crossing to Sicily Emma proved herself to be a tower of strength, ministering to the terrified royal family and even to Sir William – but on the voyage six-year-old Prince Albert, Ferdinand's second son, died in Emma's arms.

The fleet arrived in Palermo on 26 December, 1798, after a bleak Christmas by any standards. Altogether some 2,000 refugees were put ashore. The royal family settled down reluctantly in the draughty, sparsely furnished palace and Sir William, having made arrangements to leave for Gibraltar in the spring, rented a large house near the Mole. Nelson shared the expenses with him, thereby establishing for the first time the congruence of what should have been an incongruent triangle.

Life crystallized into the familiar social round. Naples had been invaded by the French; the Queen was upset, but the King was already more interested in the pursuit of hunting. Emma discovered the pleasures of gambling, for which Nelson was quite happy to provide finance. It is probable that during this interlude Emma became his mistress. Sir William was continually unwell in the bitter cold of the Sicilian winter, so that during the next two or three months Emma and Nelson were very much alone together.

In the spring an army of Italian peasants raised by a Cardinal Ruffo recaptured Naples and negotiated a treaty with the French. The terms were considered too lenient, so Nelson, Sir William and Emma went to Naples to spend two months in renegotiating the terms on more severe lines and arranging the affairs of state – in fact, paving the way for the return of the monarchy. This was duly accomplished, and when the King and Queen were reinstated, Nelson and the Hamiltons went back to Palermo. There they were greeted with almost hysterical acclaim; the Sicilian royal family showered them with gifts and persuaded Nelson to accept the Duchy of Brontë. The festivities and adulation went on for a long time, to Emma's self-gratification – indeed, she was becoming quite swollen-headed, seeing herself as a person of considerable political importance.

Nelson lingered in Palermo while the war at sea continued. It was not long before his conduct with the Ambassador's wife began to stimulate gossip, and then scandal. Emma cared for nothing; she would sit up most of the night gambling and eating and drinking to excess, with Nelson always at her elbow. This way of life duly earned him a rebuke. Lord Keith, in charge of the Mediterranean squadron, sharply told Nelson to get on with the business of fighting a war – and tartly pointed out that there were a number of ports more suitable for bases than Palermo. But Nelson, after making a variety of naval sorties, always returned to Palermo.

The rumours eventually reached the ears of his wife Fanny. She threatened to come out to Palermo to join him, but he put her off with curt determination. Emma, learning of the rumours, wrote an indignant letter to Greville emphasizing that Nelson and Sir William were the best of friends and that Nelson himself never gambled – which was no doubt true enough. Nelson's behaviour, however, was under critical scrutiny, and was considered so outrageous in some quarters that even Troubridge, one of his squadron captains, took his courage in his hands by writing to both Nelson and Emma and begging them to mend their ways.

Early in the year 1800 Emma discovered that she was pregnant by Nelson, and shortly afterwards Sir William's relief arrived to take over his ambassadorial functions, for he was in poor health. For Emma the thought of having to exchange the scene of her great social triumphs for the comparative anonymity of England was depressing in the extreme and put her into low spirits. Nelson, who was due for home leave at the same time, was refused permission to take the party home in the *Foudoyant* – perhaps a gesture of disapproval of his conduct, but more probably because the warship was required for Mediterranean service as the war with France was still raging. So an overland itinerary it had to be.

They left Palermo on 16 July, accompanied as far as Vienna by the Queen and a large entourage – but nevertheless an unwieldy confused body travelling often within just a few miles of Napoleon's advanced posts. Sir William's health improved a little, but he was still a sick man. In Vienna, Emma finally said farewell to her "beloved Queen", a woman whom many saw as dangerous, meddlesome and foolish – and promised "eternal love".

Then the Nelson party, as it was known, continued alone, progressing through the various capital cities of Europe. The scandal of the ménage-à-trois had travelled ahead of them, and they were received with reserve rather than enthusiasm. Many of the comments of people who met them during their journey were uncomplimentary. Nelson, it was observed, made no attempt to conceal his infatuation for Emma; he continually hung about at her elbow, singing her praises – and incidentally lapped up all the adulation that was showered upon himself. Emma was acknowledged to have a well proportioned figure and fine features, but was described as bold, coarse, assuming and vain – and also "ungraceful" except when performing her famous "attitudes". She astonished observers by her greed and her capacity for champagne which both she and Nelson consumed in large quantities.

In October they left Dresden by boat along the River Elbe for their final European port of call, Hamburg, where a frigate was said to be waiting to take them across to England. Their departure was viewed with some relief by the Ambassador in Dresden who had found their week's stay with him a trying round of noisy living. He escorted them to the river boat and noted with astonishment the change in their behaviour as soon as they set foot aboard. Lady Hamilton's maid began to scold in French, using words of extreme vulgarity, and Emma herself "began bawling for an Irish stew and her old mother set about washing potatoes ... They were exactly like Hogarth's actresses dressing in the barn". At Hamburg there was no sign of a frigate, and they were reduced to seeking passage on the regular mail packet to Yarmouth.

Nelson's reception at Yarmouth and in the towns and villages he passed through on his way to London was tumultuous – but society was less enthusiastic in its response. The Hamiltons were still with Nelson when he finally arrived at the London hotel where he was to meet his wife – and the reunion was distinctly frosty, for Fanny Nelson had heard all the rumours and saw little reason to doubt them. But the matrimonial facade had to be maintained; for a time the Nelsons moved into a rented house which, to nobody's surprise, was quite close to the home of the Hamiltons. During the following weeks the two families saw a great deal of each other, maintaining a charade which must have been painful for all concerned.

The inevitable break came at Christmas and was probably triggered by Fanny taking issue with Nelson about his mistress. He spent the holiday at the home of a mutual friend with Emma and Sir William (who was still maintaining an attitude of perfect friendliness with his wife's lover). Fanny was not present, and thereafter she and Nelson lived apart.

Emma was by now eight months pregnant, yet although her *embonpoint* was remarked upon in various contemporary accounts nobody seems to have guessed her secret. Her normally generous build enhanced by the high-waisted full-skirted fashion of the day would have supported the deception.

Early in the new year Nelson was appointed Vice-Admiral of the Blue, and left to join the H.M.S. *San Josef* in Plymouth. Two weeks later Emma's baby, a girl, was born. The birth took place in Sir William's house at 23 Piccadilly in London, and there Emma was confined to her room for three days with "a very bad cold". She was looked after by her mother who shared all her daughter's secrets. It is impossible to believe that Sir William did not know very well what was going on in his own house, but for reasons best known to himself he preferred to feign ignorance. Perhaps it was for the sake of peace and quiet, for Emma in a temper was a veritable force nine gale, but more likely he was genuinely fond of Emma and Nelson and chose not to intervene in a relationship which was clearly making them both happy. Emma herself rallied from her accouchement with characteristic vigour, for three days after the birth she was not only up and about, but attended a Grand Concert at the Duke of Norfolk's house – where, among the guests, she encountered again her old lovers, Sir Harry Featherstonehaugh and Charles Greville!

Nelson was unable to get away from Plymouth until the end of the following month. Meanwhile he wrote passionate letters to Emma, full of expressions of love and concern for her welfare. But he had also heard that the Prince Regent had his appreciative eye on Lady Hamilton, and this was insupportable. He wrote her letters of jealous despair imploring her to refuse to see the Prince, to reject him, and to remain completely faithful, as he was to her. These letters were, perhaps, to do her a disservice in the years to come.

At last Nelson managed to get three days leave which gave him time for a brief trip to London to see Emma and their child. The baby, Horatia, had been smuggled out of the Piccadilly house and taken to an address in Marylebone to be looked after by a Mrs. Gibson. The pretence agreed between Nelson and Emma was that Horatia was the daughter of a Mr. Thompson, serving in Nelson's ship, and that Nelson and Emma were the godparents. It proved to be an acceptable fiction.

Nelson went back to sea and to the battle of Copenhagen – the scene of the famous "telescope to his blind eye" incident. Meanwhile, Emma was to look for a house for him which could be their "peaceful paradise". She decided on Merton Place, an hour's drive from London; as a house it was large and comfortable, but by no means grand. Nelson bought it, furnished. It was to be a new home for himself, Emma, her mother and Sir William who was to share the household expenses. Nelson, who wished to regard the house as a haven for himself and Emma, was not eager to have Sir William move in lock, stock and barrel, but at no time did he ever make any serious attempt to break up the ménage-à-trois situation which had circumscribed his relationship with Emma from the start. It was not lack of courage or finance on his part, but it is possible that Emma herself, with her insecure background, was reluctant to jettison the security of being Lady Hamilton, and preferred to make the best of both worlds.

Nelson first saw the house in 1801. Both he and Emma were greeted rapturously by the local inhabitants of Merton, despite the fact that Emma was not received at Court and was frowned upon by high society. Her neighbours in Merton chose to ignore the irregular situation. The Hamiltons and Nelson were hospitably entertained, and in return Emma began to take up again her own lavish brand of entertaining which had been in eclipse since the return to England. Her parties became so numerous and noisy, and the stream of guests staying in the house so incessant that Sir William, now 70 years old, was constrained to complain to a friend that he had no peace in his declining years. He did not dare, however, to remonstrate with Emma for fear of "coming to an explosion which would be attended by many disagreeable effects, and would totally destroy the comfort of the best man and best friend I have in the world".

Emma, in fact, did very much as she pleased, whether in the Merton or London house. As she grew older she became more domineering. Nelson himself once remarked that she knew how to raise "the hell of a dust" when she could not get her own way. She continued to "cram Nelson with trowelfuls of flattery", a friend commented, and she filled the house with pictures of Nelson and herself, and of his naval battles, with pieces of plate in his honour, flags and a multitude of souvenirs – all in the height of bad taste. Nelson, however, appeared to be perfectly content. His wife, Fanny, sent him a few sad and humble letters begging him to return to the comfortable home she had prepared for him but, apart from making financial provision, he brutally ignored her.

Although the ménage would occasionally stay in London at the Hamiltons' Piccadilly house, it was at Merton that they spent most of their riotous time, and it was there that the relationship between Emma and Sir William deteriorated steadily until finally he was prompted to write an indignant letter to her, complaining of her lack of consideration for him. Emma heeded its warning tone; for a while the flood of visitors and parties subsided, and Sir William was even allowed to entertain his own friends in his own time. But he was now an old man, and towards the end of March 1803 he was taken seriously ill and died in his London home, with Emma and Nelson at his bedside.

Now that Emma's "chaperon" was dead, propriety required that Nelson should move out of the Hamilton home, and equally that Emma should not stay at Merton – but this impasse was resolved within a few weeks when Nelson was called to join the H.M.S. *Victory* at Portsmouth. His duties at sea kept him away for the next three or four years, and during this period Emma's affairs began to decline. Financially she seemed to be adequately provided for: Sir William had left her an annuity of £800 and some capital – the rest went to his nephew, Charles Greville – and Nelson had arranged for her to have £100 a month to cover expenses at Merton. She moved out of the Piccadilly house into a smaller one in Clarges Street, but the trouble was that she continued to pursue her extravagant ways.

The upkeep of Horatia was an additional expense, and Nelson was anxious to install her at Merton in the guise of a three-year-old child who had been left in his care and now needed more than the attention of just a nurse. Emma was somewhat reluctant to oblige, for she felt that to accept increased responsibility for her daughter, for whom she had little maternal feeling, would inhibit the freedom of movement which she so enjoyed. Nearly a year passed before, in May 1805, Horatia was actually moved into the Merton house.

In the meantime, in January 1804, Emma had given birth

to a second daughter, but the baby had survived for only a few weeks. Suffering from shock and illness, with Nelson far away and Sir William dead, she slipped deeper into her more discreditable faults – self-indulgence, vulgarity, extravagance and lack of discretion. She was remarkable for the vast amount of port which she could put away without any observable effect, not to mention her insatiable appetite for food and her rather scatter-brained foolishness, but for all that she was kind-hearted and generous and never forgot her old friends and relations.

She began to run steeply into debt, so much so that by the middle of 1805 she owed about £7,000 and was still spending money on quite unnecessary luxuries such as enlarging the house at Merton. She wrangled with the government for the payment of compensation due to Sir William for losses he had suffered during his period of duty in Naples, and petitioned for compensation for herself for the part she had played in aiding the war effort and in organizing the evacuation to Palermo – but her appeals fell on deaf ears. And yet, when Nelson came home for his last leave, she said not a word to him about her money troubles.

Nelson came home in August 1805 and Emma, who had been sea-bathing at Southend, hurried to Merton to meet him. He was able to remain in England for only 25 days so that he had little time to relax with Emma. Once again the house bustled with visitors, and Emma, who missed the days when she had been hostess to the most important and influential people of society, was delighted – but her delight was not to last for long. The news that the French fleet under the command of Villeneuve was at Cadiz signalled Nelson's hasty recall to sea. There seems no justification in the story that Emma selflessly and bravely urged him to return to duty as soon as possible; indeed, on the eve of his departure she was so distressed that she could hardly eat or drink and was near swooning. Their final hours together were packed with as much social bustle and comings and goings as ever. Then, late on the evening of 13 September 1805, after coming back to her no less than four times before he could finally tear himself away, Nelson left Emma for ever.

He seems to have had some presentiment of his imminent death. In a note in his diary on the day he left Emma, he submitted himself to God should his days on earth be cut short. And two days before the battle of Trafalgar, which was fought on 21 October, he wrote "The enemy's combined fleet are coming out of port . . . I will take care that my name shall ever be most dear to you and Horatia, both of whom I love as much as my own life. And as my last writing before the Battle will be to you, so I hope in God that I shall live to finish my letter after the Battle."

On 21 October, when the enemy fleet was in sight, he also made a codicil to his will. In this he pointed out that the services of Emma Hamilton to her country had never been rewarded and that, as it had not been in his power to reward them, he left Emma, Lady Hamilton, "a Legacy to my King and Country that they will give her an ample provision to maintain her rank in life". He also commended his "adopted daughter" Horatia, to his country. These, he said, were the only favours he asked of King and Country at the moment when he was about to fight their battle.

If Nelson had a strong foreboding of doom, Emma appeared to have no such apprehension. She wrote gossipy, cheerful, loving letters to him, with news of Horatia to whom she seemed to have become devoted. Three of them were duly returned to her by Captain Hardy. They had arrived too late.

Emma was in her little house in Clarges Street when a friend, hearing the Tower guns, hazarded a guess that some important victory had been won. Five minutes later a carriage stopped at her door with a message from the Admiralty. The messenger, uneasy and pale, said quietly: "We have gained a great victory." "Never mind your victory," said Emma impatiently. "My letters – give me my letters." The messenger, tears in his eyes, was unable to speak. Emma thus understood what had happened. She fainted dead away and for ten hours remained in a blank unresponsive condition, unable to speak or even weep.

For three weeks she kept to her bed, her world in ruins, but recovered her wits sufficiently to ask her mother to write to the Government, begging that Nelson's dependants whom he had supported so liberally during his life should not be forgotten. Nor could she resist dramatizing her tragic situation when receiving sympathetic friends, for she would show them the shawls, bracelets, rings and trinkets which Nelson had given her over the years. The coat which Nelson had worn at Trafalgar, with its blood-stained bullet-hole, was also proudly displayed.

Nelson bequeathed her the Merton house, its contents and land, and a grant of £500 a year from the Brontë estate, but they did little to alleviate her immediate financial difficulties. She became embittered, and went so far as to accuse Nelson's brother who had inherited all the titles and dignities which Nelson had earned, of deliberately suppressing the codicil to his will that Nelson had written just before the final battle. She made disagreeable scenes and so antagonized many people who might have been able to help her. Her appeals to the Prince Regent proved futile.

The remainder of Emma's life was a constant struggle against the debts which she incurred by her improvidence. Although some friends came to her aid, including many she had previously offended, the house at Merton had to be sold. And so began the moves from one house to another even cheaper, taking with her Horatia and her devoted mother. Inevitably her mother's death in 1810 was a crushing blow, for she had been a great support and confidante in all Emma's escapades.

Things went from bad to worse. Two years later Emma was arrested for debt and committed to a "spunging house" – a lodging adjacent to Kings Bench prison in which certain prisoners were permitted to live instead of actually going to gaol. Meanwhile she continued to write appeals to the Prince Regent, seeking recognition by and support from her country which she had served so well – but in vain. And then in 1814, as a final *coup de grace,* an unscrupulous publisher got hold of a number of letters from Nelson to Emma which had probably been stolen from her house, and published them. Among the letters were those containing Nelson's remarks about the Prince Regent. Although Nelson had asked Emma to destroy his letters to her, she had not been able to bring herself to do so – an indiscretion which she now regretted. Not only did their publication undermine her pleas to the Prince Regent, but they also made the true nature of her relationship with Nelson public domain.

On three subsequent occasions Emma was arrested for debt, and finally, after spending a whole year in a spunging house, she decided to flee the country. She was now 49 years old. To stay in England was merely to invite further writs for debt which, as she was well aware, might be served on her at any moment. So, with Horatia and less than £50, Emma sailed for Calais. She was never to set foot in England again.

Characteristically, she installed herself in the largest and most expensive hotel in Calais until dwindling funds forced her to move to another much cheaper one. From there she went to live in a farmhouse in a village outside Calais, but even this proved to be too dear for the slender remains of her allowance. She and Horatia returned to Calais, to cheap and uncomfortable lodgings – and there Emma fell ill. She had never been very well since a severe attack of jaundice a few years earlier, and her heavy drinking – which she continued until her death – only made matters worse. She had become so poor that if Horatia, now 14 years old, had not written secretly to Nelson's brother (now the new Lord Nelson) and to a sympathetic friend to borrow money, she would literally have not had one shilling to buy food, let alone drink.

She died in January 1815, unrecognized and unrewarded by the country which she claimed to have served and to which she had become merely an embarrassment. She was buried at the expense of the British Consul in the cemetery outside the town – and the cost of the funeral was later reimbursed to His Majesty's Government by one of Emma's friends.

Chapter 2 Eliza Lynch– Almost an Empress

In the heart of the South American continent lies Paraguay, one of the smallest of the colonies claimed by Spain in the sixteenth century. Its people were the gentle childlike Guarani who, though intelligent and quick to learn, tended to be apathetic and lacking in initiative, doing only the simplest work necessary to keep themselves alive. They were looked after by the Jesuits who in the two centuries before the Spanish king became jealous of their power, taught them a variety of arts and crafts. After the Jesuits were expelled from the colony the Guarani reverted to their former apathy, pursuing a slow leisurely life cut off from the turbulent events of Europe – except in so far as they were exploited by the rich Spanish colonists who lived in arrogant feudal style and jealously guarded their pure white blood.

For some time the South American states had been agitating for independence from Spain, but they were strong royalists, and it was not until King Carlos IV abdicated in favour of Napoleon's brother that their loyalty com-

Nelson's mistress had a great sense of the theatrical. Emma Hamilton liked exhibiting herself in "attitudes", as Cleopatra, Diana, or Kate Romney (*top*). She is depicted in James Graham's Celestial Bed (*left*

above), one of the wonders of that quack doctor's erotic Temple of Health which she visited in earlier years. – The Marquise de Montespan (*right above*) lived with Louis XIV. She kept greater state than the Queen.

歲萬萬歲萬萬歲萬歲太后皇母聖今當國清大

Orchid, or Tzu Hsi, was chosen for China's Imperial harem at the age of sixteen. She was an extraordinarily intelligent woman and had considerable political influence with her lover, the weak and debauched Emperor Hsien Feng, after she had been raised to a first-rank concubine (*right*). To satisfy her immense lust for power, she took to dangerous intrigues. As Dowager Empress (*above*), nicknamed Old Buddha, she practically ruled China. She contributed to China's defeat by the Japanese in 1894 by misappropriating vast sums from the Admiralty funds for her personal pleasure.

pletely evaporated. One after another the colonies broke away to join the Argentine Confederation. Paraguay, however, held out to the last – until in 1811 the Governor of the colony, realizing that a split had become inevitable, signed a Declaration of Independence and retired into private life.

A junta of five men took over the government of the colony, but one of them, a Doctor Francia, was able to persuade the others to name him as sole dictator. For the next thirty years he ruled Paraguay with an iron hand, ruthlessly disposing of anybody who dared to oppose him. A taciturn austere man, he lived a solitary and largely friendless life, and although his people feared him he did a great deal for Paraguay. By sealing the country off from the outside world he was able to avoid the tumults and bloodshed which other South American states experienced in their early years of independence, and so could concentrate on building houses, hospitals and schools and encouraging agriculture and education.

After his death Paraguay's government again reverted to a junta, but before a constitution could be agreed and a legislative assembly convoked another dictator appeared. This time it was a gross, greedy, 57-year-old man named Lopez. Of humble birth, he had been well educated and had furthered his advancement by marrying the daughter of a rich patrician family – for the reason, it was rumoured, that the daughter had become pregnant and Lopez had been bribed to marry her. Certainly their first child, Francisco, was born very soon after their marriage in 1827, and he was 18 years old when his father became President of Paraguay.

Lopez, on the whole, was not a bad president. He opened up trade with other countries and the republic prospered. Basically a benevolent man, he showed signs of brutality and ruthlessness only when his own interests or comforts were threatened. He was generous in advancing the careers and fortunes of his friends and he doted on his eldest son – which was just as well, for Francisco's *peccadilloes* sorely tried his father's patience. His swashbuckling behaviour and

B

precocious sexual appetite caused so many scandals that his father was always having to send him out of the country on one military or political mission after another.

In the event, Francisco fulfilled these missions with unexpected success, so that in 1853 President Lopez was prompted to send his son to Europe as Ambassador at large to promote Paraguay's image in Europe, to encourage immigration and buy battleships from Queen Victoria. Francisco set off with great enthusiasm. When he was snubbed by Queen Victoria he bought battleships from America instead. Then off to Paris he hastened, looking forward with excitement to visiting this Mecca of the fashionable world of the day. Naturally enough for a man of his arrogance and appetites, he had already notified the Chargé d'Affaires in Paris that during his stay he would require the companionship of an attractive young woman. The Charge d'Affaires conscientiously busied himself about this assignment. Sure enough, when Francisco arrived at the Gare du Nord a beautiful young woman with corn-blonde hair and deep blue eyes was introduced to him – a woman who, years later, was indirectly to cause his death.

This first meeting was brief and rather formal. As Francisco was driven off to the Consulate, Eliza Lynch was left looking speculatively after him. What she saw was a short, stocky, bow-legged man, by no means handsome, but powerfully built; the question in Eliza's mind at that moment was whether he would prove to be the means to fulfil her ambitions. Although then only 18 years old, she had already realized that youth and beauty do not last for ever. In order to secure her future she had determined to seek a rich foreigner with whom she could form a permanent liaison. Marriage was out of the question, for Eliza, with more impetuosity than wisdom, had married at the age of fourteen.

Her early years had been hard. Born in Ireland in 1835, she could claim bishops and judges among her relations, but her parents were poor and ultimately found themselves destitute when the potato famine hit the country. After witnessing terrifying scenes of tragedy and horror, they took their child and fled to Paris to live with their eldest daughter who was married to a musician. Unfortunately, the Parisian couple were also poor, so that the life of privation continued.

Eliza tolerated this miserable existence for four years, during which she matured from childhood and developed her own independent character. Then one day she declared firmly that she was going to marry a young veterinary surgeon by the name of Quatrefages who was attached to a cavalry regiment, and that nothing would stop her. The law very nearly did, for her youth created legal difficulties, but Eliza was strong-willed and resourceful. She achieved her aim, even though she had to journey to England to marry her vet. Her parents were compliant; they were probably only too glad to be rid of the responsibility of feeding her.

Predictably, however, for a girl so young and with ambitions, marriage turned out to be a bore, as did the military environment of garrison towns. After two years she calmly abandoned her husband and returned to her sister in Paris. Her father was dead and her mother had gone back to Ireland. But she was now sixteen and sophisticated, and she soon found men who were willing to keep her in the fashion to which she would like to become accustomed. She joined the glittering but brittle world of the courtesans, prudently putting aside the money she gained so that, before very long, she was able to open a gaming salon which she ran, with mercenary common-sense, as a profitable business. But that was still not enough. What she was really seeking was not merely a steady income from a business, but power and wealth, and with this end very much in mind she planned to extend her range of influential acquaintances by letting it be discreetly known that she was "available" through agents at hotels and embassies.

And so it came about that the Chargé d'Affaires at the Paraguayan Consulate, anxious to please his distinguished visitor, had summoned Eliza for the confrontation at the Gare du Nord. Several days elapsed before they met again. Meanwhile Francisco had been very busy meeting important people, including the Emperor Louis Napoleon and

Empress Eugenie. The Emperor, who was gracious in the extreme, conferred upon him the Legion of Honour, which so impressed Francisco that as he left the palace he made up his mind that he, Francisco Lopez, would become the Napoleon of the New World. For the presentation to the Emperor he had ordered a new uniform so encrusted with gold lace and braid that he was probably the first South American General to become the source of the old music-hall joke. And he was wearing this same flamboyant uniform when, two nights later, he was taken by friends to the gaming salon of Madame Lynch.

She was scarcely able to recognize the gorgeously caparisoned figure as the stocky little man she had met at Gare du Nord. But as she watched him gambling with arrogant panache for large sums of gold – which, incidentally, he won and then presented to Eliza – she analysed and evaluated her prey very carefully. She decided that he was vain, credulous and naive – and that flattery would get her everywhere.

At an opportune moment she drew him aside to pay him delicate compliments, an attention which he accepted complacently. But when she took him to her boudoir whose rich and tasteful furnishings fascinated him he discovered that she was as elusive as she was friendly. For a whole week Eliza managed to hold him at bay while she questioned him shrewdly about the country which she was already contemplating as her future home. By the time Francisco finally possessed her as his mistress she had him just where she wanted him. He was enslaved by her charms and deeply impressed by her air of cultured elegance. He saw her as a great lady, knowing too little of the world to realize that she was of the demi-monde.

While he was writing to his father about his studies of modern industrial and commercial techniques which would eventually benefit Paraguay, Francisco was in reality escorting Eliza proudly round Europe and showering her with expensive gifts. When the time came for him to return home he insisted that she must accompany him, for he could not live without her. She, accepting his invitation, added happily that she was pregnant with his child. And so the vast load of crates of furniture, carriages and clothes which had been bought in Europe were stowed aboard the Paraguayan ship which had come to escort them home. Francisco and Eliza sailed from Bordeaux in November 1854.

Two months later the paddle-steamer bringing the President's son and his mistress home chugged up the Paraguay river towards the capital city of Asuncion. Francisco in a mood of excitement visualized the promising future of his country; the professional men to whom he had given five-year contracts while in Europe would develop its science and culture, and he himself would lead Paraguay to greatness and domination in South America. Eliza, objectively and with little emotion, coolly assessed her future and was pleased with its potentialities.

Her first taste of Asuncion was, however, daunting. News of Francisco's return had travelled ahead of him, and half the native population turned out to offer a noisy greeting. But when they saw the golden-haired blue-eyed woman – colouring which was strange to them – they became silent, staring at her in astonishment and awe, and kneeling in reverence as she stepped ashore. Francisco led Eliza to a row of waiting carriages in which sat members of his family, but now her reception was very different. President Lopez, who had no idea that his son was bringing home a mistress and regarded the incident as just another of his irritating and embarrassing whimsies, barely acknowledged her before ordering his coachmen to drive off. Francisco's mother, brothers and sisters were even more abrupt in their departure.

Eliza was escorted to a damp and gloomy house to wait while Francisco went to the Presidential palace to report to his father, but he promised to return as quickly as possible. The servant assigned to wait on her in this shabby retreat was a woman who had suffered hideously from leprosy. Hours passed by while she waited, depressed and anxious, for Francisco's return, but still he did not come. Eventually, fatigued and dispirited, she crawled under a mosquito net into a sagging bed.

No sooner had she fallen asleep than she was startled into wakefulness by screams, scuffles and the sound of blows. Alarmed, she rushed to the door of her bedroom and found it locked. From the window she called in desperation to a passing guard, but he ran away as if from a ghost. Worried and frustrated, not to mention angry, she spent the rest of the night sitting in a chair – just waiting.

All this time Francisco had been at the palace, raging at his family for their refusal to accept Eliza and swearing that he intended to marry her when she obtained her divorce – but they remained adamant. Although his father finally unbent sufficiently to spend several hours discussing eagerly with his son the plans and prospects for the future development of Paraguay, he too steadfastly declined to acknowledge Eliza. When Francisco finally was able to return to his mistress he had little reassuring news for her, other than to explain that the terrifying noises during the night were from an adjacent prison, and to promise her a new house which she herself could design.

Her child was born at Patino, a country house built to Eliza's own specification some five miles from Asuncion. It was a charming house set in a small farm and tastefully furnished with the furniture, rugs, tapestries, porcelains and brasses which they had brought back from France. Eliza was happy enough in her new environment, and the arrival of her son, Panchito, gave her something to occupy her time. But she was also keenly interested in the embellishment of Asuncion – with Francisco and an English architect brought over to Paraguay she planned an opera house, a grandiose palace, a library, a post office and a social club. Although Francisco could obtain permission from his father to do anything he wished to improve the country, he was refused permission to have his child baptized in the cathedral by his uncle, the bishop. The ceremony had to be arranged privately, as did the funeral of their next child, a baby girl who died after a few months.

Despite efforts to become involved in social activities, Eliza's life was very lonely. About the only people who came to see her were a Hungarian colonel who was Francisco's military adviser and two women teachers whom she had invited from France to set up a finishing school for young ladies on French lines. Her effort to start a national theatre proved abortive, and the first performance staged before a bejewelled but unappreciative audience was a complete flop.

For eight years Eliza was rejected by the Lopez family and lived as an outcast, and as time went by her relationship with Francisco changed subtly. When she had had four children, all boys, it came to her knowledge that Francisco had taken as his mistress the daughter of an ambitious politician. The news came as no great surprise to her, and she was unmoved by it, for she had had enough of child-bearing – indeed, she even took steps to further the new liaison. So far as she was concerned the insatiable Francisco could, she decided, have all the mistresses he wanted. She made her tolerant attitude plain to him, and he in turn, feeling no longer obliged to conceal his amatory escapades, began to take her more and more into his confidence. The result was an increasing sense of "togetherness" – she was aware that he trusted her and loved her in a way that he had never done before. Together they would spend hours discussing his plans and dreams to develop the country which she had come to regard as her own.

One evening, when she and Francisco were together at her home, a messenger arrived from the palace: the President was seriously ill and was not expected to last the night. Francisco hurried off to be with his father during his final moments, but in fact the old man survived for nearly a month, dying slowly of dropsy. It was only at the very last minute, when a priest was administering Extreme Unction to the rapidly failing President, that Francisco burst into the room. He pushed a quill pen into his father's hand and placed a piece of parchment on the deathbed, then badgered his father to sign a codicil which had been added to his will, bequeathing the Presidency of Paraguay to his eldest son. Despite his mother's entreaties Francisco persisted until with a great despairing effort old Lopez signed. It is said that he died with the pen still clamped in his hand so that his fingers had to be broken to remove it.

Francisco did not waste time; he was only too well aware of the potential political instability of South American states following the demise of a President. He went straight to the Government buildings where he seized important documents and, needless to say, the keys of the Treasury. Troops were ordered out to patrol the streets. The next day the Assembly, faced once again with a *fait accompli*, resigned themselves to accepting Francisco as President. One voice only was raised against him, and its owner was promptly imprisoned. Francisco had begun his term of office as he meant to continue. His next act was to "desire that from this day on Madame Eliza Lynch should enjoy the same privileges as those usually accorded to the wife of a head of State".

Obediently the women came – the wives of the Diplomatic Corps and the eminent ladies of Asuncion, including Francisco's sisters – to present themselves and pay their respects to Eliza. Full of compliments and abject apologies for not having called before, they were probably chagrined to find, not a cheap woman of the streets, but a beautiful and accomplished lady who spoke four languages, and whose courteous European manners made them feel crudely provincial in contrast. Eliza was not taken in by these sycophants; she received them with cool but correct *politesse*, while Francisco for his part was watchful for those who neglected their social duties to Eliza.

Some foreign diplomats sneered at Francisco and his "Paraguayan Pompadour", but the Emperor Napoleon sent him a letter of congratulations on his accession. Reminded of the elegant glamour of the French court, Francisco immediately decided to set up a court of his own. The Hungarian Colonel was made Lord Chamberlain, and a number of socially prominent women were appointed as Mistress of the Robes and Ladies in Waiting to Eliza. Very soon she presided at the first official dinner for the Corps Diplomatique, none of whom dared refuse. She appeared hand-in-hand with Francisco from a bedroom which adjoined the dining salon – a fact which caused some surreptitious amusement – and took her place with him at the head of the table. At last Eliza's ambitions were fulfilled, and it remained only to enhance Francisco's power and glory, and hence her own.

Francisco, however, was making his own unexpected plans, one of which was to have far-reaching and dramatic ramifications. He applied for the hand of the daughter of the Emperor of Brazil – and was rejected flatly and with little tact. Francisco, who had done all this without Eliza's knowledge, was grossly offended, while Eliza, although angered by Francisco's duplicity, was if anything even more insulted by the curt Brazilian dismissal of his suit. Francisco was rather sheepish and contrite, and in an attempt to make amends to Eliza wrote to the Pope requesting an annulment of her marriage to M. Quatrefages which had been contracted when she was under age. He also decreed his sons to be legitimate and changed their names officially from Lynch to Lopez. Eliza accepted these moves with characteristic coolness – her hold on him was now even stronger.

When Brazil invaded Uruguay on the pretext of suppressing a revolution, Francisco saw an opportunity for revenge. He sent a letter of strong protest to the Brazilian Ambassador in Asuncion. This was, of course, rejected in slighting terms, to the fury of Eliza who urged military action. The Paraguayan army of 65,000 men was not yet up to strength, however, and was awaiting essential supplies. Francisco's chance to hit back came when he learned that the new Brazilian Governor of the Mato Grosso was on his way to his province by steamer, and the Mato Grosso could only be reached by the Paraguay river. He promptly gave orders for the capture of the steamer and the arrest of the Governor, and followed up this act of piracy by sending a task force to seize the Mato Grosso capital and province. This was achieved without a shot being fired.

When the news of the victory reached Asuncion the people danced in the streets. Francisco held an imposing military review, while Eliza was ecstatic. After the celebrations were over, Eliza was presented with a Patent of

Nobility looted from the house of a Brazilian nobleman in Mato Grosso while Francisco received a necklace made of Brazilian ears.

Now in a triumphant warlike mood, Francisco decided to follow up this victory by invading the Brazilian territory of Rio do Sul – but to reach it he had to cross the Argentinian province of Corrientes. As the Argentine government was not at war with Brazil, permission to cross was flatly refused. Francisco was in no mood to back down and lose face – he immediately invaded and annexed Corrientes, and so found himself at war with the Argentine as well as Brazil, and later Uruguay joined the opposition. Although he would not admit it, Francisco had bitten off a little more than he could chew, and nobody was more militant in his support than Eliza who thought that Francisco should march at once upon Buenos Aires in a kind of pre-emptive strike. But he was determined to stick to his original plan to invade Brazil because, he said, he needed an outlet to the sea – so off went a force of some 12,000 men.

At first all went well, but the army had only just penetrated the frontier of Brazil when it was surprised by a combined force of Brazilians and Uruguayans, and the General in charge of the Paraguayan spearhead promptly surrendered. In Asuncion, Francisco and Eliza were waiting to attend a ball to celebrate the victory as soon as the news was received, but instead came news of defeat. Francisco was beside himself with rage. He locked himself in his room and refused to see anyone. Eliza's reaction was more phlegmatic; she decided that the news of the surrender should not be made public until the following day, and meanwhile the victory ball would take place as planned.

She ordered her carriage and set off for the function, where she made excuses for Francisco's absence. The empty throne was adorned with his portrait, and to this the assembly was obliged to make obeisance, and the ball went gaily ahead. Eliza played her part perfectly. At midnight the ballroom was invaded by a group of women wearing in their hair the gilt combs which distinguished them as prostitutes. After a moment of hesitation Eliza democratically invited them in – a gesture which aroused some amusement. "Lavinche" – as she was now called – "is looking after her own!"

Francisco remained locked away for three days while he contemplated his future gambits. The defeat was only a minor setback. All that was needed was more imposing and spectacular leadership, and who better than himself for such a role? So he called Congress together and presented himself before them attired in a splendid new gold-braided Field-Marshal's uniform to proclaim his new upgraded rank and announce that he personally was to take over the direction of the military campaign. He would leave the capital city in capable hands – Eliza's hands, for she was named Regent of Paraguay in his absence – and depart for the battlefield to assume overall command. The members of Congress, only too anxious to please, gave him loud acclaim, voted him a salary ten times greater than that which his father had enjoyed, and ordered from Europe a jewelled Marshal's baton for Francisco and a diamond coronet for Eliza.

Francisco's field-marshalship, however, proved to be no more effective than the generalship of his senior officers. The Paraguayan forces invariably seemed to lose important engagements, and usually with heavy casualties. Francisco's reaction was always one of fury and he would punish the responsible officers for their "treachery" by imprisonment or death.

Meanwhile Eliza remained in Asuncion carrying out the ritual functions of the President but well aware that she had no real power. She watched and listened, and gradually became aware that many of the old established upper-class families of Paraguay were of Argentinian and Uruguayan origin, with strong existing connections in those countries, and their loyalty to Paraguay was such that they would probably welcome a total victory of the allied enemies. True loyalty was only to be found among the Guarani, the indigenous inhabitants of Paraguay, but they lacked fire and drive. It became only too apparent that in this war she and Francisco were also fighting for self-preservation – if they lost, all the apparently loyal people would turn upon them without hesitation. Finally, she began to learn of secret intrigues and plots directed against Francisco. There was no positive proof or tangible evidence, but she realized that the position was becoming precarious.

Elisa, therefore, began to indulge in little intrigues of her own for practical ends. For instance, by threatening the Treasurer General, the husband of one of Francisco's sisters, that she would expose the fact that he was receiving letters from the Argentine President urging him to sign a separate peace treaty, she coerced him into handing over to her four boxes of gold from the Treasury. These she immediately shipped to Paris – against contingencies. Then she left Asuncion and rode to Humaita, where Francisco had his headquarters. "I have discovered," she said to him, "that the seat of Government is wherever you are, Francisco."

Eliza was in Humaita when the town was besieged, but the war dragged on slowly for the enemy forces were sluggish in following up their victories. In 1866, when both sides had become heartily sick of the war, Francisco proposed talks and negotiations with General Mitre, the President of Argentina, but it soon became clear that Mitre would not even begin to discuss peace terms unless Francisco abdicated. As a condition this was a non-starter, and the two men separated with nothing settled.

Paraguay was now in trouble and virtually cut off from the outside world. Although Eliza had had several offers from neutral ships to take her and her children to safety, she remained staunchly loyal to Francisco and insisted on staying. Indeed, she became more unscrupulously militant. She inveigled the Bishop, a weak and pliant man, into aiding and abetting her in a foray on the shrine of Our Lady of Cacaupe, where she stripped the image of the fortune of gold and precious stones which had been put there by faithful pilgrims. Then she dressed the Virgin in the gown she had worn at the "victory" ball and substituted worthless baubles for the stolen jewels.

Her motive was patriotic and not selfish. With the money

she had thus "raised" Eliza set about recruiting a regiment
of women. Mounted on a black stallion she addressed mass
meetings of women, demanding that they sacrifice all for
the freedom and independence of Paraguay, leaving the
elderly and the young to care for themselves and each other.
The regiment began to take shape, with a mixture of
patriotic fervour and resignation, and the women were
drilled in the use of lances (but not firearms) and trained in
the routine tasks of any army that would release men for
more active duties at the battlefront.

Slowly Paraguay's wartime isolation began to show
itself in austerity. Substitutes had to be devised for basic
commodities such as soap, ink and wine. To add to the
overall malaise there was a serious outbreak of cholera –
and Francisco himself caught it. Eliza, in Asuncion, heard
the bad news from her 12-year-old son who had ridden 100
miles to tell her that Francisco was dying. She lost no time
in hurrying to his bedside, and forthwith took charge of
both the army and Francisco himself.

The Director General of the Medical Corps was a
Scottish doctor named Stewart, but Francisco took violent
exception to him and accused him of trying to kill him – he
even threatened to have him court-martialled. Eliza, never
at a loss to exploit a coercive opportunity, blackmailed Dr.
Stewart into sending £4,000 to Edinburgh for safe-keeping
for her. This accomplished, she settled down to nurse
Francisco with an indefatigable determination that lasted
day and night; cruel, fanatical and depraved he might be,
but he was her man and the pivot of her hopes. When
Francisco duly recovered, he ordered a gold medal to be
struck. It was to be the highest order in the land, and it por-
trayed the profile of Eliza with the legend: *Defensora
Paraguensis.*

Francisco returned to Asuncion to celebrate his miracu-
lous recovery at a Te Deum in the cathedral, and immediately afterwards had his brother-in-law, Bedoya, arrested
for the theft of four cases of gold from the Treasury. The
wretched man appealed to Eliza to save him, but she ignored him and allowed him to die in the torture chamber,

knowing only too well that he was completely innocent of the alleged crime which she herself had contrived.

Some time later Francisco casually asked her what was actually in the four cases which she had sent to Paris. Without turning a hair Eliza calmly replied that he knew perfectly well, for his spies were everywhere. Francisco, equally cool, admitted it; he had used the incident as a pretext to arrest and destroy Bedoya whom he had suspected of being concerned in a conspiracy against him.

In fact, Francisco was becoming increasingly ruthless with suspected enemies. Innocent people were arrested and put to death at the slightest excuse, and often without an excuse. And yet the Paraguayans continued to demonstrate what *The Times* called "unparalleled devotion" to their leader, and the paper said, "Whatever faults or deeds of cruelty may be urged against Lopez, it is impossible to maintain that he rules by mere arbitrary power or terrorism". It added that while Francisco ruled the war would never end, and suggested that joint diplomatic action was essential to terminate "a most sanguinary and uncalled for struggle".

Nevertheless, despite Francisco's despotic cruelties, despite the enormous losses sustained by the army, despite the abandoned estates, vanished cattle, the all but depopulated country, despite the epidemics of smallpox and cholera and the privations of all kinds which killed off about one third of the remaining population, the people of Paraguay continued to support Francisco. Apparently unconcerned about death for themselves, they seemed prepared to follow him to the bitter end.

It must have been obvious even to the most optimistic that the end could not now be very far away, for Francisco's enemies were relentlessly closing in on him, at home as well as within the frontiers of his country. An internal betrayal was by no means improbable, but when it came it was engineered, incredibly enough, by his own mother. She summoned the American Ambassador, Washburn, to her house, and there, in the presence of her sons and daughters, two important Government Ministers and the Bishop, she made a prepared statement to the effect that Francisco was a bastard child, fathered on her by her own stepfather. It was to her second son, Benigno, that the Presidency of Paraguay should have gone.

The Bishop, no doubt hoping to curry favour, conveyed the news of this astonishing denunciation to Francisco in his army camp. According to reports Francisco became wild with rage and threw himself on the ground, roaring like a wild animal. When he was able to speak coherently he ordered the arrest of everyone who was present in his mother's house at the time of the statement – but with the exception of Washburn whom he dared not touch. He even turned on the cringing Bishop and had him shot for venturing to defame his mother. Washburn remained a problem, and Francisco exercised his cunning mind to find a way to bring him down.

One of the grievances which Francisco had against Washburn was that he had taken into the protective security of the American Legation a number of refugees from Francisco's brutal anger. There they lived in a state of siege, awaiting anxiously the appearance of the "liberating" enemy allies – but with their customary South American lethargy the allies had not followed up their territorial gains with sufficient speed, even though Francisco had long since disappeared northward with the remnants of his tattered army.

One night the bell at the door of the American Legation rang, and Eliza walked into the courtyard followed by 40 emancipated slaves carrying cases of gold. Although to the refugees she represented the enemy, the men among them instinctively removed their hats as she greeted the Ambassador. To his astonishment she asked if she might leave the public treasure of Paraguay as well as her own personal property in his safe-keeping, to prevent it from falling into the hands of the advancing conquerors. The Ambassador, taken aback by this extraordinary request, felt obliged to agree, and Eliza waited long enough to see the gold stowed away by the slaves in the Legation vaults.

Three days later, when the threat of an imminent Brazilian invasion had receded, Eliza returned to collect the gold, but this time her manner was cold and distant. She warned him that a conspiracy against the state had been discovered among the refugees at the Legation, and that he would do well to hand over the offenders; further, she accused him of being personally involved in a plot against Francisco, employing a series of half-truths which he found difficult to deny without embroiling himself still further. Direct accusations were launched against a number of his guests, and some of them, to save Washburn embarrassment, left the Legation. They were promptly arrested and most were shot. The pressure on Washburn and the Legation continued, but very quickly an American ship arrived to rescue Washburn and his staff. Several others were arrested and tortured in an attempt to force them to testify that Washburn had been the ringleader in a conspiracy to oust Francisco.

The retreat continued and gathered pace. Francisco withdrew further into the northern country, trailing his prisoners along behind the army. On the march the President, who had now grown very fat, would ride ahead on his horse, surrounded by his personal bodyguard. Eliza and the children followed immediately behind in an ancient carriage, and next came carts containing the cases holding the gold reserves of Paraguay. Francisco's mother and sisters were in the rear along with the starving rabble of prisoners. Whenever the column stopped the prisoners would be tortured as a diversion, and Francisco divided his time between this entertainment, religious frenzies and sexual orgies which Eliza condoned and ignored.

At a place called Pirebebuy the enemy launched a sudden unexpected attack which forced Francisco to abandon camp and set up his campaign headquarters about a mile away. Eliza accompanied him. There was a further surprise attack by a body of Brazilian troops, and Francisco and his staff were obliged to take shelter in the undergrowth. Eliza, however, had different ideas. She knew that close at hand was a large contingent of half-naked Guarani women – part of her enlisted female army – and some 200 cadaverous horses which had been seized from the enemy on the previous day. Shouting at the top of her voice, she set the example by hurling herself on to a horse, ordering the others to mount, and leading the women in a frantic charge into the enemy ranks. The sight of these half-clad females with lances tucked under their arms, led by a wild Eliza with her golden hair streaming in the wind, so unnerved the enemy that they turned tail and fled. Eliza herself was injured when her horse stumbled, throwing her to the ground and falling on top of her. Later Francisco berated her angrily: "How dare you expose your life, you wilful stupid woman. My life may be necessary to lead my people to victory, but yours is necessary to me." Probably never in his life had he spoken to her such words of tenderness!

On Christmas Day, 1868, Francisco sent a despatch to his enemies reiterating his intention never to abdicate, and pointing out that if they insisted on this proviso then the continuation of the war would be their fault. But he was now feeling pessimistic, for he wrote a will in which he left all of his property to Eliza, and it is believed that in the forests north of Pirebebuy he had ordered the golden treasure of Paraguay to be thrown over a cliff, and the men who threw it to follow suit, so that none but he himself could possibly know where it lay. Since then many treasure hunters have tried to locate the gold, but Francisco's secret is still his own.

The balance of his mind was becoming more and more suspect, and his tyranny took curious twists. He prevailed upon the Sacred College of Paraguay – by shooting all those who voted against him – to have him beatified as a saint of the Christian church. No sooner was this blasphemous ceremony completed than he sent for his mother and had her tried by an Ecclesiastical Court for treason. She was found guilty, of course, and even though she was his mother he had her tied to a cross and flogged.

The horrific struggle went on all through 1869 and into 1870. In the February of that year when Francisco, now thoroughly in the grip of megalomania, had decided that his mother must die, the sleeping camp was one night surprised by Brazilian cavalry. Hurriedly he mounted his horse and galloped off into the jungle in a frenzied effort to escape. His route brought him into a valley where he was thrown abruptly when his horse stumbled. Up to his knees in water, the President of Paraguay found himself surrounded by Brazilian soldiers. A spear embedded itself in his stomach. When a Brazilian General rode up and called on him to surrender he knew already that he had received a mortal wound. He managed to stand erect to say: "I die with my country" – and then collapsed into the swamp and died.

With Francisco's death the spell he had exercised on his followers was broken. The women militia of Eliza's female regiment suddenly turned upon her, howling for blood, but the Brazilian troops came to her rescue. In the fray her son Pancho was killed. And so, finally, holding the body of her dead son in her arms, Eliza surrendered Paraguay to the enemy. She was taken to the swamp where Francisco lay, and there she and her remaining sons scraped out a shallow grave with their bare hands. In it they placed the remains of the man who, Eliza had hoped, was to have made her Empress of South America. Beside him they placed the body of her eldest son.

Eliza was treated with great courtesy by the Brazilians. They sent her back to Europe, and for a while she lived near London while she conducted a lawsuit against Dr. Stewart who refused to hand over any of the money which both she and Francisco had given him for safe-keeping. He counter-claimed that Francisco had robbed him of £20,000 during his period of duty in Asuncion. Eliza lost her case and moved to Paris, where money awaited her. Her capital sustained her for five years of lavish living until, finally, in 1875 she decided to go back to Paraguay to claim her inheritance under Francisco's will. In Buenos Aires she was greeted favourably, but when she reached Asuncion she was refused permission to land. So she ceded her estate to her second and third sons, and with her youngest son, who died on the journey, she returned to Europe.

After a transient period in Jerusalem, Eliza Lynch homed

once more on Paris. She was now almost destitute, and the wheel of fate had turned a full circle. She found employment in a house of ill repute where, as the Madame of the establishment, she presided at the gaming table. She eventually died in July 1886, at the age of 51, and she must have died in poverty for the municipality paid for her funeral.

Eliza was buried in Père Lachaise, but 50 years later her remains were taken back to Asuncion where, this time, she was received with honour. Massed bands, speeches, salvos and guards of honour combined to escort her with high ceremony to her final resting place in the Panteon de los Heroes. She had, after all, been all but Empress of Paraguay and South America!

Chapter 3 Athenais—
Mistress of Versailles

Athenais, second daughter of the Duc de Mortemart, was born in 1640 in the Château de Lussac in Poitou, and in the course of time she grew into a beautiful young woman with dark hair, wide blue eyes, a rosebud of a mouth, good white teeth and a shapely figure enhanced by a full bust. When she was 23 years of age she married a wild Gascon named Louis, Marquis de Montespan, and bore him two children.

She was a proud woman, for she belonged to one of the oldest families in France, but she was also poor. This was partly due to her own personal extravagance, and also the fact that her dowry had never been paid in full, and that her husband had lent a large sum of money to his father which was never repaid. In those days when Louis XIV, the Sun King, required the presence of all his nobles at his glittering court, life tended to be very expensive. On one occasion Athenais even had to borrow money to buy a costume for a carnival.

The King's court had just moved into the new Palace of Versailles of which he was so proud. It had been built round an old hunting lodge, and no expense had been spared in the elaboration of this elegant building. Indeed, the Minister of Finance had been forced, reluctantly, to provide vast sums of money for the project – money which, in his view, would have been better devoted to the good of the country as a whole. Le Vau, Le Notre and Le Brun were some of the great artists of the time who were responsible for the design of the palace and gardens. Louis was delighted with his new *ambience*, but the courtiers grumbled; it was some way from Paris, and as Louis apparently expected all his nobles and his ministers to live in the place it tended to become an exclusive clique isolated and divorced from the rest of the country.

In 1674, although the palace was far from finished, enough of it was habitable to accommodate the king and his court – so they moved in. Very soon more than 3,000 people were living there, all bound by rigid customs and protocol. The noblest families had spacious apartments for themselves and their entourages, while lesser lights were relegated to the attics where one might have expected to find the servants. The court was strictly bound by the daily ceremony of the King's domestic routine – his getting up in the morning, his meals, his receptions, his prayers and finally his going to bed, all conducted in the presence of as many people who could crowd into the room at the time. King Louis observed everybody and everything; all letters in and out of the palace were opened, so that he knew all that was going on. The entire court was in effect a vast family with an omnipotent, all-seeing and strict patriarch at its head. Louis would stand no nonsense, and nothing was too petty for him to notice. He was as interested in the precedence of two duchesses as he was in the progress of a war.

But the court as a whole were idle, with not enough to do; they were there simply because the King wanted to keep his eye on them. In such an inward-looking atmosphere gossip, intrigue and jealousy were rife. There was constant plotting and jockeying for position and favour. To keep his courtiers amused, Louis organized a constant round of amusements – parties, fêtes, plays, concerts, dancing and gambling. Questions of fashion became a matter of major importance, and hours were spent over dressing and toilet. The days were frittered away in endless frivolity which only just served to stem the ever-threatening boredom.

In this hot-house environment Athenais became lady-in-waiting to the Queen Marie Thérèse, a diffident self-effacing young woman brought up in the rigid etiquette of the Spanish court. Her husband was away most of the time, for he was an army officer – this was about the only reason Louis would accept for absence from court. Athenais herself was sophisticated, witty, voluptuous and self-assured, but she was also a reckless gambler and ambitious enough to try to attract the king's attention. She made jokes in his hearing about the many suitors who courted her in her husband's absence, but Louis was not at first taken by her brashness and she did not please him. He expected greater decorum and subtlety from his women.

For a while the King's amorous interests ambled elsewhere. At the age of eighteen he had a tender love affair with the Italian Marie Mancini, a reserved and thoughtful girl who was the niece of Cardinal Mazarin, but she was finally rejected by his need to make a royal marriage, and left France. Louis, perhaps reluctantly, consoled himself with his shy but – he soon discovered – dull Queen. Then he found himself attracted to his funny, sweet new sister-in-law Henrietta, sister of the English King. To distract him from this politically loaded diversion his mother, who had acted as Regent during the minority of her son, threw in his way three young ladies of the court whom she personally considered to be suitable. One of these was Louise de la Valliere, a shy country girl of seventeen years. Louis courted her for two weeks with the encouragement of all of his intimates, at which point she abandoned her shyness and became his mistress.

This was in 1661 when Louis was 24 years old. She bore him three children, and the King retained his interest in her

tor six years, and would often take the trouble to visit her
while she was recovering from the birth of her children.
Now Louise knew perfectly well that she had no facility
for entertaining small talk with which to amuse her royal
lover, and so both she and the Queen would arrange for a
friend to be present. The friend, who had a happy genius for
le mot juste, an imaginative turn of mind and a knack of
making the dullest subject interesting, was Athenais de
Montespan.

The King, although at first he had confided to his brother,
"She does what she can, but I don't want her," gradually
began to develop an interest in Athenais. Her gaiety, wit
and good humour never seemed to fail her, and although
she was determined to capture the King, she knew how to
dissemble. In May 1667 Louis decided to spend the summer
with his army, taking with him the Queen and her ladies-
in-waiting – a retinue which included Athenais – but he
persuaded Louise who was expecting another child to stay
behind, and gave her the title of Duchess as a consolation
prize.

For part of the summer the court stayed at Avesnes, near
the Dutch frontier. Athenais lodged with Madame de
Montausier, the chief lady-in-waiting. Their rooms were
on the first floor of an elegant mansion, close to those of
the King and Queen, which were guarded by a sentry. After
a while the sentry was relegated to the ground floor; the
King went around in high good humour and Queen Marie
Thérèse wondered complainingly why her husband did not
come to bed until four o'clock in the morning.

Although Louis had finally fallen in love with Athenais,
she did not climb so readily into his bed as the shy, pliant
Louise had done. Shrewdly she kept him at arm's length
while his passion for her increased. His mother had died
the year before, and Louis, freed of her restricting presence
and the poverty that had dogged the early years of his reign,
was beginning to enjoy the sensual pleasures that attracted
him so much. The voluptuous and sophisticated Athenais
appealed strongly to this side of his nature, and he had
little difficulty in suppressing the scruples, inculcated by

his mother, which made him hesitate to take a married woman as his mistress.

This desired relationship was achieved in the summer of 1668 when the King was thirty. Louise de la Valliere gently protested, for she was still in love with the King and, despite the blow to her pride, she was not prepared to part from him. For Louis it was a situation which he could use to his advantage. His *affaire* with Louise was common knowledge, so he continued to use her as a cover for his second adultery in order to avoid a scandal. He confessed to Louise that he was in love with Athenais, but still, he insisted, he was very fond of *her*, too.

The two mistresses were given adjoining rooms. Louise assisted Athenais with her toilet and was continually in her company. When the King called on Athenais he could disguise the purpose of his visit by passing through Louise's apartment first. "The King," the courtiers said with irony, "is with the ladies!" Louise accepted this embarrassing situation out of concern to be close to her youngest child who had not yet been recognized by the King.

Hardly had Athenais become established as *maîtresse-en-titre*, however, than her husband irritatingly turned up. Needless to say, the King was annoyed. Montespan, although he did not get on well with Athenais, made a great fuss. He threatened to publish a "harangue" to the King, quoting the scriptures and exhorting His Majesty to release his wife. Monsieur de Montespan was persuaded not to do this, but nevertheless he took to bursting unexpectedly into the bedrooms of Athenais and Madame de Montausier to hurl insults at them. When rumours began to circulate that he was plotting with another wild Gascon nobleman to kidnap his wife and carry her off, the King was quite prepared to believe them. Only a few months previously Montespan had seduced a peasant girl and placed her, dressed as a man, in his cavalry company. A bailiff, acting on behalf of the girl's family, had rescued her and lodged her in prison for safety – but he had been beaten up by Montespan's cavalry for his pains.

King Louis had little alternative but to have Monsieur de

Montespan arrested. He imprisoned him for a short time on some minor misdemeanour and then banished him to his estates. Montespan was furious – he declared that his cuckold's horns were too high to allow him to pass through any but the great gate of his own castle. When, a year later, Athenais gave birth to the King's child, he held a mock funeral of his wife and dressed himself in mourning. But a few months later he kidnapped another girl from a convent.

Athenais could now settle down to enjoy and exploit her new status. Unlike her predecessor, she was out to get all she could from the King. She would refuse a small gift only in order to wheedle a more valuable one out of him. By shrewd deployment of her resources she managed to pay off all her debts and buy a house. Nor did she forget her relations, for she was able to beg favours of titles and position for them and use her influence to arrange advantageous marriages.

For six years the mistresses, Athenais and Louise, lived constantly in each other's company. Whenever the King travelled he drove in a coach with "the three queens" – his wife and mistresses. The Queen was able to accept the situation without much difficulty because Louis always insisted that his mistresses should treat the Queen with every respect. Then, in 1670, Louise fell ill and began to turn to the consolations of religion. When her son was safely settled she asked the King if she could retire to a convent. He, fond of his gay life and the wit and beauty which surrounded him, and no longer enamoured by the melancholy piety of Louise, her good looks jaded by illness, granted permission. On her last night at the court she dined with the King and the woman who had supplanted her in his affections, and the next morning she was conveyed to the convent where she remained for the rest of her life. The court instantly forgot her.

For Athenais, this was the moment when she could really come into her own. Now that Louise was no longer there to look on sadly, the King could give her all kinds of magnificent gifts. Athenais, of course, would accept nothing but the best. Louis built her a chateau at Clagny, which took ten years to construct and cost nearly a million pounds (it later passed to Louis XV's daughter-in-law and was demolished after her death). The gardens were stocked with thousands of beautiful plants and the adjoining farm with pedigree animals. Athenais was courted by everyone; the gentlemen and ladies of the court spent hours trying to think of new ways to please her and so gain her approval.

She freely spent a great deal of money, travelled about in magnificent carriages with a huge entourage, and kept greater state than the Queen herself. As the years went by the King seemed, to everyone's astonishment, to dote on her as much as if not more than ever. The physical hold she seemed to have over him was such that he appeared to tire himself out every night, and complain in the mornings to his doctors of dizziness and headaches.

Athenais spent much time and money on her clothes and her body. She became famous, so much so that visiting diplomats would bring her gifts in addition to those they gave to the King and Queen. On the credit side she was an intelligent and courageous woman. She would cheerfully put up with discomfort when on journeys with the King and still retain her good humour, even when she was ill or pregnant. She never lost her gambling fever – on one occasion she bet £500,000 on three cards, and lost. She became increasingly proud and arrogant, so that even the Queen found her more and more difficult to tolerate. Everybody at court feared her wit. In a single sentence she could demolish a reputation, often only to amuse the King.

In 1675 Athenais suffered a setback and was obliged to retire to Clagny for a while. What happened was that the King's religious scruples got the better of him when Bossuet, the Bishop of Meaux and "keeper of the King's conscience", spoke to him sternly about his continuing adultery. While Athenais languished at Clagny, Louis went off to the wars, but in due course his baser instincts overcame his religious fears. On his return to Versailles, Athenais was recalled and the pair fell indecorously into each other's arms, much to the chagrin of the long-suffering

Queen. After this worrying episode Athenais found herself standing in higher favour than ever.

Athenais had six children of whom four survived – a good record in an age when so many died in infancy. Both she and the King were concerned that Monsieur de Montespan might try to claim the children, for they were legally his as he firmly refused to divorce Athenais. So they were held in the greatest secrecy and smuggled out of court as soon as they were born, to be kept in a nearby house.

When they were old enough to need a governess, Athenais recommended an intelligent young widow named Françoise Scarron whose husband had been a successful playwright, though paralysed from an early age by polio. Madame Scarron gratefully accepted the appointment offered to her, and when the children were older they were brought to court and acknowledged by the King.

Madame Scarron pleased Madame de Montespan so much that the King was continually prevailed upon to make her liberal gifts of money, so much so that by 1675 the governess was able to buy Maintenon, a small estate with a pepper-pot turreted castle which had just come up for sale, and thereafter she called herself Madame de Maintenon. Louis was displeased; he did not like Madame de Maintenon, and he actually lost his temper with Athenais. Of Madame de Maintenon he said, according to a witness, that he could not abide her, but that he was prepared to give her money provided he never saw her or heard her name mentioned. Even so, he considered that far too much had already been done for "that sort of trollop". And yet she was the woman who eventually was to replace Athenais in the King's affections. Meanwhile Athenais, distressed at having vexed the King, continued to plead for her friend. The governess's devotion to the children and her undeniably intelligent teaching slowly lessened the King's aversion to her.

The slow transition of the King's interest from his mistress to the woman who was to supplant her was partly the fault of Athenais's own character, for she was becoming more and more volatile and bad-tempered, and had never really learned to control her mercurial nature. Frequently she directed her fury against the King himself, which was presumptuous, but he minded because he still loved her. Madame de Maintenon used to reproach Athenais for her bad behaviour. Naturally, in gossipy Versailles this was instantly reported to the King.

Gradually Louis fell into the habit of telling Madame de Maintenon what to say to Athenais on his behalf, and then to confiding his sufferings to her and asking her advice. Inevitably Madame de Maintenon became the direct *confidante* and go-between in the King's intimate relations with his mistress, and she was able to turn the situation to her own advantage. For her it was a simple matter to appear calm and wise in contrast to the violent emotional scenes created by Athenais, whose increasing lack of self-discipline was aggravated by her growing jealousy of the governess who was enjoying so much of the King's intimate confidence.

Louis XIV was an indefatigable lover. During the years of Athenais's reign as his mistress he had been interested in many other women and had had a number of transient affairs. Athenais was always furiously jealous and did her best to bring about their downfall. She would create angry scenes with Louis and ridicule his other mistresses with her clever, biting tongue or tell him downright lies about them. The amorous liaisons never lasted for very long, and Louis always came back to Athenais – but at the time when Madame de Maintenon appeared on the scene he was already becoming bored with his temperamental and unpredictable mistress.

To make matters worse, in 1680 a scandalous affair exploded in court circles. While Louis was dallying with Mademoiselle de Fontanges, the latest of his temporary *inamorata*, the activities of a certain Madame de Brinvilliers attracted the attention of the police. Investigations had resulted in her arrest. She was accused of poisoning husbands, brothers and lovers with a free hand and a total lack of conscience. Her trial and subsequent execution were watched with interest by a number of high-born ladies, who hoped that the matter would end there. But police investigations continued, and a further series of arrests followed. The scandalous culmination was an order for the arrest of several fashionable ladies of the court – who promptly made themselves scarce.

It transpired that a middle-aged Parisienne known as La Voisin had been selling poisons to these high-placed ladies. Starting out in her professional life as a beauty specialist, La Voisin had graduated from making skin tonics and rejuvenating creams to love philtres, charms and poisons. In the scandal, La Voisin was one of those arrested and executed, and although she kept her mouth shut her daughter talked freely to the police – and among the names she mentioned was Madame de Montespan. She told the police that Athenais had first visited her mother in 1667, the year when she had accompanied the King on his visit to the army while Louise de la Valliere stayed at home.

Athenais, the witness alleged, had commissioned La Voisin and a fortune teller named Lesage to make spells for her with the object of undermining her rival and winning the King's affection. Black Masses were performed, some of which were intended to procure the death of the unfortunate Louise. Over the years, said La Voisin's daughter, Athenais had also bought aphrodisiacs to put in the King's food and drink, and a selection of poisons including arsenic and sulphur with which she had impregnated Louise's clothes in the hope of destroying her.

A further accusation was that Athenais had consulted a depraved old priest named Guibourg who performed Black Masses on the naked bodies of women, and Guibourg confessed that he had indeed performed a Black Mass for Madame de Montespan and that he had acquired the body of a still-born baby for use in the ritual (rumour had it that Guibourg in fact used living babies and had murdered hundreds in this way). Finally, it was stated that Athenais had impregnated with poison a petition which she had promised to deliver to the King, and had thus even attempted to murder Louis himself.

The King was terribly shocked by these disclosures, unsubstantiated as they were. He was fundamentally pious and God-fearing, but more than that he was only too well aware that it was dangerous in the extreme to have in a position of such power a woman thought capable of such hideous acts. And as for the allegation of love philtres and aphrodisiacs – whether true or not, no doubt he equated them with his too frequent headaches and his sleeplessness.

Even so, Louis had the evidence against his favourite suppressed. But he never felt quite the same about her. His boredom and antipathy increased, encouraged by the prissy Madame de Maintenon and his confessor, Père de la Chaise. More and more he indulged in long and serious discussions with Madame de Maintenon and reached the conclusion that she took better care of his children than did Athenais. It did not take Madame de Maintenon long to evaluate the King's growing interest in herself, and she began to behave extremely badly to her benefactor who had rescued her from poverty and introduced her to court circles. Whenever the opportunity presented itself she snubbed and humiliated Athenais and sought to usurp her place. As time went by it was to Madame de Maintenon that the King turned for relaxation as well as for sensible advice.

Athenais was only too well aware of what was happening, but she hung grimly on. Nobody dared point out to her that she was no longer wanted when even the King himself flinched at the task. It was the Bishop of Meaux who finally persuaded Louis to deal the final blow, by convincing him that he should give up his adulterous practices for the sake of his immortal soul. Athenais was still installed at Versailles and the King continued to visit her each day – but between mass and dinner so that he could not stay for very long. At the same time Louis spent many hours in the apartment of Madame de Maintenon, the former governess who was not yet his mistress but in whose apartment all the affairs of court and state were discussed.

It was the eldest son of Athenais, the Duc de Maine, who brutally pointed out to her that she was no longer needed at court, and that the King was too polite to tell her that she was now merely an embarrassment to himself and the erst-

while governess. Athenais retired from the court (says the
Duc de Saint-Simon, a chronicler of the time) on a storm
of tears. She never forgave her son, who found his reward,
perhaps, in the grateful devotion which Madame de Maintenon thereafter accorded him.

For a long time Athenais could not reconcile herself to
her fate, but after much restless travelling she finally settled
down in her own house to an actively Christian life. Her
prayers and penances increased day by day. Nevertheless,
she continued to live in the regal manner of her days at
court. All society called on her, for somehow it was *de
rigueur* to do so, and in fact she held her own private court,
yielding not an inch of precedence and only permitting
such visitors as the King's brother or sister to sit on chairs
in her presence. Others had to make do with stools, as at
Versailles. She remained attractive and witty, and always
hoped that one day her rival would die and that she would
be summoned back to court – but it was not to be.

In fact, Madame de Maintenon actually managed to persuade the King to marry her. The Queen had died, and by
resisting his amorous advances Madame de Maintenon left
him with no choice but marriage. In any case he had sworn
to give up mistresses, yet he could not do without women.
Even when he was seventy and she seventy-four the King
continued to make his sexual demands, sometimes twice a
day, to Madame de Maintenon's annoyance.

While Athenais hoped to outlive her rival, she also feared
her own death, even though she was a remarkably healthy
woman. Saint-Simon records that as the years wore on she
gave away much of her property to the poor and insisted
on working in their service sewing rough shirts, and so on.
So afraid of death did she become that she slept in her huge
bed with the curtains open, surrounded by lighted candles
and hired watchers, for if she awoke in the night she liked
to find herself with company.

On the night of 27 May, 1707, at the age of 67, she awoke
feeling so ill, choking and congested that friends who were
staying with her gave her an emetic. The effects were so
alarming that they promptly gave antidotes, and it was

probably this drastic treatment which precipitated her death. In those days one needed an iron constitution to survive the traditional medical cure-alls – bleeding, purging and emetics. Athenais died soon after her "treatment", consoled by a confessor and the last rites of the Church. Her children – all save the Duc de Maine who, according to Saint-Simon, was overjoyed to be at last rid of an embarrassment – were consumed with grief. Perhaps they too had hoped to see their mother restored to the court.

Even Madame de Maintenon suffered from remorse for the vicious way in which she had treated her former benefactor. Indeed, so upset was she that she had to retreat to her *chaise-percée*, the only place in crowded Versailles where she could find a little privacy; even there, however, she was pursued by the Duchesse de Bourgogne, daughter-in-law of the King, who later gleefully expressed to the whole court her astonishment at the spectacle of Madame de Maintenon's grief.

The King himself appeared totally insensible and unconcerned. When the inquisitive Duchesse de Bourgogne expressed her surprise to him he replied calmly that when he had sent Athenais away he had never expected to see her again – and thus she had already been dead to him.

The constant companion of Hitler's hours of leisure was a round-faced, blue eyed blonde. Hitler rewarded her loyalty with marriage, which was solemnized to the thunder of the approaching Russian guns in the bunker of the Reich Chancellery before their deaths by suicide. The photo from Eva Braun's album (*below*) shows them together at an earlier, happier time. – The gentle and patriotic Polish Countess Marie Walewska (*left*) had been married off to a rich man in his seventies when Napoleon's visit to Poland changed the course of her life. She surrendered to the passionate Emperor after his promise, "Your country will be even dearer to me if you could take pity on my poor heart".

Cleopatra pleading Egypt's and her own interests before Caesar, by an unknown French painter (*above*). – Gabrielle d'Estrées (*right*) and Henri IV felt a deep and lasting love for each other. The portrait of her in her bath (*left*) is a French painting of the sixteenth century. Robert Cecil, the English Ambassador reported that she was "stout but really pleasant and gracious".

Chapter 4 The Concubine who ruled China

Orchid was the name given to a baby girl who was born to the wife of an obscure Manchu official in China in 1835. Although her parents could not have predicted it at the time, this humble child was destined to become Empress of all China via the beds of the Manchu rulers. When her father died Orchid and her mother went to Peking to live with their relations, the Muyanga family. There, some years later, when she became of nubile age, Orchid became betrothed to her cousin Jung Lu who was an officer in the Imperial Bannermen, an elite regiment of guards.

Jung Lu for his part fell deeply in love with Orchid at their first meeting. She had grown into a girl of unusual charm and intelligence, but she also possessed boundless ambition. Although her life up to that point had followed a conventional pattern, the marriage was never to take place, for Orchid's fate was to become an Imperial concubine.

China at that time was ruled by the Manchus, who had

C

overthrown the Ming dynasty some 200 years earlier. The occupant of the Dragon Throne and ruler of China was a young man named Hsien Feng – a weak character of poor physique, thoroughly debauched by the eunuchs in accordance with tradition. The dynastic rulers took their sex seriously. The eunuchs were the only men allowed within the precincts of the incredible Forbidden City, a vast and fabulous treasure house protected by walls four feet thick. For generations the eunuchs had wielded power over their Emperors by initiating them and exercising them in all the forms and arts of vice and debauchery. Hsien Feng had been an easy and vulnerable prey, but his health had been ruined by his excesses.

Feng was a widower. His Empress, an elder sister of one of Orchid's Muyanga cousins, had recently died, and so an edict was issued by the Dowager Empress, Feng's mother, ordering district officials to despatch to the Forbidden City comprehensive lists of suitable Manchu girls from which she would select concubines for her son. After casting and consulting the all-important horoscopes of the candidates, sixteen girls were "short-listed" and summoned to the Forbidden City so that the Emperor and his mother might inspect and interview them.

Among the fortunate girls thus invited to the Imperial tea party were Orchid and her cousin Sakota – the latter a reserved and rather dull girl, although the Emperor is said to have paid her alone the highest attention and honour. In the event, both Sakota and Orchid were among the girls chosen to join the Imperial harem. Sakota was appointed a concubine of the second rank, and 16-year-old Orchid a third-rank concubine. Inevitably this promotion meant that Orchid's engagement to her fiancé Jung Lu was automatically nullified, and that she would spend the rest of her life in the distinguished seclusion of the Imperial harem.

Orchid, although in love with Jung Lu, was already ruled by her head rather than her heart. She accepted her destiny with equanimity and was shrewd enough to realize the importance of winning the favour of the all-powerful Chief Eunuch. This she set out to do with commendable success.

But nearly four years went by before she was summoned from the harem, bedecked with jewellery, to be escorted and laid naked at the foot of the Emperor's bed to await his pleasure.

In this sense she got off to a late start, for her cousin Sakota had already achieved the desirable state of pregnancy and had been elevated to the rank of Empress Consort. Unfortunately she gave birth to a sickly girl who soon died. Orchid did better; when in 1856 she produced a healthy son she was raised to the first rank and known as the Yi (meaning "feminine virtue") Concubine. Malevolent gossip of the day alleged that the 25-year-old Emperor, half paralysed from a decade of debauched living was probably impotent and that the real father was Jung Lu, whose assignations with the Yi Concubine had been arranged by the co-operative Chief Eunuch.

Nevertheless, the birth of this son put Orchid into a position of power and influence. The Emperor quickly discovered that she possessed a natural flair for politics and was avidly interested in affairs of state. Before long she found herself permitted to read confidential diplomatic papers and advising the Emperor on questions of policy.

At that time China was involved in a great deal of trouble with the French and British, the legacy of some fifty years of dispute, strife and occasional armed conflict – including the infamous Opium War of 1839 – based on the question of foreign trading agreements. In 1858, as the result of another war, the Manchus were forced to sign a number of treaties which gave the British and French certain trading and diplomatic rights. It was the view of the Chinese rulers, however, led by Hsien Feng and the Yi Concubine, that the agreements had been made under duress, and therefore they refused to honour them. Inevitably there was further trouble, and when the "foreign devils" sent an embassy under a flag of truce to negotiate with the Emperor, the envoys were seized and tortured by the Chinese who neither knew nor cared about the rules and conventions of honourable warfare.

Such an atrocity clearly demanded retaliation. With brisk despatch British and French troops advanced swiftly on

Peking. The Emperor and his Ministers took fright and, against all the advice of the Yi Concubine, left Peking hurriedly on what was face-savingly described as "a tour of inspection of the realm". In a panic-stricken and disorderly rout the Court fled to Jehol, leaving Prince Kung, the Emperor's brother, in Peking to deal with the foreign devils.

At Jehol the Emperor fell ill and it became apparent that he might die. Certainly his jaded sexual appetite failed completely, so that he was no longer moved by his favourite's charms and in consequence Orchid's influence declined. His assistant secretary was a man named Su Shun who, before the emergence of the Yi Concubine, had wielded great power over the Emperor. Now he saw his chance to overthrow her and so became her implacable enemy. The Emperor's health deteriorated and so did Orchid's status in the court – for the four months preceding his death she was refused audience with him at all.

The jockeying for position and power became more intense and cunning. Su Shen and his fellow conspirators removed the young prince, Orchid's son, to the care of one of their wives, and persuaded the dying Emperor to sign an edict proclaiming themselves as Regents to the prince, and also to order the imprisonment of the Emperor's brothers. What they had overlooked, however, was Orchid's longstanding friendship with the eunuchs. One of them had stolen the Imperial seal and given it to her, and without the seal no edict was legally valid.

All the conspirators could do was to hope for the best, but after the Emperor's death it was clear to them that the greatest threat to the success of their plot was Orchid herself, and so they decided to murder her on the return journey to Peking with the funeral cortege. The procession, a pageant of colour, pomp and ceremony, progressed at snail's pace, and protocol demanded that the self-appointed but illegal Regents accompanied it. Orchid and Sakota, in accordance with Chinese custom, had been proclaimed Western Empress and Eastern Empress respectively, the names referring to the palaces in which they lived, and they rode ahead of the procession. In theory assassination should have been simple, but Jung Lu, now head of the Imperial Guard and escorting the funeral cortège had his own suspicions. He galloped off with his men to surround and protect the palankeen bearing the Western Empress and so thwarted the attempt at murder.

In such a manner the two Empresses returned to Peking and won the active support of the Emperor's brothers, who were in danger of imprisonment under the illegal edict of the Regents. It was uncompromising political defeat for the would-be Regents, for the Western Empress simply issued further edicts bearing the full authority of the Imperial seal, in her son's name. She appointed herself and Sakota as Regents and, with more humanity than perhaps was justified, merely stripped the conspirators of their rank, titles and fortunes.

An uneasy peace had been agreed with the "foreign devils" who, as part of their reprisal, had utterly sacked the beautiful Summer Palace of the Emperor. Prince Kung had negotiated a new treaty with the British and the French; although its terms were harsh, he had recognized that foreign aid would be essential if the Manchu dynasty was to survive. Nevertheless violent incidents, particularly involving foreign missionaries, were to continue for many years, and the mere presence of foreigners in China was to be a cause of constant conflict.

Once in power as mother of the young Emperor, Orchid, the Western Empress, became known as Tzu Hsi, and she dealt competently with the many problems of administration and affairs of state, though not without intrigue and opposition. As her son, Tung Chih, grew up and reached maturity he followed tradition in his dissolute search for pleasure in the brothels and opium dens of Peking – with the inevitable adverse effect upon his health. His mother made no effort to restrain these activities, so that Tung Chih became gradually more independent and self-indulgent.

It was only when the time came for the young Emperor to take a wife and concubines that Tzu Hsi made any attempt to regain her ascendancy over him by seeking to provide him with a wife of her own choice. But the bride eventually chosen by Tung Chih was a girl selected by the Eastern Empress, and Tzu Hsi's power and influence was therefore in serious danger.

This setback was of short duration, however, for very soon the Emperor contracted smallpox in its most virulent form and died. This, it was suggested, may have been contrived by his unscrupulous mother with the assistance of a eunuch, because she saw in her uncompliant son a threat to her own status and security. The young Empress Consort was pregnant, but it was not possible to await the birth of her child in order to determine the succession, for by law the Dragon Throne could not remain unoccupied. A new struggle for power was unleashed to fill the monarchical vacuum, and this was a situation which Tzu Hsi, with her shrewdness and subtlety, could exploit to her own advantage.

The two Dowager Empresses and Prince Kung all put forward their own favoured candidates. Tzu Hsi's protégé was a child of four years of age, the son of her sister who had married a younger brother of Hsien Feng and was therefore a first cousin of the dead Tung Chih. His name was Kuang Hsu, and by all the laws and customs of lineal descent in China he was ineligible since the succeeding monarch, in order to be able to perform the necessary rites for the dead Emperor, was required to be of a younger generation than the last. Tzu Hsi overcame this particular hurdle in a pragmatic fashion by emphasizing that as soon as the young Kuang Hsu had fathered a son, Tung Chih would automatically be provided with a rightful heir. Until this time, according to Manchu beliefs, the soul of the unfortunate Tung Chih would exist desolately in a kind of limbo.

The dominating power and personality of the Western Empress, backed by the dedicated support of her favourite eunuchs and of Jung Lu and his guards, was such that her opponents had to capitulate in the end. Kuang Hsu was accepted as the infant Emperor, and Tzu Hsi's power and influence was restored and assured – and even further reinforced when the young Empress, still awaiting the birth of her child, committed suicide, perhaps because she felt usurped or more probably due to further devious machinations by Tzu Hsi.

But hers was not the only suicide. Tzu Hsi's arrogant action in thrusting aside old traditions shocked the Chinese nation and drove one important member of the mandarinate to hang himself after publishing a protest condemning the Empress's activities. This second major suicide shook the people and even disturbed the conscience of the superstitious Tzu Hsi herself. Severely practical though she was, she secretly believed that all the disasters which later befell China could be traced to the wrath of the gods on behalf of the slighted ghost of the late Emperor Tung Chih.

However, for a long time Tzu Hsi was able to wield her power undisturbed. On the evidence she became more and more single-minded and ruthless. When she reached the age of 45 she learned that her lifelong lover Jung Lu was having an affair with a court lady, so she immediately exiled him by putting him in command of a far-distant military post. Some time later the Eastern Empress made a number of serious complaints about Li Lien-ying, the Chief Eunuch, and so incurred Tzu Hsi's lethal wrath – at least, it was certainly lethal in that the Eastern Empress died under mysterious circumstances shortly afterwards. The only remaining opposition lay in the person of Prince Kung, her onetime ally, and although he did not die, she succeeded in displacing him from his various official positions until finally he was forced to retire from public life altogether.

Having thus disposed of her principal rivals, Tzu Hsi then turned her attention to the young Emperor, Kuang Hsu, who was nearing marriageable age. She had no great affection for her nephew and sought to ensure her power over him by marrying him to her niece – even though the two cousins hated each other. The Empress also knew that a genital defect would preclude the Emperor from ever conceiving a child. Nevertheless, when at the age of nineteen Kuang Hsu became Emperor in fact as well as in name, Tzu Hsi had no alternative politically but to retire to the rebuilt Summer Palace.

The Empress was now 54 years old, but far from thoughts of relinquishing power, to which she had become accustomed. Her years of dominance and intrigue had established her securely in a position of authority which she had no wish to abdicate. She had a love-hate relationship with her people. She was simultaneously feared and venerated, and none dare gainsay her. The extravagance and vice that she had permitted, – indeed, encouraged at her courts, her long clandestine association with Jung Lu, and rumours of the sinister ways in which she had disposed of her rivals were common gossip among the masses, but the people of China nevertheless loved her. It was a superstitious nation; when, in the matter of rain-making, her intercessions with the gods were inundatingly successful, she was given the half-affectionate and half-reverent nickname of "Old Buddha". She was known by this name for the rest of her life.

At her beautiful and beloved Summer Palace life became more and more a matter of amusement and self-indulgence, with diversions such as amateur theatricals, water picnics and gardening. She spent vast sums of money on her own personal pleasures, much of which was misappropriated from Admiralty funds with the assistance of the Chief Eunuch, still her loyal friend and aide. This was partly responsible for the disastrous results when China was soundly beaten in the war with Japan which broke out in 1894.

Old Buddha's life, however, was by no means all pleasure, and she continued to take an active part in politics. Even the Emperor Kuang Hsu was obliged to make frequent visits to the Summer Palace to report to her and receive counsel on state affairs, while the young Empress kept her Imperial Aunt well informed of all his activities.

Times were changing, as they do, inexorably. While Old Buddha was a confirmed reactionary imbued with the ritual conventions, laws and customs of her honourable ancestors, Emperor Kuang Hsu was beginning to realize the need for reform, and even trying to introduce into his country some of the ideas borrowed from the much hated foreign devils who lived, worked and preached in their midst. But in these enlightened efforts he was continually thwarted by Old Buddha.

Obsessed by this problem, he decided to make a bid for absolute power. It was the only way in which he could hope to restrain her activities and political interference. Unfortunately, his plot was naive and foolish in the extreme. He sent one of his supporters to Jung Lu who, now returned to favour, had been made Viceroy of the province of Chihli. The envoy had orders to restrain Jung Lu by force, and kill him if necessary; but the important thing was to bring back the crack foreign-trained regiments stationed in the province. They would then be deployed around the Summer Palace, so putting his "Imperial Mother" under indefinite house arrest while he pressed on with his programme of social reform.

The Emperor was too optimistic. He over-rated his envoy and under-rated his Imperial Mother. On arrival at Chihli the Emperor's envoy, no doubt fearful for his own life as the result of the consequences of this brash scheme, reported the entire plot directly to Jung Lu himself. He in turn hurried to Old Buddha, his life-long girl friend to whom he was still loyal and told her all. The wrath of Her Imperial Majesty was beyond description, and she set forth with great pomp and circumstance and a tremendous entourage for the Forbidden City and the wretched Emperor.

Kuang Hsu was utterly demoralized when he learned that his plans had been betrayed, and that he was considered of having committed what, to the Chinese, is the most heinous of all crimes – raising his hand against the Holy Mother and his Honourable Ancestors. With typical oriental fatalism he made no attempt to escape his punishment. When Old Buddha arrived in all her majesty he crouched humbly before her. In a sense she was merciful. She spared his life, but ordered him to abdicate the Dragon Throne, and returned herself to supreme power. And to prove her earnestness she also ordered his imprisonment.

The imprisonment took the form of house arrest. The Emperor was confined to four tiny and rather dreary rooms in the Winter Palace where Old Buddha could keep an eye on him. His death would probably have followed quite quickly – from natural causes, no doubt! – had it not been for the unprecedented degree of alarm and despondency displayed by certain protesting high officials and, more annoyingly, the heads of the main foreign legations in Peking. Kuang Hsu was allowed to live, and Old Buddha took it upon herself to deal with the heads of the reform movement and seize the reins of government again. From time to time, when necessary at social or official functions, the imprisoned Emperor was produced to satisfy protocol.

Old Buddha was now 63, and slowly her intuition and cunning seemed to be deserting her. Even her favourite advisers were proving to be reactionaries. One of them was Prince Tuan, a first cousin of Emperors Tung Chih and Kuang Hsu, and it was this Prince's son which Old Buddha, at last redeeming her promise to provide an heir for Tung Chih, appointed as heir apparent to the Emperor. It was an unfortunate choice, for the young man soon turned out to be a trouble-making layabout and a rampant lecher.

This was bad enough, but Old Buddha was burdened with more serious problems involving politics. One of the most important and ominous concerned the secret society known as the Boxers which was rapidly growing in strength and beginning to direct its energies against the hated foreign devils dwelling and trading in China. Old Buddha who also hated foreigners hardly lifted a finger to restrain the activities of the Boxers. Throughout China the score of isolated incidents of violence gathered pace and heat to culminate, in 1900, in the Boxer rebellion.

The story of the rebellion is known well enough. Foreigners were tortured and murdered, and thousands of Chinese Christians were put to death. Amid scenes of bloody butchery in Peking, the city was set on fire. One by one the legations were burnt down until the foreigners were besieged in the British legation. During this crisis Old Buddha, hoping that the Boxers might be successful in driving out the foreign devils and yet not daring to be too openly on their side, pursued a vacillating, double-edged policy while Jung Lu, more in touch with the realities of the insurrection, constantly urged moderation to her.

After several weeks foreign troops came to the aid of the besieged legation and marched in force into Peking. Old Buddha's pride and arrogance deserted her. She disguised herself as a peasant woman and fled the city. But first she ordered the Emperor to accompany her, against his will and better judgment. When his favourite, the Pearl Concubine, the only woman Kuang Hsu had really ever loved, begged her to allow him to remain in Peking, the Empress ordered the wretched young woman to be thrown into a well. Then she set off with the Emperor and Empress and a handful of courtiers in three common travelling carts. A month later Old Buddha set up her court again at Sianfu in the province of Shensi, well out of reach of her vindictive foreign enemies in Peking, though still in their power and obliged to comply with their victorious demands.

The foreign devils were uncompromising in their requirements. They insisted that severe penalties should be imposed on the Boxer faction at court. Old Buddha had no alternative but to obey. Prince Tuan and several other prominent leaders were exiled, dishonoured or executed, and Prince Tuan's son was disinherited as Emperor-elect. She herself stayed well away from Peking until the military situation had settled down and new treaties had been signed. Then, choosing her moment with her usual intuitive sense of good timing, she returned, with the greatest possible pomp and panoply, in triumph to Peking and succeeded by her charm and magnetic personality in completely disarming her former enemies.

One of her first tasks was to repair the palaces which, to her intense anger, had been considerably damaged and looted by foreign troops. That done, she settled down with unimpaired vitality to several more years of active rule. For the first time she travelled throughout the length and breadth of her own kingdom – something which protocol had never before permitted her to do. And once more she was able to hold her sumptuous water picnics and her private theatricals in the beautifully restored gardens of the Summer Palace. It was as if the clock had been turned back and the violent years had never been – but time was advancing remorselessly just the same.

One day, to her great sorrow, her faithful and apparently only love, Jung Lu, died. He was buried with full national honours. Seven years later, in 1908, the feeble Emperor Kuang Hsu became very ill. For the past decade he had been retained in the Dowager Empress's personal entourage, a mere puppet, broken in spirit and health. As he grew weaker, even Old Buddha relented slightly and allowed him to forgo some of the exhausting physical ritual of the court such as the "kotow".

When it became clear that Kuang Hsu was dying, Old Buddha informed her statesmen that she had chosen a new Emperor to succeed him: the infant son of Jung Lu's daughter and one of the Imperial Princes. Old Buddha herself was now ailing, and Emperor Kuang Hsu's death when it occurred was suspected by many to have been expedited by the old Empress herself in her determination to outlive him and thus ensure the continuing supremacy and political domination of her own relations.

And then, finally, Old Buddha herself was suddenly taken ill and died within a few hours. But with her usual shrewd foresight she had first issued edicts designed to further the interests of her own kinsfolk. She was the last great ruler in the tradition of ancient China, and with her died an epoch of culture and history. China was destined never to be the same again.

Like China itself, she was a subtle combination of charm, culture, benevolence, cruelty and fantasy, divorced from, yet dependent on, the outside world with its foreign devils – and perhaps the same behaviour pattern is true today, for even the new China is to some extent based upon and conditioned by the ancient conventions and rituals of its ancestry.

The funeral ceremony of Old Buddha, who started life as plain and humble Orchid, was as spectacular and impressive as she herself would have wished. At vast expense she was buried in the costly mausoleum built for her many years before by her faithful Jung Lu.

Chapter 5 The Führer's Plaything

Adolf Hitler, the Führer of the Third Reich, was a man who seemed to have as little luck with women as he had with war. The first and perhaps the only true love of his life was his niece, Geli Raubal, who with her mother and sister formed part of Hitler's household for several years. Although she was twenty years younger than him, his infatuation for her was possessive and extremely jealous. He kept her strictly under his eye, refusing to allow her any personal life of her own, and on one occasion he became incensed when he believed that she had allowed his chauffeur, an old friend of the family, to make love to her.

Geli for her part was said to be secretly in love with another man who lived in Vienna. Whether it was for this reason or because she could not abide Hitler's emotional tyranny is not precisely known, but in September 1931 she killed herself. Only a few hours earlier she had said goodbye to Hitler when he left Munich for Hamburg; at that time she had seemed quite normal and contented, and she left no letter to indicate the motivation for her suicide.

To Hitler her death was a staggering blow. For days he was in such a state of despair that his friends seriously thought that he might take his own life too. He recovered from the shock very slowly, but he never forgot Geli; he ordered that her room should be kept exactly as it was and that flowers should be placed before her portrait on the anniversary of her birthday and death. It was almost certainly the traumatic experience of Geli's suicide which influenced his behaviour in his relationship with Eva Braun a few months later.

Eva was the second of three daughters of Fritz Braun, a master craftsman of Simbach, a town on the other side of the River Inn from Hitler's own birthplace, Braunau. She was a pretty, round-faced, blue-eyed blonde, not over-endowed with brains. At the age of nineteen, after taking a commercial course, she took a job with Heinrich Hoffmann who was Hitler's personal friend and official photographer. Hitler had often met Eva in Hoffmann's shop and, as was his custom with women, he paid her gallant compliments, gave her flowers, and from time to time invited her on social outings. Even so, it is unlikely that he gave any serious thought to the girl; she, however, in her empty-headed way, developed an obsessive hero-worship for him.

At this time Hitler was 43 years old, and the shining hope of the Nazi party in Germany. He was certainly the most powerful political leader of the post-war years, and, indeed, in the following year he became the Reich Chancellor. To 21-year-old Eva Braun he was a figure of glamour, and she indulged her daydreams to the extent of telling her friends that Hitler was in love with her and wanted to marry her. If her dreams eventually came true it was under circumstances which she could never have foreseen nor consciously desired. Hitler for his part paid no more attention to her than he did to the other women with whom he associated; he liked women and was very much at ease in their company. Eva, resenting his attitude, decided on a melodramatic gesture. In the summer of 1932 she attempted to kill herself because (she said) of his indifference towards her.

Hitler was considerably upset by this second suicide episode so soon after the first. In compensation he visited Eva's
bedside to comfort her and reassure her of his devotion and
made a point of spending more time with her. When she
had recovered, Eva and her mother moved into a small
house close to Hitler's, and he began to associate with her
and take her about with him with increasing frequency. In
due course she moved into Hitler's home. Heinrich Hoffmann
put on record that she became "the constant companion
of his leisure hours", and that "Eva became his mistress
some time or other before the end . . . but when, neither I
nor anyone else can say". There seems little doubt that to
Hitler Eva was a decorative plaything of whom he was
very fond and for whom he felt responsible, but it was
probably proximity rather than love which brought about
their closer and more intimate relationship. It was Freud
who said that love is "90 per cent association".

On the whole Eva kept discreetly in the background and
was never seen publicly in Hitler's company in Munich, or
later in Berlin. When official functions, receptions and
dinners were being held in Hitler's home she tactfully remained out of sight in her own room. The Führer's im-
maculate reputation had to be preserved at all costs, and it
was only after Eva's sister married Fegelein, Himmler's personal representative with Hitler, that she was permitted to
appear in public – as Frau Fegelein's sister.

At the Berghof, however – Hitler's country home high in
the mountains above Berchtesgaden – Eva lived a more
normal life. She joined Hitler there whenever he was in residence and slowly she took over the running of the household. This led to resentment and difficult relations with Frau
Raubal, the mother of the dead Geli; she was still keeping
house for Hitler who was her brother, and she regarded Eva
as a common little upstart who was striving to take the
place of her deceased daughter. There were inevitable rows
and recriminations in which Hitler, who in common with
many men disliked being involved in domestic arguments,
refused to take part, and eventually Frau Raubal departed
leaving Eva in charge of the Hitler ménage.

Martin Bormann, who held the influential post of personal secretary to the Führer, controlled the economics of the household and helped the inexperienced and therefore inefficient Eva with the complicated arrangements and protocol for state and social occasions. Bormann, always a tactician, was careful to make himself obliging and even indispensable to Eva, thereby strengthening his own position and status with Hitler – for he was only too well aware that his Führer was extremely sensitive on the subject of Eva.

The girl herself made no pretensions to any intellectual or sophisticated attainments. Her interests in life were simple and superficial – clothes, cinema, sport, animals and sex. She read cheap novels and preferred trashy romantic films, and on these she based her concept of life and living. Hitler was no great shakes as an author, but his single-minded, dedicated and prophetic literary effort, *Mein Kampf*, was in complete contrast to Eva's "woman's magazine" view of life. His determination never to marry caused her constant unhappiness, and she suffered agonies when she learned that he had been in the company of other women. One woman who provoked her into making a number of jealously acid comments was Britain's aristocratic Unity Mitford, daughter of Lord Redesdale, whom Hitler saw as the personification of perfect Germanic womanhood. Hitler was particularly fond of Unity and yet she was another who, when war broke out between Germany and Britain, tried to kill herself – but it was, in fact, at that time that many of Eva's fears were allayed. Hitler became so absorbed in planning and directing the war that he had less and less time to pursue social activities, and so Eva's rivals gradually disappeared from the scene.

Throughout her association with Hitler, Eva longed for the respectability and status of marriage, though it was not until the bitter end when the Third Reich was crumbling in ruins that she was to have her dearest wish fulfilled – for a short time. There is no doubt that as time went by Hitler developed a genuine fondness for Eva although he was well aware that with her petite figure she was not the generously built Aryan beauty of the specification which was his proclaimed ideal. But she was pretty enough, and if she was somewhat shallow-minded, well, the Führer did not care much for intellectual women. In Eva's company he could always be at his ease, cosseted by her unswerving devotion and doglike loyalty.

Eva herself, although admittedly dominated and even tyrannized by Hitler and always subject to his possessiveness and petty jealousies, was not forced into frustration and misery as had been the unfortunate Geli. She smoked heavily, but in secret, and she danced whenever she could do so without alerting him, for Hitler disapproved strongly of both relaxations, but she was always loyal. Indeed, Hitler himself said that the only two who remained faithful to him to the end were Eva Braun and his dog, Blondi.

Over the years Eva developed from an ordinary little shop-girl with a pretty face into a woman of acceptable intelligence and strength of character. Under the stress of the historical events, political and military, with which she was inevitably closely associated, her frivolity and vanity disappeared; she abandoned her earlier romantic daydream in which she had seen herself as a kind of modern Madame de Pompadour, and her character acquired depth and seriousness. Even so, any ambitions she may have had to influence the course of men and events were never realized, for Hitler declined to discuss affairs of state with her and she never even became an active member of the Nazi party.

There was one field in which she was able to exercise influence, however, and that was in the matter of new films for the cinema. When Goebbels arranged for new films to be previewed at the Berghof, he soon discovered that Eva was acting as an amateur film critic with considerable executive influence. It was often as a result of her displeasure at some scene or actor (or actress) that Hitler would order expensive cuts and modifications. Eventually Goebbels stopped sending new films, so that the long-suffering guests at the Berghof had to watch old films over and over again, for they formed a regular part of the entertainment at Hitler's country home. Hoffmann relates that he protested to Goebbels that he was fed up with seeing the same old films. "And I, my friend," retorted Goebbels, "am not in the least interested in hearing critiques of my films from some stupid little flapper."

This biting dismissal of Eva is over-harsh, for although she was far from intellectual or sensitive she was also far from stupid or incompetent. She learned to carry out her role as *Hausfrau* at the Berghof with more than adequate grace and efficiency, and she acted successfully as hostess at all the formal and informal gatherings there. Her own friends and relations were welcome to visit her there, and they often formed part of the many cosy and informal week-end parties.

As the progress of the war became more and more disastrous for the Germans, Hitler became increasingly tense, neurotic and difficult. His frequent rages – which, it has been suggested, could have been a symptom of tertiary syphilis from which some of his biographers have claimed he was suffering – became more violent and irrational. Eva was not antagonized by his tantrums, however, and the evidence is that Hitler always seems to have treated her kindly. While one after another his henchmen and advisers, and even his military commanders, were turning away from him, she never wavered in her devotion to him.

The single-mindedness displayed by Eva is probably the only remarkable feature in the long liaison between this unlikely couple. The image of Eva that is, without exception, presented by those who knew her is of a frivolous and shallow character who was more interested in the ill-cut suits her lord and master wore than in his political activities and planning. Nevertheless, towards the end when it became obvious to everybody – even to Hitler himself – that the Third Reich was tottering and that a violent finale was imminent, she did not hesitate in her decision to share her Führer's fate, however disastrous it might prove to be.

During the key years of 1943 and 1944 when the Russian campaign was going badly, when North Africa had fallen into the hands of the Allies and military strength was being built up for the D-day landings in France, Hitler spent nearly all his time in his headquarters in Berlin, obsessed with tactics and strategy and cursing the enemy – and even cursing some of his own senior officers. Meanwhile Eva remained at the Berghof, though the days so often spent in idle talk and amusements in the country had gone for ever. Hitler rarely went there; instead, according to Goebbels, he had become a recluse. "He never gets out into the fresh air. He does not relax. He sits in his bunker, worries and broods."

More and more Hitler shut himself up in a private megalomaniac world of his own in which he could shut out the unpleasant facts of what was really happening to the party and the régime that he had created. It was, perhaps, only in such a way that he could continue the management of the war that was already lost, though he did not realize it. In this self-imposed deception Martin Bormann did everything possible to pander to his leader, suppressing unwelcome and, indeed, alarming information and quite undermining the efforts of all those, led by Goebbels, who tried to force the Führer to face reality, to comprehend the gravity of Germany's situation and take appropriate action.

But all Hitler's paranoiac delusions could not hold back the flood tide of his advancing enemies. Slowly but inexorably they closed in, from east and west, until they were upon the soil of Germany itself, and the great Nazi empire was shrinking visibly day by day. First the Russians overran Poland and pushed on to threaten Berlin and Vienna. Three months later the British and Americans crossed the Rhine. In a few weeks Hitler's Reich had shrunk to a narrow corridor about one hundred miles wide, and now even he had to face the fact that there was no way of saving it.

It was at this critical time that Eva, of her own volition, decided to go to Berlin. She insisted on staying there, defying Hitler's orders to leave immediately, and she refused to listen to Hoffmann and others who at Hitler's request tried to persuade her to return to the comarative safety of Berchtesgaden. In the event her presence in the bunker seemed to soothe and sometimes even cheer the anguished Führer, and she herself remained perfectly calm and controlled throughout the harrowing days in which the imminent catastrophe loomed ever closer.

"You know better than anyone," she told Hoffmann, "what close ties bind me to Adolf Hitler. What would people say if I deserted him now in his hour of greatest need? No, my friend – where the Führer is concerned I can stand fast to the very end."

What that end was to be had not then been decided. Plans had been made for the government to move south to the Bavarian Alps, to Berchtesgaden itself, the birthplace of the Nazi movement. Many military and administrative departments had already been transferred, and if Hitler and his establishment were to join them while the way was still open then it had to be done quickly, for time was getting short.

On 20 April, 1945, Hitler celebrated his 56th birthday. His plan was to make his departure to Bavaria after the celebration was over – but still he hesitated. At a conference attended by all the top Nazis such as Ribbentrop, Goebbels, Bormann, Speer, Goering, Himmler and the Service chiefs, he ignored their advice to leave at once. Instead, still looking ahead to some infinitely remote and fantastic victory, he ordered the establishment of a Northern and Southern Command in the event that the Allies should cut Germany into two halves, and suggested that he himself might go south to take over that area himself.

Then, the following day, he ordered an all-out attack on the Russians, threatening with death any commander who held back his troops. But the attack never took place, for the next day the Russians broke through the weakening defences in the northern sector of Berlin. Chaos reigned. Nobody could discover what was happening because even field intelligence services had broken down. And in the afternoon of that day – 22 April, 1945 – Hitler held his last famous conference. For three hours he stormed and raged at his staff, denouncing them as incompetent and treacherous cowards. He was utterly determined, he said, not to leave Berlin. Those who wished to escape could go south, but he personally intended to remain in Berlin and to die there if necessary.

Nothing would make him change his mind. In his diary

Koller, the Luftwaffe Chief of Staff, relates what General
Jodl told him of those times. "Hitler declared that he had
decided to stay in Berlin, lead its defence, and then at the
last moment shoot himself. For physical reasons he was
unable to take part in the fighting personally, nor did he
wish to, for he could not run the risk of falling into enemy
hands. We all attempted to bring him over from the decision. His answer was that everything was falling to pieces,
anyway, and that he could do no more. He spoke all the
time of treachery and failure, of corruption in the leadership and the ranks."

Having thus, in effect, abandoned his armies to their fate,
Hitler then arranged for an announcement to be made over
the radio stating that he would remain in Berlin until the
end. Calmer, and probably in a fatalistic and possibly mystical mood, he set about burning his papers. He also invited
Goebbels to join him in the final drama which was to take
place in the underground *Führerbunker*.

The *Führerbunker* was naturally the safest spot of all. It
was the lower of the two storeys of the Chancellory air-raid
shelter, and consisted of a single central passageway with
small rooms on either side. There, fifty feet below ground,
Eva had a "bed-sitter" with dressing room and bathroom,
while Hitler had a study and bedroom. Most of the other
rooms were used for administrative purposes, but two
rooms were reserved for Hitler's personal doctor and another two for Goebbels. On the floor above lived Frau
Goebbels with her six children, adjacent to the dining room,
kitchen and servants' quarters.

In this cramped claustrophobic environment, dominated
and unsettled by the unpredictable personality of the Führer,
fear and hysteria brooded only just below the surface of
the mind. In that steel and concrete hole in the ground
Hitler had been living for many months, and in the few days
that remained before his death he seemed to those who
observed him to be growing ever closer to total insanity.
His moods varied swiftly from raging anger to confident
hope, from wild accusations and charges to vain optimism.
He still did not fully realize that the end had finally come;

he continued to hold conferences, make contingency plans and issue orders and dispositions.

He sent for Greim, the commander of an Air Division, simply to tell him that he had promoted him to command of the Luftwaffe in place of Goering. In order to receive this not entirely welcome news, which could in any case have been delivered quite well by telegram, Greim had to make a very dangerous flight into Berlin with the help of a young woman pilot named Hanna Reitsch. During this pointless journey a number of escorting planes were lost and Greim himself was wounded. Hanna later described Hitler's theatrical and irrational behaviour when he greeted them in the bunker on 24 April. He gave her a vial of poison, telling her that she was privileged to belong to the group of loyal supporters who were to die with him – and in the next breath said he still had hopes of rescue.

It was to Hanna that Eva railed against the members of Hitler's entourage who had fled from Berlin – "the ungrateful swine who had deserted their Führer and should be destroyed". Without doubt Eva had wholeheartedly adopted Hitler's own attitudes; her view was that the only good Germans were those who had remained in the bunker, and that all the others were traitors because they had not elected to stay behind and die with their leader. "Poor, poor Adolf," she wailed, "deserted by everyone, betrayed by all. Better that ten thousand others die than that he should be lost to Germany."

Apart from her indignation on Hitler's behalf, Eva herself remained quite calm during these final days. There were no doubts in her mind and she made it clear that she had no desire to exist without Hitler. While she waited patiently for the Führer to determine the hour and means of her end, she passed the time in changing clothes and making up her face, meanwhile maintaining a cheerful air in the hope of keeping Hitler in good heart.

On 26 April the demoralized and exhausted German armies were fighting street by street in Berlin, inexorably driven back by the Russians who were now barely a mile from the Chancellory. And yet Hitler was still expecting his General in the south to mount the counter-offensive and rescue-operation that he had promised Hanna. Two days later he was radioing demands for information on the progress of his armies in the south. One of these had been wiped out and the other was in full retreat, but it was not until the arrival of a message stating that Himmler was negotiating peace terms that Hitler really accepted that the end had come. He exploded into insane rage and then, abruptly, subsided into a silent stupor. Later, when he had recovered his composure, he ordered Greim and Hanna Reitsch to try to get out of Berlin and arrest Himmler at all costs. They were not to fail, for Hitler was determined that *that* traitor should not succeed himself as Führer.

Then, when Greim and Hanna had gone, Hitler turned his attention to the closing arrangements of his turbulent life. His first decision was that he should reward Eva for her unfailing devotion and loyalty. His continued refusal to marry her over the years had been on the grounds that it might interfere with his career, but that argument was no longer valid. Goebbels was asked to find somebody with the proper civil and legal authority to perform the ceremony, and he produced a municipal councillor who was serving in the German equivalent of the Home Guard.

The marriage was finally solemnized in the map room of the bunker, with Goebbels and Bormann as witnesses. It was a brief enough ceremony which ended with Hitler and Eva Braun swearing that they were both of pure Aryan descent. They then signed the register. Eva began to write her maiden name of Braun, but crossed it out and wrote instead *Eva Hitler, née Braun*. It was the first and last time she ever signed herself by the name which for so many years she had coveted for her own.

Despite the forbidding circumstances the doomed bride and groom then retired to their suite where they were joined by Bormann, Goebbels and his wife, two of Hitler's secretaries, his personal cook and his adjutant. They drank a toast in champagne to the newlyweds and for a while talked quietly of the old days.

While the "celebration" continued, Hitler retired with his

secretary to write his will and his "Political Testament", in which he defended his career, explained his decision to take his life, and made various provisions and recommendations for the future of Germany. The will first spoke of Eva: "Although I did not consider that I could take the responsibility during the years of struggle of contracting a marriage, I have now decided, before the end of my life, to take as my wife the woman who, after many years of faithful friendship, of her own free will entered this town when it was already besieged in order to share my fate. At her own desire she goes to death with me as my wife. This will compensate us for what we have both lost through my work in the service of my people."

He left his possessions to the party or to the state, and his pictures for the establishment of a gallery in his home town of Linz. He then requested his executor, Bormann, to hand over to his relations "and especially my wife's mother and faithful fellow-workers" anything of sentimental value to them, or which they might need to maintain a modest standard of life. Finally he wrote: "I myself and my wife choose to die in order to escape the disgrace of deposition or capitulation. It is our wish to be burned immediately in the place where I have carried out the greater part of my daily work in the course of twelve years of service to my people."

This completed, Hitler settled down to try to rest, while Goebbels set about writing his own political manifesto. In the morning the documents were despatched by messengers to Command Headquarters. Soon afterwards the news arrived of the death of Mussolini and his mistress, Clara Petacci. The details of the final indignity to which their dead bodies were subjected – they were hanged upside down in public – strengthening Hitler's determination to make absolutely sure that nothing similar could possibly happen to himself and Eva.

He made his arrangements with meticulous care. On the morning of 30 April, after his dog Blondi had been destroyed, he lined up his staff in the passage of the bunker and walked slowly along, shaking each one silently by the hand. At this time the Russians had advanced to within two blocks of the Chancellory, but in the last hours of his life Hitler, for once, behaved calmly.

At about two o'clock in the afternoon he lunched with his secretaries and his cook, behaving impassively as though nothing unusual was about to happen. Eva stayed in her room, but she joined him after lunch, and together they again said goodbye to everyone who was still in the bunker. Hitler and his wife returned to their suite and closed the door. Presently a shot was heard. When those waiting outside went into the room they found Hitler lying on the blood-drenched sofa, with Eva by his side. She had swallowed poison; he had shot himself through the mouth.

This at least was the official version of the suicide pact until the Soviet Union recently released from their archives the documentation and autopsy reports which apparently prove that both Eva Braun and Hitler took poison (cyanide) after first trying it out on the dog to test its efficacy. Then, just in case the poison failed to do its lethal job, Hitler arranged to have himself shot as a kind of "coup de grace".

Hitler's detailed instructions for the disposal of their remains were carefully carried out. The two bodies were taken out of the bunker and into the Chancellory garden where, earlier, a shallow depression had been hollowed out. Five cans of petrol lay waiting. The bodies were placed in the shallow grave and inundated with petrol. Hitler's SS adjutant ignited the blaze with a lighted rag. With a roar the flames leaped skywards and, while Russian shells fell constantly on the Chancellory, the small group of mourners withdrew to watch the funeral pyre as the body of Eva burned steadily beside that of the man to whom she dedicated, and finally sacrificed, her life.

Chapter 6 The Girl who defied Napoleon

In the winter of 1806 all Poland – a country which no longer existed politically on the map of Europe – shivered in the icy winds sweeping from Russia and waited hopefully for the arrival of Napoleon, the conqueror who had terrorized the rest of Europe but on whom Poland pinned all hope of national survival and independence. A decade earlier, when France was still absorbed with her own problems arising from the revolution, Russia, Prussia and Austria who for a long time had occupied most of Poland divided up this unhappy land yet once more between them adjusting the portions to which each laid claim and finally swallowing up the last remaining fragment of free Polish territory. The King was deposed and sent into exile in Russia, and the entire country came under the heel of foreigners whom the Poles were powerless to overthrow.

When Napoleon defeated Austria in 1801, entered Berlin in victory five years later, and then marched eastward to where the Prussian and Russian troops were still holding out behind the River Vistula, the Poles saw in him a chance for their country to regain its independence. While they anxiously awaited his arrival, patriotic Poles worked feverishly to whip up support for the French Emperor and his military campaigns. Such was the situation in subjugated Poland that national and political problems and enthusiasms took the place of the normal domestic issues which would concern the people of more settled nations.

Many of the Polish ladies were as politically minded as their men, and among them one of the most ardent patriots was the young woman who was destined to become Countess Marie Walewska, but started life as Marie Laczynski. Her attitude had no doubt been established and conditioned by the circumstances of her childhood, for her family had been virtually ruined by the long years of strife and occupation. As a family the Laczynskis were of the lesser nobility – one-time wealthy landowners whose possessions had gradually been reduced to one estate at Kiernozia which was slowly crumbling under the erosion of time, poverty and debts.

During the war years Matthieu Laczynski had vanished without trace, leaving his wife with six children and the arduous responsibilities of a large estate to attend to. The eldest son had joined Napoleon's army, but he too was constantly in debt. When, therefore, Count Atanase Walewski, a neighbour and a local governor, began to show a marked interest in Marie, the eldest daughter, it seemed like the answer to all problems and prayers.

However, there were serious difficulties. For one thing the wealthy Count was nearly seventy years old; he had been twice widowed and, in fact, his youngest grandchild was ten years older than his prospective bride, sixteen-year-old Marie. For another, Marie was imbued with the romantic ideas natural to her youth, she wanted to marry for love. In this ambition she had the support of her closest friend, a young married woman named Elzbieta Abramowicz who lived in Paris and was anxious for Marie to go and stay with her. But Marie's mother and her brother Teodor, with both eyes on the rich Count, conspired to frustrate these hopes and to keep Marie at home so that Count Walewski could pursue his courtship.

Only too aware of the disadvantages of his age in the eyes of a romantic young girl, the Count enlisted the help of an old friend, the Countess de Vauban. She was a French-woman of some influence and the mistress of the late King of Poland's nephew and heir, the handsome Prince Joseph Poniatowski. To his surprise and dismay Madame Vauban refused to intervene – indeed, she expressed romantic senti-ments that seemed rather out of place on her cynical and experienced lips.

The Count realized that he would have to do his own wooing. Knowing Marie's precocious interest in politics he would spend hours talking to the girl about Poland's future and the potential influence of Napoleon, but whenever he tried to lead the conversation into more personal channels she pretended not to understand his purpose. In the end he was obliged to turn for support to Marie's mother who, he was confident, would listen to him with understanding and sympathy.

Eve Laczynski's understanding was instant and her sym-pathy practical. She promised to do all she possibly could to persuade her daughter to accept the old man. But Marie proved stubbornly intractable and in the end was so upset by the pressure being brought to bear on her that she fell ill and suffered a nervous breakdown. The only person she could bear to have near her was her friend Elzbieta who had left her husband because she could not tolerate his possessive jealousy. Apart from Elzbieta nobody seemed to understand Marie's inner feelings.

Slowly Marie recovered, but still her mother would not relent and was seeking a further convincing argument to beat her daughter's weary spirit into submission. It came when the doctor advised that Marie should be sent to a warmer climate to recuperate. The family's impecunious position made such a convalescence quite impossible, and this was the opportunity Eve had been waiting. Firstly she pointed out to Marie that if she were to marry Count Walewski this problem could easily be solved to the benefit of her health quite apart from the family's fortunes. Marie angrily countered by asking her mother if the family had now lost all sense of honour to sink to such miserable scheming. At this retort Eve also lost her temper – honour, she shouted, was a luxury she could not afford, and she listed all the hardships and privations to which the entire family was being condemned by her daughter's selfishness. Eve's vehemence was too much for Marie; at last, with the listlessness of despair, she agreed to marry Walewski.

And so, in February 1805, the ill-assorted couple were quietly married in the chapel at Kiernozia. Elzbieta, who on the previous night had sent Marie a secret letter offering to help her escape if she wished, formally congratulated her friend in a voice close to tears, for she was sure that the marriage was doomed to failure. Madame de Vauban, to whom Elzbieta had now become companion, also attended the wedding, and her compliments, too, were modified by gloomy forebodings.

In fact, the Count could not have been kinder to his new wife. For their honeymoon they went to Rome, and when Marie took to going off for long expeditions in the company of the Baroness de Staël-Holstein (a lively and entertaining lady to whom Madame de Vauban had given them an introduction) he made no complaint. He paid all the outstanding debts of the Laczynski family and financed the necessary upkeep of the estate. Marie's reaction to her marriage was one of relief, gratitude and pleasant surprise. She enjoyed her honeymoon in Rome, returned to Warsaw in excellent health, and in due course gave birth to a son. The child, however, was weak and puny and Marie rarely saw him, for he was instantly taken over by the numerous female relations who lived in the Walewski household.

Now, with much more idle time on her hands, Marie turned once more to politics. With Elzbieta and a number of other women friends she set up an organization for the dissemination of pro-Napoleonic propaganda. When the news was received that the Emperor Napoleon was marching eastwards and on his way to Warsaw, the excitement was intense. Napoleon's first visit to Warsaw, however, had to be secret, for there were political rifts to be evaluated. Many Poles preferred not to regain the country's independence, and some believed in absolute submission to Russia who, they thought, would be bound to be indulgent for fear that Poland might be annexed by France; others, for motives of personal gain, favoured an alliance with Prussia. So, before he entered Warsaw openly, Napoleon wished to ascertain and consolidate his position.

He called a secret meeting of leading Polish statesmen and set up a provisional government. At the same time he directed the mopping-up operations of his army with such efficiency that the last remaining Russian and Prussian troops were quickly cleared from the area. Marie was bitterly disappointed that her husband, because of his advanced age, was not included in the new government, but her first reaction of disdain soon turned to pity when she observed that the Count was even more disappointed than she was.

Having made his political arrangements Napoleon retired to his headquarters some distance outside the city and announced that he would enter Warsaw formally on 1 January, 1807, when the citizens would be able to greet him in proper style. But Marie and Elzbieta, carried away by patriotic fervour, made their own personal plans to greet the conquerors. Very early on the morning of 1 January they met secretly at the house of a servant from whom they borrowed cheap cloaks and a dilapidated cart. Thus they travelled to the village of Bronie, the final halt before Warsaw, where Napoleon was due to change the horses of the Imperial carriage just before entering the city.

When they reached the village the Emperor was already there. A large and excited crowd clamoured round the coach in which Napoleon was sitting, grim and unheeding, accompanied by Duroc, the Grand Marshal of the Palace. Napoleon ignored the cheers of the crowd, the salutes of the Polish soldiers and even the Polish national anthem – he only wanted to get the tedious journey over.

It was Duroc who first noticed the two pretty young women frantically struggling to push their way through the mob. He stood up to see what was happening, at which Marie called out excitedly to him. Duroc descended from the coach and gallantly helped her through the crowd towards the Emperor. Elzbieta, less impulsive than the eighteen-year-old Marie, remained in the background as her friend, completely forgetting the adulatory speech of welcome she had prepared for her hero, stammered out a few incoherent sentences of welcome and gratitude that came from her heart rather than her head. Napoleon stared at her in astonishment, and then doffed his hat, for she was clearly a lady of rank despite her clothes. Her flushed and eager face with its big blue eyes under a tangled mass of fair hair was appealing and, indeed, beautiful. Although well accustomed to such outbursts, Napoleon was nevertheless touched and delighted – but he forgot to ask the girl her name.

The Emperor duly made his ceremonial entry into Warsaw and was installed in the Royal Castle. All hastened to do honour to him, including Prince Poniatowski who had been given an important post in the provisional government. The Prince found himself in a somewhat difficult position; more Austrian than Pole by birth, and hostile to France by upbringing, the recent hope of achieving his country's independence reminded him that he was, after all, Polish, and he had now turned wholeheartedly to Napoleon's support. Nevertheless, it was important that he should not only prove his honesty and integrity to the people who were inclined to mistrust him, but also gain the personal friendship of Napoleon, if possible.

When Duroc told the Prince about the mysterious young woman who had pushed through the crowd at the relay post, and to whom the Emperor had been so attracted, he briefed his spies to identify and locate her. Some time went by, however, before his enquiries proved successful, and it was probably Elzbieta who gave away her friend's secret, on hearing of the search for the unnamed beautiful girl. Prince Poniatowski promptly arranged a lavish ball in Napoleon's honour to which he invited Count Walewski and his Countess.

Marie, in her volatile way, flatly refused to go anywhere near the ball, and it required considerable persuasion by her husband, Elzbieta and Madame de Vauban, not to mention the Prince himself who saw his little image-building plot in jeopardy, before she finally assented to attend the ball with the Count. There, at a suitable moment, Prince Poniatowski introduced her to the Emperor. To her confusion and dismay Napoleon, who had been told of her reluctance to come to the ball, fiercely demanded what the devil she meant by such behaviour, why she had acted thus after taking so much trouble to address him at the relay post in the village of Bronie, and why she had gone there, anyway, in the first place. It was a typical Napoleonic verbal attack – frontal and flanking. Marie was utterly taken aback by such a barrage of direct questions and found herself unable to think of any coherent answers, for, of course, her behaviour had been motivated by whims and they were difficult to explain in logical terms.

Having launched the assault, Napoleon's manner softened; nobody could remain impatient with Marie for long. She was small, dainty and gentle, her disposition apparently yielding (once you had overcome the initial stubborn barriers), and with her graceful manner and soft attractive voice she could disarm anybody. She was a charmer, as Napoleon discovered when he hastened to reassure her in apologetic terms. He said he would see her again the next day – and then, before she could reply, ordered Durec to have her sent home in one of his personal carriages. The Emperor Napoleon had fallen in love.

Naturally, the brief and rather terse encounter between Napoleon and the Countess had been covertly observed by many curious eyes, and the next morning, when Marie awoke, it was to find Elzbieta and Madame de Vauban already in the house – and a note for her from Napoleon accompanied by a large bouquet of flowers. Marie found the note alarming. "I had eyes only for you," The Emperor had written, "I admire only you and I desire only you. Send an answer immediately in order that the fire consuming me may be appeased."

The Girl who defied Napoleon

If Marie was flattered it was not apparent. She appeared
to be very indignant and upset. And, to the shocked horror
of her friends, she insisted on showing the note to her husband. He would probably have preferred not to have seen
it, and certainly seemed unable to cope with this formidable
turn of events, for Napoleon was not a man to be trifled
with. Elzbieta and Madame de Vauban, fascinated by the
affair, insisted that it was perfectly normal for a French-
man to write in such an amorous fashion and urged her
to acquiesce. Since it was Marie alone who had been invited to dine with the Emperor that night the Count had
little alternative but to give his assent.

The dinner, arranged by Prince Poniatowski's sister, was
a nightmare for Marie. Napoleon observed protocol and
went through the conventional social actions and formulae,
talking to the company at large, but his eyes hardly ever
left Marie. By now she was aware that everybody seemed
to be joined in a conspiracy to procure her for the Emperor,
and she felt angry, afraid and powerless. The next morning
another note arrived from her would-be Imperial lover:
"Have I displeased you? Your interest seems to lessen as
mine increases. Vouchsafe a little joy, a little happiness
to the poor heart that is ready to worship you." But again
Marie remained defiant and sent no answer to the man who
was used to women responding to his slightest nod.

The situation to Prince Poniatowski was nothing short of
alarming – that a Polish girl should ignore and reject the
Emperor Napoleon, particularly when he himself had
traced her and introduced her to him! The political ramifications did not bear thinking about. Two days later the
Prince and some colleagues in the government called on
Countess Maria at her home and begged her to use her
influence with the Emperor on behalf of Poland. They
stressed that the Emperor would listen to her with attention,
and that so far as he had not been so indulgent as they had
hoped towards their concept of a free and independent Pol-
and. If Marie were to sacrifice herself to the desires of this
man it would be a noble sacrifice for her country, such as a
man might make on the field of battle – if not quite in the

D

same way! Immediately on top of this appeal came another letter from Napoleon. This time he wrote of the heavy burden of his high position which could be so much relieved by her presence, and added shrewdly: "Your country will be even dearer to me if you could take pity on my poor heart."

Marie surrendered. Late that same evening she presented herself as instructed at a side door of the Royal Castle and was escorted to Napoleon, much to everybody's relief. For several days Napoleon had been brooding in frustration, continually pacing about and refusing to attend to business. He greeted her with unrestrained eagerness, but she was still afraid and reluctant. During most of the three hours she spent with him she was in tears. With immense patience Napoleon restored her calm, and she discovered that the feared ogre of Europe could be a gentle and tender wooer who even allowed her to depart with his own desires still unsatisfied. But she promised to return the next night, provided Napoleon agreed to discuss Poland's affairs with her and to continue to be calm and patient.

The following day Napoleon sent her an opulent brooch and another impassioned letter. Marie's immediate reaction was that he was now trying to buy her, having misconstrued her motives for continually rejecting him. Her tender honour was again injured – Poland was demanding too great a sacrifice of her. She decided to escape from the whole intolerable situation.

That night, dressed in dark clothes and taking with her only her jewels and a small bag of spare garments, she stole from the house intending to make her way towards France and lose herself somewhere in that great country. But a chance encounter made her change her mind. She met a ragged child who trustingly confided in her the hopes of all his family that Napoleon would give them back their country and bring about a new prosperity. The idea of disappointing all these humble people proved to be even more horrifying to Marie than the thought of losing her honour. So she turned back and made her way to the Royal Castle.

The Girl who defied Napoleon

Napoleon was furious. He had been waiting for hours. But now that she had finally arrived he nevertheless fulfilled his part of the bargain and allowed her to plead Poland's cause. Then he explained his own attitude and reasoning: he was not convinced that from a strategic point of view it would be right to give Poland independence, surrounded as she was by enemies of France. Nor could he be sure that Poland would ever be strong enough to preserve her independence. Marie argued with him and Napoleon became angry. Everyone, he shouted, was constantly demanding this and that of him – even Marie herself, and yet she would not in return even give him her love. Overwhelmed by his anger, by his ardour and by her own sense of patriotic obligation, Marie at last allowed the Emperor to become her lover.

She was installed in the Royal Castle, for she felt she no longer had a husband or a home. She wrote a letter to her mother explaining what had happened and insisting that she could no longer have any contact with either Elzbieta or Madame de Vauban. And she also insisted that her mother must disclose the truth of the situation to everyone immediately concerned, including her husband; as for the rest of the world, she now had powerful friends who would do all the explaining for her.

It was not long before Napoleon had to leave her. The Russians had attacked on the Baltic, despite the fearful winter weather, and Napoleon was obliged to lead his weary troops into battle. Before leaving he told Marie to worry about nothing – Duroc and Prince Poniatowski would take good care of her. Count Walewski had been apprised of the position concerning his wife, and he had agreed to a separation. In fact, during Napoleon's absence Marie went home to her mother, and then together they travelled to Vienna for a short holiday. Hardly had they arrived there, however, when the news of Napoleon's victory at Eylau reached them – a shattering defeat for the Russians which would force them to abandon what had been known as Prussian Poland. Full of joy the two women abandoned their trip and hurried back to Warsaw to share the rejoicings, although these were to prove somewhat premature.

As Napoleon was still absent on his campaigns, Marie and her mother went to stay at Kiernozia, their family estate. There Marie lived quietly, reading and sewing and, as spring came, walking in and around the estate. Her only serious occupation was writing long letters in reply to Napoleon's brief but affectionate notes.

The Russian campaign made slow progress and was by no means successful. Napoleon was forced by the persistent bleak weather and the lack of food in the already plundered countryside to retire to the Prussian castle of Finckenstein. At this time Marie received a visit from General Zayon-czek, accompanied by Elzbieta who had become his mis-tress. Although Marie refused to soften her attitude towards Elzbieta, whom she no doubt felt had been one of the chief procurers in the conspiracy to deliver her to the Emperor, she listened carefully to the General's suggestions. He wanted her to make the journey to Finckenstein, to ask Napoleon for a directive that the corps of 6,000 Polish men which the General had helped to levy should be assigned to him for active service. The General was convinced that the fighting which had temporarily subsided would flare up again at any moment, and he could not bear the thought that he might not be in the firing line.

While Marie certainly sympathized with General Zayon-czek's patriotic zeal, she probably saw the project as a good excuse for rejoining the Emperor at a time when there was a comparative lull in the fighting, and he would therefore not be too preoccupied. So she undertook the long journey, running the gauntlet of the jokes and jibes of the encamped soldiers along the route. When she arrived at the castle Napoleon was openly delighted to see her and she stayed with him for about a month, waiting quietly, with her books and her sewing, in the room next to his until he had com-pleted his day's business and could spare the time to relax with her. He took all his meals with her alone, and there is little doubt that he must have found Marie – the only woman he had ever known who had asked nothing of him for herself – a charming and restful companion, and in turn he, the fierce conqueror, could release the gentle side of his nature. It was perhaps inevitable that Marie should soon fall deeply in love with him.

By now the Empress Josephine had heard rumours about Marie and the Emperor's infatuation for her. Predictably she wrote to him a number of times suggesting that she should join him in Warsaw or elsewhere, but equally predictably he had written her off-putting letters. The fact is that although Josephine was probably the only woman Napoleon ever truly loved, he was now seriously considering divorcing her. Her fault was that she had failed to produce a child for him, and he was anxious to ensure the continuation of the dynasty which he had created. Josephine had had two children by her first husband and so was indisputably fertile, but Napoleon had also proved that he was capable of becoming a father when a young woman he had previously taken as his mistress produced a son.

Napoleon, always a strategist, though not always successful, had to consider what he would want to do if Marie became pregnant; a marriage with her would be by no means impossible. However, when she left Finckenstein at the end of May she was still not pregnant. The Emperor resumed his campaign against the Russians, while she continued to live quietly at Kiernozia, awaiting the promised call to rejoin him once more. As a souvenir she took with her a small piece of material which she tore from the hangings of her bed in the castle. The hole is still there to this day, and the rooms are furnished just as they were during Napoleon's occupation.

By the end of July Napoleon was back in France, but still the promised call did not come and the brief notes he sent from time to time hardly consoled her for his seeming lack of need to have her with him. And, against her better judgment, she found herself becoming strongly attracted to a young French Colonel named d'Ornano who was stationed in Warsaw. But when the long-awaited call from Napoleon came at last, Marie easily dismissed her young suitor from her mind. In January 1808 she hastened to Paris.

A house was bought for Marie in the same street in which Josephine had lived when Napoleon first met her – perhaps a touch of retrospective sentiment – and there he would go whenever he could get away from his duties. Marie in her characteristic way lived a quiet life, keeping out of society and always ready to receive her lover at any moment. Meanwhile, perhaps to some extent because of Marie's influence and certainly against the advice of his allies and generals, Napoleon had insisted on creating an autonomous state in Poland called the Duchy of Warsaw and under the control of the King of Saxony. The state had its own government, its own army and civil facility to enable it to expand and develop. Although the area was small, it was at least a start, and to this extent Marie felt that she had been successful in her mission with Napoleon, though she continued to plead with him for the full restoration of her country. When he was in a calm and patient mood, Napoleon would answer gently, explaining in detail the intricacies of European power politics and the reasons why he could not at present grant her wishes.

In April Napoleon departed again for Bordeaux. This time it was Spanish politics. The abdication of the Bourbon king and his replacement by Josef Bonaparte called for his attention. The Empress Josephine was to join him, so Marie was obliged to remain in Paris for a few weeks before she decided to return to Warsaw. In the months that followed she continued to write long letters to Napoleon detailing the progress of political affairs in Poland, but he was busy elsewhere and gave little indication of interest. Life in Warsaw was gay, however, and Marie, with a new sense of freedom, joined enthusiastically in all the social events.

The interlude did not last for long. In April 1809 Austria rose again against Napoleon and marched against Poland. The Polish army was defeated with little difficulty and the Austrians entered Warsaw. Meanwhile Napoleon was attacking Vienna and Prince Poniatowski, with the remants of the Polish army, had marched south and successfully engaged the Austrian forces. Poniatowski took Cracow and Napoleon took Vienna. He established quarters in Schönbrunn and took the trouble to find for Marie a house in a village a few miles away. The Austrian armies were finally beaten and scattered at the battle of Wagram, and Napoleon returned to Schönbrunn, and to the waiting arms of Marie.

For three months Napoleon and Marie were together, but the hours when they could be alone were brief, and it was always difficult for him to get away from his responsibilities of command and the demands of his retinue. Nevertheless, during the ensuing weeks the lovers managed to find a great deal of happiness together. Marie was by now completely devoted to Napoleon and quite miserable when she was away from him.

When the time came for him to return to Paris, she did not know that he had already made up his mind to divorce Josephine – and even less was she aware that he had decided to set in train negotiations for the hand of the fifteen-year-old Grand Duchess Anne of Russia. This was a political move which he hoped would produce an alliance that would bring him not only a son but also peace between Russia and France. Marie for her part went back to Warsaw – to discover that she was now pregnant! When Prince Poniatowski heard of Napoleon's new marital plans he hurried at once to Marie and urged her to go to Paris, but she firmly refused. She felt that her presence there would only embarrass Napoleon and, anyway, she had already done as much as she could for Poland.

Two months went by, and then Marie received a letter from her husband, Count Walewski, inviting her to use the family house of Walewice if she wished to do so. Somebody, perhaps Prince Poniatowski or even Napoleon himself, had informed Walewski that his wife was to bear the Emperor's child and that there should be no social stigma attached to its birth. Marie, no doubt gratefully, moved into the Walewski home; there, with a completely new staff which knew nothing of her past history, she lived quite alone awaiting the birth of her child. The days passed peacefully enough, one by one, and she found that she no longer cared very much what was happening in Paris. Napoleon's negotiations to marry Anne of Russia had failed; instead he had married the Grand Duchess Marie Louise of Austria.

A son was born to Marie on 4 May, 1810 as a legitimate child of the house of Walewski. Congratulations poured in from her husband's family and all her friends. But Napoleon, who up to the time of the birth of his son had been sending messengers almost daily for reports on her progress, suddenly appeared to lose interest. The messengers ceased and no further letters arrived from him. Marie could not understand this at all, for marriage had made no difference to Napoleon before. So in November Marie decided to move to Paris and reopen her house, and this she did – but still Napoleon remained distant, and to her repeated pleas for an appointment he sent messages by Duroc to say that he would not see her at present.

Marie begged her friends to help her. Their advice was that the Emperor might be better pleased to see her taking her place in society as a lady of fashion and title rather than hide herself away as she had done during the weeks she had been in Paris. Nevertheless, a friend was able to arrange to present Marie at court. The event took place at a small evening party at which only a few of the Empress's friends were gathered. Marie was formally presented to the Empress who was already stout through pregnancy, and then Napoleon approached and told his wife that the Countess Walewska had been one of the most popular ladies at his court in Warsaw a few years ago. The Empress, who in fact knew precisely who Marie was, greeted her blandly and maintained conversation with her husband's former mistress on a formal level.

It was only as the Empress was leaving that Napoleon took a brief opportunity to speak privately to Marie and ask about her. Tremulously she begged the Emperor to come and see his son. He promised to do so, and then the Imperial couple retired. The soirée was over, and Marie had achieved nothing. But from that moment on she circulated in Parisian society and was received everywhere, and she herself did a certain amount of entertaining.

Two months went by before Napoleon decided he would see her at her home. He sent a message warning her of his arrival and requesting that all the servants should be kept out of the way. In the event, the visit was brief and depressingly formal – his coming and going were marked with a dispassionate kiss and the conversation was centred wholly around the ten-month-old baby. But he visited her again a few weeks later, and this time he talked of his work and his plans, but he gently discouraged her when she tried to comfort him. Finally he told her what she had already feared – that everything was over between them, and that nothing could be allowed to mar this most important marriage. What was more, he explained, he was actually in love with his Austrian princess, but he hoped that Marie would always remain his friend, and if there was anything she needed at any time she had only to ask him. To Napoleon's great relief Marie accepted this moment of truth quite calmly; that Napoleon still had a place for her in his heart was perhaps reward enough, and she still had her beloved country to fight for and keep her mind occupied.

Some time later Napoleon sent for Marie and discussed with her in detail as to how she should work to re-establish Poland, and in due course she went back to Warsaw. But it was at this time that Napoleon embarked on his disastrous Russian campaign which was to signal the end of his career of conquest. As his armies were pushed back into Poland, Napoleon, returning to his headquarters, found himself near to Marie's home at Walewice, near Warsaw. He despatched a message to say that he would spend the night there. After playing for a while with Alexandre, his small son, he retired and asked Marie to come to his room. There he sat exhausted on to his bed and, with Marie clasped gently his arms, began to talk quietly about the events of the few months, the failure of his campaigns and the impossibility of re-establishing Poland at the present time. There was nothing more she could do, and he urged her to go to Paris where she would have no need of money, and she could enjoy her own life, putting all thoughts of aside – and in addition he promised to give her son and estate of a French count. When he left with dawn she truly felt that her life of purpose was that there was nothing more she could do for Poland. She decided to take the Emperor's advice and return to Paris.

There she lived the life of a carefree lady of fashion. She renewed her acquaintance with d'Ornano, her old admirer of Warsaw days, who was now a General, and he became her accepted escort. From time to time she met Napoleon – she was often at court and occasionally the Emperor sent for her to hold a private conversation. Once she met the little King of Rome, Napoleon's son by Empress Marie Louise, now aged two and a half years. Napoleon was clearly devoted to the child who romped unchecked in and out of his father's rooms. At the same time he was so kind and gentle with the woman whose own son by him could never possess such honour and status that Marie wept.

Napoleon kissed her affectionately, and for a while her hopes that they might renew their love were revived. She spent less time with d'Ornano, just in case Napoleon might need her, but two months later he had departed again for the battlefield to pursue his last and most disastrous campaign. Defeat followed defeat, until inevitably Napoleon was forced to abdicate.

As he waited in Fontainebleau for the escorts who were to take him to exile in Elba, Marie went to see him. She handed in a private note to be delivered to the Emperor, and then sat down to wait in an obscure corner of the gallery outside his room. All night long people hurried to and fro, not recognizing the melancholy woman who sat so quietly in the gloomy corner, and in the end, towards dawn, Marie gave up and left. When Napoleon later discovered that she had gone he sent a member of his staff to apologize to her and ask her to write to him.

Marie did write, asking permission to visit Napoleon in Elba, and telling him too of her present difficulties; in the present unsettled state of Europe nobody knew what would become of the Walewski fortune – the old Count was now seriously ill – while Alexandre's estate in Italy had been confiscated by the King of Naples. In reply she received a friendly letter from the former Emperor. He begged her not to worry or be unhappy when she thought of him, and he promised to receive her and her son with "great and particular interest" should they come to Elba.

In the months that followed Marie joined the faction that was working actively for Napoleon's return, and she travelled the length of Italy in pursuit of this object. In addition she negotiated and argued to have her son's Italian estate restored to him. Eventually she succeeded in arranging a visit to Elba, where she sailed with her brother and sister and two servants. For two days she remained in the Hermitage, the house where Napoleon and his suite were living. To her surprise, when she saw Napoleon, he would discuss neither the past nor the future; his conversation was almost banal, and his interest appeared to be centred only on her own affairs and her child. When Marie discovered that Napoleon was desperately short of money she offered him all her jewels, but he refused to accept them. Two days later Marie left the island. Her visit had been a well guarded secret, for Napoleon had been trying to persuade the Empress Marie Louise and their son to join him in exile and was anxious to avoid giving her possible grounds for declining.

Hurt by Napoleon's attitude and by the realization that he was still noticeably in love with his Austrian princess – who firmly kept her distance – Marie returned to Italy and Naples. There she eventually succeeded in having her son's title and estate restored, and she continued to work politically for Napoleon's return and reinstatement. In France, Louis XVIII, brother of the French king who had been executed in the Revolution, was now on the throne, but not for long. After eleven months Napoleon escaped from Elba and returned to France, to the acclamation and support of his old armies. King Louis XVIII fled, and Napoleon returned in triumph to Paris.

Marie, hearing this joyful news, immediately hurried to Paris and sent Napoleon word of her arrival, but she received no reply or invitation from him whatever. His mind was occupied with other matters, and in particular the threat from the British and Prussian armies deployed in Belgium under the command of the Duke of Wellington. Napoleon decided to attack, and on 18 June, 1815, the fateful battle of Waterloo was fought and lost in total defeat for the French. Napoleon became a fugitive, and returned briefly to the Elysée Palace in Paris. Once more Marie hurried there to see him with her child in her arms, and this time she was received at once. Napoleon was preoccupied and had little to say, but he played cheerfully with the little boy for a while before sending them away.

The next day he abdicated for the second time and left the Elysée Palace for Malmaison, the home of Josephine who had died the previous year. There Marie was able to visit him once again, but this time was appalled to learn that he had made up his mind to retire for ever from the public and political scene. It was necessary, he insisted, for the good of his country and the peace of Europe. Marie wept, unable to believe that she might never see him again – and yet she knew that, although not long ago she would have followed him to the ends of the earth, now she would have gone with him only from pity, or perhaps a sense of duty. In fact, Napoleon, unable to escape from France, gave himself up to the British and was exiled to the lonely island of St. Helena in the South Atlantic, where he died six years later.

Marie, desolate and without hope, began to pick up the threads of her life again, and now she began to listen more earnestly to the pleadings of Count d'Ornano who had for so long wished to marry her. Slowly she came to love him, and on 7 September, 1816, they were at last married. Marie, to the delight of her husband, very quickly became pregnant and in June of the following year gave birth to another son. But the pregnancy and birth proved too much for her. The kidney ailment which she had managed to keep under control by dieting and "cures" for many years became aggravated and her condition deteriorated. In spite of the attention of the best doctors available and careful nursing she slowly sank, until she died on 11 December, 1817, only 29 years old. Her heart was placed in an urn in the family vault of the d'Ornanos. Her body was taken to Poland and buried there, according to her wishes.

Chapter 7 Mademoiselle of the Harem

The Empress Josephine, wife of Napoleon, once related that as a child in far-off Martinique a fortune-teller had predicted for her a disastrous marriage, two children and widowhood, but that her second husband would be a dark and apparently insignificant man whose glory would one day resound round the world, and that she would become his queen, only to die unhappily in the end. As a prophecy, if true, it was very close to the mark. She also told of another prophecy concerning her cousin, Marie-Marthe Aimée Dubucq de Rivery, who had been her close friend in Martinique – the same fortune-teller, gazing into the future, foresaw that Aimée would be captured by pirates, to become a concubine in a royal palace, but that her son would reign gloriously while she, when happiness was within her grasp, would die from a lingering illness. A grim prediction, perhaps, but again one which was to prove precise enough over the years. The fortune-teller's name was Euphemia

David, and Josephine's story is regarded as too well authenticated to be dismissed as mere legend.

The crystal-gazing occurred in the year 1775, a year or so after the ill-fated Louis XVI had ascended the throne of France. Josephine and Aimée were both twelve years old and inseparable friends. Josephine's family had an estate at Trois Islets, about fifteen miles from Pointe Royale, quite close to where the famous fortune-teller lived. Aimée had been born in Pointe Royale. Her family was of noble Norman stock, but an ancestor, exiled for killing his adversary in a duel, had fled to Martinique in the West Indies where he had established a large family estate. Like many islands in the West Indies, Martinique was full of superstition, black magic and witchcraft; fortune-tellers abounded and were generally taken seriously. No doubt the young girls were sceptical about the respective futures prophesied for them, but Josephine, when she had become Empress of France, remembered the old woman who had so accurately foretold her fate – and that of her friend also.

Three years later Aimée was sent to France, to be educated in a convent at Nantes which was regarded as a finishing school for fashionable young ladies. In such an atmosphere of religious dedication, needlework, music and not very arduous learning, Aimée probably forgot all about the melodramatic future that had been promised her.

She stayed in the convent for several years – much longer than had been planned – for war had broken out between France and England over the question of the American colonies, and it was not considered safe for Aimée to return to Martinique. It was not until 1784, when she was twenty-one, that she finally sailed for the West Indies. Accompanying her was the devoted old mulatto nurse who had looked after her throughout her travels. On the quayside to see them off were most of the sisters of the convent, weeping and praying for her, for Aimée had made herself extremely popular during her six years among them.

Disaster struck very early in the voyage when the old and leaky ship ran into a violent storm and began to founder. Hope had almost been abandoned when a large

Spanish trading ship appeared and took on board the passengers and crew of the doomed vessel. The Spaniard turned for the Balearic Isles to set down its unwanted passengers and, in fine weather, was actually in sight of her destination when a sail was sighted which brought terror to everyone aboard. Pirates, the dreaded Algerian Corsairs, were in hot pursuit of the Spanish ship. No escape was possible – the faster pirate vessel was soon alongside and Aimée, no doubt in an agony of fear and apprehension, found herself a prisoner with the rest of the passengers sailing south to Algiers.

The Dey of Algiers, which at that time was under Turkish domination, was a cunning septuagenarian named Mohammed Ben Osman. His policy was to encourage and protect the pirates of the Barbary Coast, organize and co-ordinate their raiding sorties and support them against the angry foreigners who periodically but unavailingly attempted to sail into Algiers and destroy the Barbary pirates. His headquarters was located in a palace in the heart of the Kasbah, an area of fearsome repute, and it was to this palace that the Corsairs would bring the choicest of their booty as a gift for their protector. When the pirates saw Aimée they realized at once that they had acquired a highly desirable prize, for she was indeed a beauty, with large oval blue eyes, a fair complexion and a mass of flaxen hair. She was clearly destined for the Dey's exclusive attention and amusement, and therefore she had to be segregated from the other worthless captives. She was locked in a cabin and carefully guarded. What happened to her mulatto nurse is not recorded, but she would certainly not have been allowed to return to Europe to tell of the girl's misfortune.

When the Dey saw Aimée he too recognized her unique value – she was a rarity worthy of the Sultan himself. Slave trading flourished all along the North African coast, and white women always brought a good price, particularly blondes who were regarded as something of an exotic luxury among the black-haired swarthy Arabs. Boys, both black and white, were supplied to Turkey to be castrated and trained as eunuchs. Supplying the needs of the harem and similar establishments was a large and profitable industry. On this occasion, however, the Dey of Algiers put mere mercenary considerations such as money out of his mind – he would send the blonde mademoiselle to Constantinople as a gift to the Sultan for his harem, and thus earn himself the certain gratitude of his master, Sultan Abdul Hamid I, Caliph of the Faithful.

And so Aimée was carefully locked away by herself in a room in the Dey's palace and cared for with every attention until a ship was available to take her to the capital of the Ottoman Empire. Then she was dressed in the richest and most elegant clothes of Turkish style, veiled in the approved Muslim fashion and sent off on her journey to join the Caliph's harem. At the end of the long voyage, as the ship anchored in the port, Aimée could see on the promontory between the seas of the Bosphorus and the Golden Horn the great mass of the Seraglio – the royal palace which was to be her future home. It was a vast conglomeration of smaller palaces, pleasure gardens, temples, and mosques, with kitchens, stables, prisons, torture-chambers and barracks. The outer walls were high with battlements, planted about with tall black cyprus trees, all in severe contrast to the filigree-like marble lattice-work of the windows and the elaborately carved walls of the dwelling houses.

Feeling like a shapeless bundle in her Turkish clothes, Aimée was escorted through the crowded and noisy streets of Constantinople to the Seraglio, passing through the Gate of Felicity which opened on to the area occupied by the harem. Here she was received by the Chief Eunuch, the *Kizlar Aga*, a huge black Nubian gorgeously robed with a towering turban adorned with flamingo plumes. He alone was enough to strike terror into Aimée's heart, but worse was to come. Close to him in the courtyard lay a heap of severed heads, some old and putrescent and stinking, and others so newly severed that they reeked of fresh blood. For convent-trained Aimée it was all, not surprisingly, too much too soon. She passed out.

When she recovered she found herself already installed in the harem, one among hundreds of nubile young women from the age of twelve upwards who had been hand-picked for their beauty and virtually imprisoned to serve the pleasure of one man – and inexplicably they regarded it as a privilege. Their names and even their natural personalities were altered with only this one object in view, and their lives were devoted to the enhancement of their beauty and the cultivation of the sensual arts for the better enjoyment of the ageing Caliph. It was a bizarre environment for a young woman who had just spent six years in a convent. True, the society of women was nothing new to Aimée – indeed, the gossiping and giggling, the rules and conventions, the petty feuds and spiteful secrets of the harem must have seemed somewhat familiar. But everything else was quite different; here there was no question of dedication to duty and high moral principles, of self-abnegation and self-sacrifice for others, no conventional academic lessons to be studied and learned, no tedious sewing and no reading or writing. There was strange and exotic food, and the days were spent in idle gossip, nibbling sweetmeats and self-adornment – a mixture of luxury, constraint and boredom. The only lessons Aimée learned were those of voluptuousness.

There in the grand, ornately furnished apartments of the harem Aimée had to reconcile herself to the fact that she might have to spend the rest of her life as an odalisque. In the early weeks she must have hoped to persuade the Sultan to release her, or that friends might hear of her plight and perhaps use diplomatic pressure on her behalf, but before long she was obliged to accept the inevitable truth – that there was no escape, that nobody cared what happened to her, and that very few people even knew, least of all her friends and relations in France and Martinique. Surrounded by hundreds of girls, none of whom spoke her language, Aimée was obliged to dry her tears and adapt herself to her new life. One can only imagine how her convent-bred soul reacted when she fully appreciated that henceforth her entire future lay in becoming accomplished in the arts of beauty, seduction and copulation so that she might for a fleeting moment please the jaded senses of one ageing man, and all that in competition with some five hundred other girls who were only too anxious to succeed in their enforced careers. For the aim of every odalisque was to become the Sultan's favourite, and above all to give birth to a son who might eventually become heir to the throne, and thus bring to his mother the coveted status of *Sultana Valideh* – the Veiled Crown.

The harem and the *selamlik* (the men's quarters) were at the heart of the Seraglio, and between the two were the apartments of the *Sultana Valideh*, from which she could wield enormous executive power. Among the rabbit warren of rooms, passages, staircases and secret tunnels lay the corridor of the Bath, the pivot-point of daily routine life. Elsewhere was the Golden Path along which the chosen favourite was escorted to the Sultan's bed. But there was much more to the Seraglio than the harem; the maze of buildings included the slave lodgings, the Janissary guard house, the council chambers, the dormitories of the court jesters, the Chief Eunuch's rooms, the torture-chambers and place of execution, the hall of circumcision, and the Cage – a pavilion where the heir to the throne remained incarcerated until his accession. In addition there were the quarters of the myriad court officials, including the esoteric Nightingale Keeper, the Tent-Pitcher, the Chief Turban-Winder, the Keeper of the Pedigree of the Prophet's Descendants, and so on, not forgetting the multitude of messengers, gardeners, scribes and other servants needed in the vast palace.

Over this teeming mass of servile humanity the *Kizlar Aga*, or Chief Eunuch, ruled supreme, his rank equal to that of the Grand Vizier himself. His power was absolute and all-embracing. He was responsible for the administration of the harem, and therefore ranked higher than the chief white Eunuch who ruled over the *selamlik*, and he was not only in charge of the household and all the ceremonies which took place in it but was also the Sultan's confidant and completely loyal to his master.

The present *Kizlar Aga*, in whose hands Aimée's future lay, was a kindly and reasonable man, completely incorruptible, and well liked and respected by his master. Aimée soon realized that it was he who had the power to determine her destiny, and it did not take her long to recognize that there was something special about herself. It became obvious that the Chief Eunuch was taking a particular interest in her, visiting her every day to check on her welfare and comfort, but – and her hopes that he might be persuaded to help her to escape were soon dashed – gently but firmly insisting that she must follow the inflexible rules of the harem.

Her favoured status could hardly have pleased her fellow odalisques – nor, indeed, could the new name she was given, Naksh, the Beautiful One. Undeniably her golden hair, fair skin and blue eyes made her unique in that harem full of dark oriental beauties. She regained a measure of self-assurance, perhaps because of the self-control instilled by her convent training, and perhaps because of the vague memory of the old fortune-teller's prophecy that one day she would reign supreme in a great and splendid palace. The prophecy seemed to be crystallizing around her.

First with resignation, then with patience, she struggled through the first few months in the harem, making an effort to learn the Turkish language. In due course she was required to study all the protocol and etiquette of the harem community, as well as the arts and techniques of love-making. She had to accept the strange notion, completely alien to her upbringing, that she now enjoyed an honoured and privileged position and was extremely fortunate in having been accepted as suitable to join the Sultan's harem, and more – the even greater incentive that because of her unique beauty she was likely to catch the eye of the great ruler himself. The odalisques, she learned, lived only for this; many of them never even saw the Sultan, let alone shared his bed, and they had to pass their time as best they could with trifling domestic arts or looking after their more fortunate sisters' babies. Some of the girls in their boredom became involved in liaisons with the eunuchs – frequently castration was not entirely effective – but most of the time was spent in quarrelling among themselves, in adorning themselves, and in trying to attract the Sultan's blasé attention. All were luxuriously imprisoned in the Seraglio for life, unless they were given away by the Sultan to some man he wished to honour – or even to eliminate, for the odalisques were sometimes ordered to kill their new lords and were duly rewarded.

In this totally alien world Aimée slowly learned to make her way, relying only on the friendship of the *Kizlar Aga* who had his own professional reasons for taking a special interest in her. She represented the remote and strange outside world; the Sultan's other concubines were nearly all slave girls from Greece, Circassia, Georgia and Rumania, countries as backward as Turkey, but this girl with the golden hair came from cultured and civilized France – never mind that at that time it was undergoing a particularly bloody revolution.

The *Kizlar Aga* was a man of progressive ideas, and he had sympathizers in a small group of courtiers which included the Mufti Verly-Zade and a beautiful Circassian *Kadine*, or wife, once the favourite of the late Sultan and mother of his son Selim, the heir apparent. In Turkey succession did not proceed by direct descent from father to son, but by age – the eldest surviving son of the family succeeded to the throne. This was an arrangement which often caused bloodshed when ambitious younger sons of the reigning monarch decided to murder older claimants standing bebetween them and the throne. In this context Selim's life was in constant danger from his cousin Mustapha, son of the present Sultan Abdul Hamid.

Mustapha's mother was naturally as ambitious as her son, for if he became Sultan she would acquire the coveted status of *Sultana Valideh* and so, next to the Sultan himself, carry most power in the intricate petty internal politics of the Seraglio which were the boundaries of her life. Consequently the Circassian *Kadine* had to be constantly on the watch to guard her son's life, and her job was made even more difficult by the fact that Selim was not confined to the Cage, the pavilion or little palace in which the heir to the throne was traditionally kept. Sultan Abdul Hamid, having spent forty-five years of his life thus imprisoned, had no desire to wish such a fate upon his heir.

Selim, however, was not only the object of a murder conspiracy, but he was also the centre of the new progressive and liberal movement in which his mother and the *Kizlar Aga* so firmly believed. They in turn were violently opposed by the Janissaries – the infantry which formed the Sultan's bodyguard – who favoured Mustapha's cause, seeing him as a puppet ruler continuing the ancient customs and traditions.

The Janissaries were an ancient and unique formation of soldiers who had become not only reactionary but also corrupt. The corps was made up of Christians who as children had been forcibly abducted from the many provinces of the great Turkish empire to be converted to the Moslem faith, and given a long and rigorous military training. The élite among them were appointed to the Sultan's personal bodyguard, but all lived tough austere lives. In the course of time, as successive rulers had failed to keep them in check, the Janissaries had become very powerful. They terrorized the citizens and waxed fat on the proceeds of intrigue, corruption and protection rackets, and even the Sultan and the Grand Vizier were afraid of them. The sound of the ruthless Janissaries drumming on the kettles and cauldrons which had become their symbol, awoke fear in everyone who heard it. These were the men who formed the chief stumbling block to the hopes of Selim's progressive party.

Aimée soon realized that the *Kizlar Aga* could or would do nothing for her, and she could only await her fate. It was not long before she received a messenger in her luxurious apartment where, surrounded by her own slaves, she had been pampered and groomed for this moment. She was informed that she was to be taken to the Sultan's bedchamber. Her reaction to this royal summons filled the *Kizlar Aga* with dismay and her envious sister odalisques with astonishment, for Aimée, far from being delighted by the honour, fought, bit, scratched and screamed in vigorous protest. She flatly refused to be dressed up in the sumptuous garments prepared for her visit to the Sultan's bed – she was a civilized woman and not a human sacrifice for a savage heathen, she said, with the wrong kind of passion. As the *Kizlar Aga* could do nothing with her, he sensibly sent for the Circassian *Kadine,* and somehow this woman, who had been born a slave but had grown wise in the ways of the harem, persuaded Aimée to surrender. She pointed out that if Aimée could win the Sultan's favour she would have a high place in court, and if she allied herself with the *Kadine's* faction could improve her own lot a great deal.

When Aimée overcame her hysterical revulsion, her practical nature served her well. It came as a great relief to her to find that the Sultan, far from being a savage, was practised and considerate in the arts and graces of love. In turn, the Sultan's jaded palate was stimulated and delighted by Aimée's unusual blonde beauty, her western outlook and her educated mind, all of which made a striking change from the usual run of harem girls.

In a remarkably short time Aimée was installed as favourite and in June 1785, little more than a year from the time when she had left the convent, she gave birth to a son, Mahmoud. The Sultan was delighted; he ordered the entire Seraglio to be illuminated in honour of the occasion, and the festivities went on for days. Despite his five hundred wives and concubines, the Sultan now had only two surviving children, Mustapha and Mahmoud (the other offspring had presumably died natural deaths or had suffered from the attentions of the Court Executioner or the Court Abortionist). As a reward for her success, Aimée was elevated from the rank of *Ikbal* – one who had enjoyed the royal favours – to *Kadine,* or wife (the Sultan had four so-called wives, but the status was nominal and none of them was ever legally married).

Now Aimée began to enjoy real power; her apartments were among the most elegant and luxurious in the palace and her retinue of slaves expanded to include such functionaries as her Lady Water-pourer, Lady Coffee-server, Mistress of the Sherbets, and so on. Her circle of influential friends grew wider and, apart from the *Kizlar Aga* and the Circassian *Kadine,* also embraced a number of enlightened court officials and administrators and, perhaps most important of all, Selim, the heir apparent.

In the course of time she learned to settle down and adapt herself to this strange and exotic environment. She was obliged to adopt the Muslim faith. But under duress, as it were, and in due course, by being co-operative and complaisant, she found opportunities to introduce French ideas and western customs into this eastern court. As her son grew older she taught him to speak French and told him stories of the legends and histories of the "civilized" world. And she developed a close friendship with Selim, a man of about her own age who listened with avid interest to her accounts of western societies and cultures whose freedom and liberal philosophies he was so anxious to put into effect in his own country.

With everybody in the Seraglio (except Mustapha and his mother) Aimée was highly popular and her influence quickly spread. For example, the letter which Selim wrote to King Louis XVI of France in October 1786, expressing friendship and admiration, could only have been inspired by Aimée – it certainly surprised the French court which had virtually no diplomatic relations with the Sultan and could not imagine why his heir should have written such a letter. They did not reply for many months. Aimée also had the chance to send a letter to her uncle in France relating what had happened to her, but what he thought or felt about it nobody knows. No action was ever taken, and for Aimée it was already too late anyway.

Then, in 1789, Sultan Abdul Hamid died. He was succeeded by Selim who immediately found himself confronted with troubles with the truculent Janissaries at home and with Russia abroad – a situation which he found intolerable. One of his first acts was to form a new army along French lines whose loyalty he could trust. French officers were brought to Turkey to teach modern military techniques, reorganize the cannon foundry, train the navy and modernize the ship-building yards. The *entente cordiale* increased when the Turks actually sent an ambassador to Paris, and, surprisingly, a French weekly newspaper was published in Constantinople. Again, the influence of Aimée was undeniably behind these events.

This new east-west axis was disrupted for a period when Napoleon attempted to capture Egypt from the Turks, but in the event the French Emperor's dreams of oriental conquest were shattered, and by 1801 friendship was resumed. Meanwhile Selim had been able to effect some minor reforms and a little progress. A printing press, the first in Turkey, had recently been installed, and he had imported masses of books to create a central state library. Other imports included western musicians, odd plants, French furniture, food and wines, and even – to satisfy Aimée's whim and childhood memory – Montgolfier balloons which sailed over the domes and turrets of Constantinople to the astonishment of the populace.

But in the Seraglio the atmosphere remained tense. The Janissaries were biding their time and would occasionally strike and murder a loyal member of the Sultan's party. When the Circassian *Kadine* died in 1805 the Janissaries recognized that one of their strongest enemies had been eliminated, and they were backed by Mustapha and his mother. Selim was in himself a kind and gentle man, shy and rather introspective, and so revolted by the Seraglio's common practice of strangling newly born infants that he neglected his harem and refused to risk the responsibilities of parenthood. He was, in terms of cold ruthlessness, no match for Mustapha, his mother and the Janissaries. Aimée, concerned for him and for her own son whose life she knew to be in peril from Mustapha, implored Selim to make overtures to the friendly French, for they needed a powerful ally. Mustapha's supporters had also been making overtures – to the Russians and the English. When Napoleon heard that the Russians were marching south and that the British were sending a fleet to the Eastern Mediterranean, he acted with lightning speed and despatched General Sebastiani post-haste to Constantinople.

Sebastiani was a brilliant soldier and very much a live-wire. As soon as he reached Constantinople he proceeded to organize and deploy the army and navy, and review the defences of the city and the Sultan's policies. Naturally the British Ambassador was consumed with indignation; this amounted on the part of the supposedly neutral Turkey to an act of war. But the British were sadly outmanoeuvred, and by the time their fleet arrived to demand Sebastiani's recall the city had already been turned into a virtually impregnable fortress.

Aimée persuaded Selim to take a strong line and stand firm by demanding the withdrawal of the British fleet beyond the Dardanelles before any negotiations could take place. While this was being put into effect the final fortifications of Constantinople were completed to such an extent that the British Admiral decided that nothing could be done about this city which only once in its long history had fallen under siege.

Sebastiani's arrogation of power in the city, although tacitly supported by the Sultan, inflamed the anger of the Janissaries and the reactionaries, with the inevitable result that when the French contingent at last went home a wave of intense nationalism set in. The Janissaries rose in insurrection, with the result that Selim was forced to abdicate and proclaim Mustapha as Sultan in his place. As soon as the new Sultan had been installed, Selim tried to poison himself, but was prevented from doing so by Mustapha himself. Selim, Aimée and Mahmoud were imprisoned, in daily terror of their lives, while Sultan Mustapha turned back the clock by restoring all the old reactionary customs. Cruelty again reigned in the Seraglio and the city, and many of Selim's followers were seized, tortured or killed.

Mustapha and the Janissaries made one mistake, however. They overlooked one of Selim's strongest supporters, a single-minded man named Baraiktar who was Pasha of a Bulgarian province on the Danube. As soon as he learned of Selim's downfall he gathered an army of 18,000 men and promptly marched upon Constantinople to restore Selim to his throne. The *Sultana Valideh,* Mustapha's mother, responded to this threat by ordering the murder of Selim and Mahmoud, for by ancient custom the sole survivor of the royal house, which would be Mustapha, was sacrosanct. Selim was therefore murdered, but he died like a lion, fighting his assassins so ferociously that Mahmoud had time to escape and hide. When Baraiktar arrived at the walls of the Seraglio with his army and demanded Selim, Mustapha had his cousin's corpse thrown over the wall. Baraiktar, who had hoped for a peaceful solution to the confrontation, then ordered that the Seraglio be stormed and occupied, and this was duly accomplished in the bloody fashion of the time. Mahmoud was discovered, Mustapha and his mother were imprisoned, and Mahmoud became Sultan.

Aimée now became the *Sultana Valideh*, and the prophecy of the Martinique fortune-teller was fulfilled. Her rank was second only to that of her son. Together they introduced many reforms and many western customs such as sitting on chairs instead of squatting on cushions, eating with knives and forks instead of with the fingers, and – this shocked their Muslim compatriots – drinking champagne of which Mahmoud became inordinately fond.

His own innovations included not only such relatively unimportant things as more simple styles of dress (he introduced the fez in place of the turban) but also new forms of taxation and more efficient administration; he introduced quarantine, which saved the city from a fearsome outbreak of plague, and he founded hospitals and schools of anatomy to train physicians.

Unfortunately many of these new ideas and concepts were contrary to the teachings of the Koran, and certain of Mahmoud's policies began to anger the population. The Janissaries exploited this resentment, stirred up as much trouble as they could, and threatened to overthrow Mahmoud unless he abandoned or at least slowed down his reforms. Mahmoud reacted in the true Turkish tradition. He had Mustapha, all the women who were pregnant by him, and Mustapha's mother bound and thrown into the Bosphorus. The threat was temporarily over, but it was not until 1826, after Aimée's death, that Mahmoud finally succeeded in breaking the power of the Janissaries once and for all by the simple expedient of having the bodyguard slaughtered to a man.

When Mustapha's despotic régime ended, Aimée who had probably resigned herself to the cruelties which had surrounded her for so long, settled down to a relatively quiet and peaceful life. Contemporary accounts record that she loved precious stones and always dressed in the height of elegance and luxury. Her long blonde hair fell loosely around her shoulders and interwoven with it on almost invisible gold wires she wore tiny diamonds. Aimée's Creole background no doubt explains her love of flamboyant display, and the opulence of the Seraglio probably suited her tastes. At any rate, she surrounded herself with every luxury that the vast revenues she now commanded could buy.

Aimée was also behind her son in every foreign policy decision he had to make. As the years passed by Turkey's standing among the nations of Europe and the Middle East became more secure and more imposing – and also more peaceful. He continued his programme of liberalization and remained on the whole kindly and simple in his own tastes. He is known in history as Mahmoud the Reformer.

On a winter night in 1817 a priest from the convent of Saint Antoine at Pera was roused from his devotions and given an Imperial summons. Escorted by solemn guards the priest went down to the harbour where a splendid craft of the royal household was waiting. Swiftly he was conveyed across the dark waters of the Golden Horn. At the far shore he was led through starlit gardens into a luxuriously appointed room where a dying woman lay on a bed. A Greek doctor and slaves were in attendance, and nearby stood a dark bearded man of commanding presence overwhelmed with grief.

The bearded man ordered the others in the room to leave, and when they had done so he ushered the priest to the bedside. Addressing the woman as mother, he told her that her wish to die in the religion of her fathers would be granted. The priest moved forward, prayed with the woman, then gave her Absolution and Extreme Unction.

As the priest left the room, still without having spoken a word to anyone but the dying woman, the bearded man dropped to his knees beside the bed, lamenting loudly, and the priest was escorted back to his convent to spend the rest of the night in prayer for the soul of Aimée Dubucq de Rivery, *Sultana Valideh* of Turkey.

Chapter 8 The Calculating Queen

Cleopatra! Her very name evokes a mystical dream of enchantment and power. She is for many women even today the embodiment of a personal fantasy, an incarnation of passion, glamour, ecstasy and tragedy. Heroine of one of the world's greatest love stories, her tale has been told hundreds of times and is still, two thousand years later, as fascinating as ever. From Caesar and Plutarch to Vivian Leigh and Elizabeth Taylor, men and women have tried by description and portrayal to capture the essence of this remarkable woman.

In fact, there is very little documentation. Nothing survives of Cleopatra's personal letters, and there are no remaining Egyptian papyri of her reign. But the three famous Romans with whom her life was linked have their places in history, and their careers were recorded in adequate detail by the contemporary historians and authors. Even so, a great deal of legend and exaggeration has grown up around the story of Cleopatra's life, and her classic love affair and tragic end have been too often dramatized at the expense of truth.

On all the available evidence, Cleopatra was a shrewd, intelligent and ambitious young woman, and one of the last members of the Ptolemaic dynasty whose Greek founder had been made King of Egypt, which was then a province of the vast empire built up by Alexander the Great. The first Ptolemy built the capital of Alexandria and founded its famous library. He was a wise ruler and the country prospered owing to his enlightened and civilized ideas. During the next three hundred years of the dynasty, however, the moral fibre of the family degenerated drastically; although they continued to encourage the restoration of old buildings and the construction of new ones, and subscribed to the arts and culture and the preservation of the national heritage, their viciousness grew. This may have been due in part to the incestuous marriages between brother and sister, a custom which was intended to preserve the purity of the divine royal blood.

It is perhaps remarkable that the Ptolemy history does not contain more of the crimes of fratricide and infanticide, of treachery and murder than it does. Cleopatra's father, Ptolemy XIII, came to the throne as the result of a particularly bloody period in the annals of the family when a number of violent deaths left him and his brother in the line of succession. Ptolemy Auletes (the Fluteplayer, as he was popularly known) acquired Egypt and his brother took over Cyprus which then belonged to Egypt.

Ptolemy Auletes was a weak and shiftless man, caring only for drinking and playing his flute. Moreover, he held his position only by the goodwill of Rome, to whose increasingly powerful empire the late Egyptian king had, according to the Romans, bequeathed his kingdom as a gesture of gratitude for setting him securely upon his throne during a troublesome period in his reign. Consequently, Ptolemy had to play his hand carefully, and he went about it by trying quietly to buy recognition in the Roman Senate of his claim to his land and his title. This proved to be an immensely expensive plan, and not very effective, but fortunately Egypt was a wealthy country.

Meanwhile the people of Alexandria, more Greek than Egyptian in outlook, were provoked by Ptolemy's continuing subservience to Rome, and there was increasing unrest. Ptolemy became alarmed and sent an invitation to Pompey, the great Roman general who was then pursuing his trail of conquests in the East, to visit Alexandria. But Pompey did not come – instead the Romans annexed Cyprus, and Ptolemy's brother killed himself.

The Alexandrians were incensed. They insisted that Ptolemy should demand the restitution of Cyprus. In the year 58 B.C. Ptolemy, afraid of annoying the Romans on the one hand and his people on the other, reluctantly set out for Rome where he complained that he had been turned out of the city. While the Romans were willing enough to push Ptolemy Auletes back to power, the Senate could not agree among themselves as to whom they could trust with such a mission – not to mention the pickings of a wealthy Egypt. The *impasse* continued for three years, during which Julius Caesar, Pompey and Crassus formed their famous Triumvirate through which they planned to rule Rome together. At last Ptolemy received the news he had been waiting for: Gabinius, the proconsular governor of Suria, had been appointed and briefed to restore Ptolemy's throne by military force. Delighted, Ptolemy promised a generous bribe to Gabinius who, equally delighted, agreed to march at once for the Egyptian frontier. He sent Mark Anthony, a young cavalry officer, ahead of the main army to secure the isthmus of Suez.

In the meantime, behind Ptolemy's back, the Alexandrians had installed his eldest daughter Berenike as Queen of Egypt. A husband was recruited for her, but she found his coarse manners and behaviour disgusting, and after a short while he disappeared in a mysterious fashion. (According to a contemporary account by Strabo she had him strangled). Her second husband was more to her liking, but he only survived six months, for at that time Gabinius and Ptolemy rapidly overcame the defences of the Egyptian capital and

Berenike and her new husband met a violent and sticky end at Ptolemy's hands.

Ptolemy was left with two sons and two daughters, one of which was Cleopatra, aged fourteen. It is said that it was at this time that she first met – and remembered for many years – the handsome young cavalry leader Mark Anthony. Gabinius, mission accomplished, returned to Rome, leaving behind him some troops to act as bodyguard to the newly restored King who was obliged to set about gathering the money to pay the bribe and the cost of the Roman operation. The task proved troublesome, however, for the people were beginning to resent this constant drain on their resources. However, the imposition was not to last for long; in 51 B.C. Ptolemy Auletes died, leaving his debts as well as his kingdom to Cleopatra and his elder son. He made the Romans his executors and sensibly sent a copy of his will to Rome.

In such a way the seventeen-year-old Cleopatra and her eleven-year-old brother Ptolemy XIV began their joint reign over Egypt. According to Plutarch Cleopatra was an intelligent and well-educated young woman who would and could "easily turn her tongue, like a many-stringed instrument, to any language she pleased". Of her appearance he said: "Her beauty was not altogether beyond comparison, nor such that one could look upon her without being struck by it. But familiarity with her had an irresistible charm, and the attraction of her person, combined with her persuasive manner of speech and with the peculiar character which was evident in all that she said or did, was something bewitching. There was a sweetness also in the mere sound of her voice."

But if there was sweetness in her voice, there was little in her personality. By the time she came to the throne she had already succeeded in making herself unpopular in Alexandria. She had discarded her tutors and guardians and was intent on pursuing her own ambition – that of ruling Egypt herself. Nevertheless, she had her brother to reckon with; he was under the care of his eunuch guardian Pothinus who had for allies Achillas, commander of the King's troops in Alexandria, and Theodotos, young Ptolemy's tutor, all of whom were equally determined to rule Egypt in the name of their ward.

Unfortunately, little is known of the events during the first three years of the new régime. Cleopatra had a brush with the new proconsular governor of Syria over the question of the troops left behind by Gabinius, and in 49 B.C. she was said to have had an affair with Cnaeus, the son of the Roman general Pompey. Caesar and Pompey had by then become enemies, and it was in anticipation of war that Pompey sent his son to Egypt to procure men, ships and corn. Cleopatra was generous to Cnaeus in every respect, and when he left Alexandria she gave him fifty ships to use as transports for some five hundred men drawn from the former Gabinian troops. It seems likely that this action, in surrendering ships and men to the Roman oppressors, increased Cleopatra's unpopularity. Young Ptolemy's faction would certainly have made most of the opportunity in political terms. Although there are no records to explain why the twenty-year-old Queen had to fly from her capital, there seems little doubt that incidents such as this, aggravated by the impetuosity and ambition of an inexperienced girl, led to her flight across the eastern borders of Egypt. By her own efforts, she managed to raise an army and began to advance towards Pelusium, where the army of Ptolemy awaited her.

The odds are almost certainly that at that point Cleopatra would have been defeated and murdered, had it not been for fate and further intrigue which brought the Romans back into the scene. The expected confrontation between Caesar and Pompey had taken place, resulting in Pompey's defeat at the battle of Pharsalia. Pompey fled, having decided that Egypt offered him the best chance of a haven, but on the question of offering him hospitality and asylum Ptolemy's council was divided. Theodotus finally solved the problem in relatively simple terms. If they received Pompey, he said, they would have Caesar as an enemy and Pompey as a master, and if they refused him entry into Egypt then Pompey would become an enemy and Caesar would probably be hostile, too, having been given the trouble of pursuing his

E

adversary. But if they received Pompey and then killed him they would please Caesar and solve the problem of Pompey at the same time. Accordingly, the strategy having been agreed, a welcoming message was sent to Pompey and a small boat was despatched to take him off the trireme which had brought him to the Egyptian coast. As soon as he was out of reach of help, Pompey was murdered and his head cut off.

Caesar followed Pompey to Egypt and arrived in the inner harbour of Alexandria with a handful of ships and less than 4,000 men. Only then did he learn of Pompey's death. Having arrived, however, he decided to stay and settle the quarrel between the two rulers of Egypt in the interests of long-term political stability. With such a small garrison this was no easy task. The people of Alexandria did not take kindly to Caesar's arrival and the presence of Roman soldiers in their city, and there were demonstrations and riots amounting almost to open warfare. In his own account Caesar laconically recalls that "crowds gathered day after day, and many outbreaks took place, and many soldiers were killed in every quarter of the town". But despite the danger, Caesar was determined to stay, and he summoned Ptolemy and Cleopatra to Alexandria to "decide their quarrel judicially rather than by force of arms".

Theodotus was the first to arrive, bearing the head of Pompey, but far from being pleased Caesar turned away from him and wept. Ptolemy and Pothinos appeared soon after, having left Achillas in charge of the army. Cleopatra, still with her army on the border, was unable to make up her mind whether to obey the summons or not. On balance, Caesar seemed to offer the only practical way out of her difficulties, and from what she had heard of him it seemed more than likely that she might be able to charm him into helping her.

Caesar was, she knew, a great connoisseur of women, renowned for his conquests and three or four times married – yet the scandal of a homosexual liaison with King Nicodemus in his youth was still whispered about him. He was fantastically extravagant and always lived in expensive luxury; to pay his many debts he robbed the temples of conquered lands. But he was also extremely generous and possessed of a certain humility – he was undoubtedly loved by the people and by his armies, and during military campaigns he willingly shared the hardships of his troops. He was an enigma, a contradictory character who loved children, longed for a son, surrounded himself with handsome young boys and seduced maidens.

It is not surprising, therefore, that Cleopatra, brooding over the character of this man who was now in his mid-fifties, decided that she could successfully use her charms on him. She had been brought up in an eastern court which knew all the erotic secrets of the East and which possessed a near inexhaustible supply of silken luxuries and beautiful slave girls. One practical problem, however, was how to reach Caesar. First she had, in some way, to get past Achilla's army and then pass through a city full of her brother's troops in order to reach the palace occupied by the Romans. Plutarch says she solved the problem by the famous ruse of having herself delivered to Caesar rolled up in a bed-sack – a kind of bag in which bedclothes were tied up. Dion Chrysostom, another historian, suggests that her cause was first argued by her friends, but that on learning of the amorous character of Caesar she decided to see him herself, begged for a personal interview, and went secretly by night to see him.

Whatever the truth of the matter, Caesar was instantly charmed – by her courage and initiative as well as by her physical attractions. So successful was she in her gambit that a few hours later Caesar sent for Ptolemy and tried to reconcile the two, but the boy was so infuriated at his sister's sudden reappearance that he flung his crown to the ground and rushed out of the room shouting that he had been betrayed. Much confusion followed. According to Dion Chrysostom, Caesar came out of the palace and prudently standing "in a safe place" managed to calm the crowd, and then called a meeting in which he reminded the assembly of the terms of Ptolemy Aulete's will relating to succession to the throne.

Pothinus now started to spread gossip and slander – although no doubt there was truth in it – of Cleopatra's harlotry with Caesar, and of Caesar's weakness as a soldier. For his part, Caesar realized that he had not enough troops to be able to march against Achillas who was now moving his army towards the capital, but he succeeded in persuading Ptolemy to send two messengers to parley with Achillas and demand the disbanding of the army. The messengers were seized and murdered, and Caesar used the incident as an excuse to hold Ptolemy as hostage.

Achillas now decided to march into the city, and Caesar prepared to defend the royal quarter in which the palace was situated with his few well-trained soldiers. The fight was bitter and brief. During the battle Caesar's men succeeded in setting fire to the Egyptian ships in the harbour beyond the palace. The flames eventually spread to the town, and the famous and unique Alexandrian library, with its 400,000 scrolls, was burnt to the ground. But the destruction of the Egyptian ships and the capture of the island at the entrance to the harbour, on which stood the Pharos lighthouse – one of the seven wonders of the ancient world – gave Caesar total command over the sea approaches to Alexandria and enabled him to send off for reinforcements.

Even then the situation in the city was not entirely resolved, and Caesar still had to cope with troubles and intrigues from within. Cleopatra was apparently the only one who was concerned to keep Caesar in Egypt, while the rest of the royal family and their adherents constantly plotted to get rid of him. Typical of the type of cloak and dagger incident involved was the escape of Princess Arsinoe with her eunuch guardian Ganymedes to join Achillas and his army, thus providing a rallying point for the loyalists. Pothinus continued with his subversive activities until Caesar, discovering that he had been secretly writing to Achillas to encourage him in his struggle, seized the opportunity to put him to death. Meanwhile Arsinoe and her eunuch Ganymedes quarrelled with Achillas, with the result that Ganymedes arranged for him to be assassinated and took over command of the army himself.

Ganymedes and the army now set out to besiege Alexandria. They cut off the fresh-water supplies to the royal quarter and prepared to assault the entrenched Romans. A confused battle, half on land, half at sea, ensued; Caesar himself nearly lost his life, and the Romans sustained hundreds of casualties among the legionaries and seamen from the ships which had brought reinforcements. Caesar, rather outwitted and outnumbered, achieved nothing, so that when the Alexandrians professed to be tired of the domineering Ganymedes and Arsinoe and asked him to release Ptolemy as their leader, he willingly agreed, for he regarded Ptolemy as an ally. Ptolemy, with many protestations of friendship and support, departed, and promptly joined the Alexandrians to press the war even more vigorously against the Romans.

At this point help finally arrived in the shape of a massive force of Jews and Syrians which had been mustered by one of the commanders whom Caesar had sent out soon after his arrival in Alexandria. An army deployed by Ptolemy to meet the new invaders was soundly defeated. When Ptolemy, licking his wounds, withdrew his army from Alexandria to avenge the defeat, Caesar promptly marched off to join with his reinforcements. A vicious two-day battle took place on the banks of the Nile, but the Egyptians were thoroughly beaten. They attempted to retreat and escape by water, and it was during this panic-stricken withdrawal that the fifteen-year-old King Ptolemy was drowned when the boat he was in, overloaded with refugees, sank.

Caesar returned in victory to Alexandria where Queen Cleopatra was anxiously awaiting the return of her lover. Five months had gone by since Caesar first arrived in Alexandria, and while Cleopatra was concerned to maintain her position, her power and her life, another factor had entered the picture – she was pregnant. For nearly half a year she had managed to keep Caesar in Alexandria, and although he was not the type of man to leave without completing his military and political assignment it was nevertheless unlike him to abandon the affairs of the rest of Europe – in so many ways far more important than Egypt

– in order, as Mommsen remarks in his *History of Rome*, to "fight along with Jews and Bedouins against a city rabble". The main reason for Caesar's reluctance to detach himself from Egypt was undoubtedly Cleopatra, and she was now consolidating her hold upon him by quietly convincing him that she was about to give him a son – which he had always wanted.

Predictably, Caesar was spellbound. For months he had lived in close intimacy with this woman who could change from an Amazon to a Queen and to a courtesan in the space of a few hours or even minutes, as it suited her whim. He knew only too well that she was a firm and, within the limits of her vengeful nature, a just ruler. For her sake he upheld the customs of Egypt and proclaimed her second brother, the eleven-year-old boy known as Ptolemy Neoteros, as king-consort. Her sister Arsinoe was, to Cleopatra's satisfaction, imprisoned and the future of the Queen of Egypt seemed secure enough.

But still Caesar lingered in Egypt, unable to drag himself away from his mistress. In Spain, Illyria, Asia Minor and Italy itself trouble was brewing within the vast Roman Empire, and the position of the Caesarian party seemed to be in jeopardy. But while the crisis grew, Caesar (according to Appian, writing a century later) was occupying his time "exploring Egypt in company with Cleopatra and enjoying himself with her in other ways".

Caesar by nature was an active man, and idleness to him was anathema. Cleopatra, determined to keep him with her for as long as she possibly could, had devised this method of keeping him interested, occupied and apparently active – for what could be more active than exploration? They embarked in the fabulous royal *thalamegos* ("carrier of the bed chamber"). This ornate ship, 300 feet long, 45 feet wide and 60 feet high, propelled by hundreds of slave oarsmen, was a floating palace. In its two decks were bedrooms, anterooms, a vast banqueting saloon which could seat sixty people, and a chapel dedicated to the Greek goddess of love, Aphrodite. Furnishings and decorations were in the finest Greek style which the Ptolemys had preserved

134

The Calculating Queen

throughout their dynasty, and only one dining-room was designed in the Egyptian fashion. The great banqueting saloon was built of cedar and cypress wood, with cypress columns decorated in gold and ivory. Mosaics and painted friezes decorated the other rooms. The decks were shaded by elegant awnings which shaded the passengers from the sun, and there was even a small garden.

Cleopatra was shrewd enough to appreciate that her restless guest would need more than a succession of lazy days of eating, drinking, sleeping, and gazing at the sights on the river banks to keep him entertained and his conscience quiet. Deliberately, therefore, she set out to exploit her charm and intelligence, talking of art, politics and literature, while at the same time surrounding him with the sensual pleasures which he liked, but which she took care should not be too gross for his refined tastes.

The *thalamegos* ship was followed by four hundred boats containing a small army of legionaries – for one never knew what might happen. Scholars and local officials were always at hand to answer any questions Caesar might choose to ask about the country through which they were passing. In fact, Caesar was genuinely interested; he enjoyed the problems of governing a country, and he spent many hours discussing Egypt's future with Cleopatra. The voyage was prolonged for two months while the rest of the world waited for the Roman ruler to remember his duties and responsibilities and tear himself away from his fascinating Egyptian queen.

In due course they returned to Alexandria, and there Cleopatra gave birth to the son she had promised. The boy was named Ptolemy Caesar, and popularly known as Caesarion, or "Little Caesar". But since, according to Egyptian tradition, Cleopatra was legally the wife of her young brother she invented, with the aid of the priests, the legend that the child was the son of the god Amon, who had assumed human form for the purpose of procreation. Nobody believed the story for a moment, but it satisfied the conventions of the time, and Cleopatra herself never pretended that the child was any but Caesar's.

Finally Caesar departed at last to take up his neglected Imperial duties, leaving behind him three Roman legions in Egypt to protect Cleopatra. In Alexandria all remained quiet. The people accepted the reign of Cleopatra and her boy husband without demur. They were tired of war, destruction and debauchery, and it seemed to them that Cleopatra had, at least, the interests of her country at heart. Caesar meanwhile set about putting the affairs of his empire in order, and in the summer of 46 B.C. he went to Rome for the celebration of his triumph over Gaul, Egypt, Pontus and Numidia. Vercingetorix, the brave chief of the Gauls, Ganymedes and Arsinoe were among the captives who were dragged along in chains in the triumphal procession, and as part of the festivities they were put to death – with the exception of Arsinoe who was spared to meet her death at Cleopatra's hand five years later.

Caesar then went off to Spain to put Roman administrative affairs in order. The following year he celebrated his second "triumph". And about this time, in 45 B.C., Cleopatra with her boy husband, Ptolemy XV, and her two-year-old son came to Rome. Her spectacular entry into the capital, with all its pomp and splendour, created a sensation. Romans gazed in stupefied amazement at the exhibition of costly clothes and the myriad of luxuriously dressed servants. Even wealthy Rome had seen nothing like it.

Cleopatra was greeted formally by Caesar, who was surrounded by officials of the Republic, and then was conveyed to an elegant villa beside the Tiber. Here she held court, attended by those who wished to please Caesar and visited by all the leading political figures of the day. But even so, Cleopatra was far from popular. The Romans resented such a public flaunting of their dictator's mistress. It offended the dignity and pride of the ancient city of Rome, even though it hardly registered on the social morality of a people who were notorious for their adulterous conduct. Perhaps more significant was the act that she was an Egyptian, and in those days Egyptians were regarded rather as Jews were in the Middle Ages. Her Greek descent was ignored, and in any case, the Romans despised all foreigners.

Cicero, who visited Cleopatra, found her insolent and said he detested her. Rumours went around that Cleopatra had come to Rome to persuade Caesar to marry her, declare Caesarion his heir, and rule over Egypt. Caesar himself quite helplessly annoyed the Romans by openly displaying his infatuation for the Queen of Egypt. When he built a temple in Rome to his divine ancestress Venus Genetrix, as he had vowed to do after the battle of Pharsalia, he erected a statue of Cleopatra beside that of the goddess.

The rumour went around that Caesar intended to introduce a new law allowing him to marry more than one wife, provided the second wife was a foreigner. Cleopatra became more arrogant as Caesar became more dictatorial, and at some time around that period her brother-husband disappeared. He was an obvious obstacle to Cleopatra's plans to marry Caesar, for he could not have abandoned his status as king in order to agree to a divorce, and it is more likely that Cleopatra quietly got rid of him. But there is no record as to just how or when the unfortunate young King vanished.

Whatever secret plans, encouraged by Cleopatra, Caesar may have arranged for a marriage between them, or for declaring his son legal, will never be known for certain. Before he could properly concentrate on arranging the future he had one more battle to fight. In 53 B.C. the Parthians had slaughtered Crassus and inflicted a humiliating defeat upon the Roman legions. This still had to be avenged, and everyone looked to Caesar to obliterate his stain upon Roman honour. Caesar planned to march eastwards on 19 March, 44 B.C. But four days before this Brutus and his fellow senators had violently put an end to the growing tyranny of the weak dictator.

Caesar's will made no mention of Cleopatra or of his son Caesarion. Cleopatra's last hope vanished. With Caesar's assassination her dreams were in ruins, and she hastily departed for Egypt for there was nobody to protect her from the hatred of the Romans. But thanks to the obedient

Roman legions, her throne still awaited her, even if she received a cool reception from her courtiers. For more than two years she reigned quietly with her little son, Ptolemy XVI, the last of his dynasty, by her side. And then into her life came another Roman – Mark Anthony – and by her infatuation for him Cleopatra was to bring him, her small son and herself to a violent end, and deliver her country into the condition of a vassal state which has continued throughout the centuries until this day.

Chapter 9 La Belle Gabrielle

In the mid-16th century, while Pizarro and Cortes were conquering South America and the voyages of many explorers gave the century the name of the Age of Discovery, Europe was torn with internal problems and dissensions. Corruption in the Roman Church, for example, was the subject of endless protestations from the faithful. While the Pope had an emerald Venus inlaid in his cross, the prelates lived a life of depravity and systematically enriched themselves, and the clergy generally were ignorant and coarse. In such an environment the protests and ideas of men like Luther and Calvin flourished, and the Reformation – which broadened into a major social revolution – shattered Europe and divided her nations into two bitterly opposing factions.

In France, Protestantism spread rapidly and became firmly established in Picardy, Normandy, Poitou, Dauphine and Languedoc. The Roman Catholic princes suppressed the Protestants with a severity which led to civil war and culminated in the notorious massacre of Saint Bartholomew when, for three days, Huguenots were relentlessly pursued and murdered by the Catholics. But the massacre only hardened the resolution of the persecuted, and in the end they succeeded in obtaining the rights of full liberty of conscience.

Then the Protestant leader, Henry of Navarre, who had gathered the Huguenots in the Calvinist Union, became heir to the throne through the death of the French king's only brother, and civil war broke out again. As it was only too obvious that the pederastic King would be unlikely to produce a child, the influential Guise family set up the Catholic League, an organization which became so powerful that the King, Henry III, had to call on Henry of Navarre for help in besieging his own capital. In 1589 Henry III was stabbed to death by a Dominican monk, and Henry of Navarre, now King of all France, had to set about conquering the large part of his own kingdom. This pursuit was to take the next ten years of his reign before the religious wars came to an end after thirty-six bitter years.

It was against this background of strife and insecurity that Gabrielle d'Estrées was born in 1570. She was the fourth of five sisters, and had two younger brothers. She came of a long line of "dames galantes". Some thirty of her female ancestors had been notorious for their love affairs, and one of them had been in turn mistress of the French King Francis I, the Habsburg Emperor Charles V and Pope Clement VI. Gabrielle's eldest sister was married. The second sister had become an abbess when her mother took Gabrielle and her third sister to Paris, to the court of Henry III.

Gabrielle, with her clear blue eyes, golden hair, pearly skin and all the fresh charm of her seventeen years was a great success with the courtiers. The Cardinal de Guise, the Duc de Longueville, and Roger, Duc de Bellegarde and Grand Equerry of France, all paid court to her – encouraged by her mother who, not content with furthering her daughter's love affairs, proceeded at the age of 48 to fall madly in love with the Marquis d'Alegre.

When her lover became governor of Issoire in Auvergne,

Madame d'Estrées, without a single backward thought for her husband and children, departed with him. The father of the girls, Antoine d'Estrées, then asked his sister-in-law, Madame de Sourdis, to chaperone his daughters. But since she, too, was at heart a rake she turned as blind an eye on the amorous activities of her nieces as did their mother. So, after a brief liaison with the Duc de Longueville, Gabrielle became the mistress of Roger Bellegarde, a charming young man of 28 who was already famous for his success with women.

In the spring of 1588 the ineffectual Henry III fled from his capital and the influence of the Guise family to beg the help of his heir, Henry of Navarre. In view of the disordered political situation, Antoine d'Estrées ordered his daughters to return to their home at the Château de Coeuvres, near Soissons and some 60 miles from Paris. Her lover followed her and continued to pay court to her although she was watched over by an alert and puritanical father. But in the following year, when Henry of Navarre succeeded to the throne of France, Roger de Bellegarde was one of the first Catholic noblemen to rally to the new King, and he, unwisely, boasted to his sovereign about the beauty and shapeliness of his young mistress. This was indeed asking for trouble, for the King was famous for his amours. He had been separated for several years from his wife, Margaret, the sister of Henry III. Apart from his frequent *passades* or amorous adventures, the heroines of which according to a contemporary chronicler were "too numerous for their names to have been recorded", he had also had one or two semi-permanent mistresses. His most recent affair, with the Countess of Grammont, had lasted eight years, and although he had sworn his eternal fidelity in passionate letters, by the time he first met Gabrielle he had stopped writing to her altogether.

In the autumn of 1590 Henry suggested that they should use the pretext of a hunting party to call in at the Château of Coeuvres so that he could take an exploratory look at his Grand Equerry's beautiful mistress. He was delighted with what he saw – so much so that some weeks later, although the forces of the Catholic League were searching for him, the King disguised himself as a peasant and went again to Coeuvres to see Gabrielle. At the time Antoine d'Estrées was away from home and the King was received by Gabrielle and her sister Diane. Gabrielle was not impressed, however. The King was nearly forty, and his ragged clothing did nothing to enhance his swarthy complexion, his lined face and his untidy hair. The truth was that Henry had led a hard life, often in his childhood facing the threat of imprisonment and death; furthermore he was always short of money, and continually on the move in fighting for himself and his kingdom. He had none of the cultured airs and graces of Roger de Bellgarde, the elegant, suave and perfumed young man with whom Gabrielle felt herself to be in love. Henry – tall, beaky-nosed and eagle-faced – left the pretty Gabrielle unmoved, despite his regal air of courage and pride.

Early in the following year Henry laid siege to Chartres. Madame de Sourdis, Gabrielle's chaperone, had special links with that part of France. For one thing, sticking to the family tradition, she had a lover who had been governor of the area, and secondly, her husband had been governor of Chartres under Henry III and was hoping to regain his appointment. She knew of the King's pointed interest in her niece and failed to understand the silly girl's preference for a mere fop of a duke. Now she saw the chance of introducing Gabrielle again into the King's ambit, and on the pretext of rejoining her husband who was with the besiegers, she brought her niece to Chartres. There they were greeted with joyous enthusiasm by the King, who could hardly take his eyes off Gabrielle, and installed in an inn outside the city.

King Henry's double siege – of Chartres and of Gabrielle – lasted for several weeks, but with equal patience and perseverance he pressed his twin attack and at the beginning of April experienced the happiness of achieving a double victory. While Gabrielle had held out vigorously, her gentle and passive nature was not designed for prolonged struggle. Although the King's negligent appearance and clumsy advances did not please her, his violent and sincere passion at last touched her heart.

The exigencies of war soon tore Henry from his new mistress, and she was obliged to return to Coeuvres to meet with a frosty reception from her disapproving father. Actually, Antoine d'Estrées had not done too badly for himself, for Henry, in an attempt to win his support and disarm his straight-faced hostility, had appointed him governor of the town of Noyons which had just surrendered to his army. Although d'Estrées took up his new post with some alacrity, it did not buy his complacency. While he could do little to thwart the royal will, he could not bring himself to forgive his daughter. Indeed, he had already decided that a comfortable lesser establishment would be a better provision for her future than the speculative and risky position of royal favourite, particularly with a master so volatile and insecure.

By this time Roger de Bellegarde had tactfully disappeared from the scene. Although Gabrielle was convinced that she still loved him she was forced to admit to herself, when she heard that he was now having an affair with Mademoiselle de Guise, that there was no more hope in that direction. To emphasize the point Antoine d'Estrées introduced to his daughter as an eligible husband the elderly Seigneur de Liancourt, a widower with four children. King Henry was far away, fighting near Rouen, and Gabrielle did not dare to appeal to him for help in escaping this obnoxious marriage. She protested, implored and wept, but her father remained adamant, and in June 1592 the nineteen-year-old Gabrielle was duly married to de Liancourt. (Gabrielle's mother did not bother to attend her daughter's wedding. If she had she might have saved her own life, for one night in June, exasperated by the harsh policies and brutalities of her lover, the Governor of Issoire, a handful of local people forced their way into the governor's residence, murdered him and his mistress, and threw their naked bodies into the street.)

The dramatic news of her mother's violent death reached Gabrielle at the beginning of her unwanted and unhappy marriage. It was, however, a great relief to her when her ageing husband turned out to be impotent. Neither on their wedding night nor on any other night thereafter, despite the most praiseworthy efforts, was Seigneur de Liancourt able to perform his conjugal duties. Gabrielle, relatively unsullied, remained a docile wife while she awaited the return of the King, and when Henry finally returned from the wars to find his mistress married he was quite unconcerned – a complaisant husband might prove easier to deal with than a puritanical father. He installed himself at nearby Noyons, where he could visit Gabrielle to declare his passionate love and protest his undying fidelity. With every visit he begged her to come and live with him.

Gabrielle needed little persuasion to surrender. Within three months of her marriage she calmly abandoned her husband to join the overjoyed King. Faced with a *fait accompli*, her father and her husband abandoned the unequal struggle against the King's power and prerogative, and were duly rewarded with honorary titles and advancement. To Gabrielle Henry gave a château and its lands, and a generous *dot*, or dowry.

Now Gabrielle was able to take her place among Henry's court. Due to the unsettled times and the fact that the capital was in the hands of the antagonistic Catholic League, the court was of necessity itinerant. Nevertheless Gabrielle, with her undeniable beauty and charm and lack of ostentation – a happy contrast to the brash allure displayed by most of the great ladies of the period – was a great success, and she became immensely popular at court.

Henry was necessarily away a great deal of the time, always striving to unite his war-torn kingdom by the simple expedient of conquest, as and when it could be achieved. It was during one of his absences that Gabrielle's old lover Roger de Bellegarde turned up again. Precisely what went on between them is not known, but when Roger too went off to the wars Gabrielle was indiscreet enough to write to him. Inevitably, kind friends told the King all about this misdemeanour. For perhaps the first time in his life Henry found himself torn by the agonizing pangs of jealousy. It was a new and unpleasant experience for him. His Queen's flagrant affairs, and the women whose affections he had occasionally shared with another man had caused him no suffering, but to Gabrielle he wrote anguished letters demanding that she must make up her mind to have but one *serviteur*.

"My love," he wrote, "can be altered by nothing in the world – except a rival." Gabrielle's response was genuine enough; she promised not to see Bellegarde again, and it is probable that it was at this time that she really began to feel true love for the man to whom, until now, she had merely submitted. Henry appeared to be deeply in love with her. He wrote to her constantly and upbraided her when she did not write to him with equal frequency. Whenever possible he would send for her to join him, and he chafed at any delay in her arrival. "Come, come," he begged her in writing, "and honour with your presence one who, were he free, would travel a thousand leagues to cast himself at your feet, never again to stir from them . . . I do not know what charm you have used, but I did not bear previous absences so impatiently as I do this one. It seems to me that a century has passed by since I left you."

On one occasion, when Gabrielle was on her way to join her lover, the horses which drew Gabrielle's coach took fright and bolted. The road was flanked by a steep escarpment, but luckily a wheel hit a large stone on the road and the carriage came to a sudden but merciful halt with a broken axle. Gabrielle was shaken but unhurt. When the King heard of her narrow escape he went pale with fear in a manner that had never before been observed even in moments of greatest danger on the battlefield.

In 1593 Henry decided to renounce his Protestant faith and become a Catholic – a course of action which had been pressed upon him for a long time by his advisers and by Gabrielle herself. His famous observation, "Paris is well worth a Mass," is often quoted as evidence of the cynical fashion in which he adopted his new faith, but in fact it was certainly in a far less captious mood that he at last made up his mind to take what he described to Gabrielle as "the most perilous leap". He did it in the hope of finally uniting his country. But while his conversion certainly brought to an end the "wars of religion", it did not bring peace to his country. The Catholic League continued to foment trouble, and they now had the backing of King Philip of Spain whose support for the League was politically motivated.

Henry's strategy was to offer the towns dominated by the Catholic League a three-month truce in which to consider and re-assess their positions. Meanwhile he bribed the governor of Paris into opening the gates of the city to him and his army. Thus the French capital was seized and occupied without a shot being fired. Henry magnanimously issued a mass pardon to all those who had previously opposed him, and even allowed the Spanish soldiers in the city to depart with their lives. Nobody in that vicious and turbulent age was accustomed to such generous treatment, and throughout his reign Henry achieved far more by his generosity and good humour, by his clemency and understanding, than by any amount of violence. Such a king was out of context in the Europe of that day; his contemporaries regarded him as a great man and far ahead of his time. His civilized outlook and humanitarian attitudes made him one of the most outstanding monarchs of history.

Towards the end of that same year Henry's happiness was boosted by the news that Gabrielle had become pregnant. It was by no means the first time that he was to experience paternity, but when in June 1594 Gabrielle's son was born the event was "welcomed with transports of joy by the father". The child, healthy and vigorous, was named César.

Meanwhile, one town of the Catholic League after another was surrendering to the King, and in September Henry decided to make a formal triumphal entry into Paris to celebrate both the birth of his son and the increasing security of his kingdom. Gabrielle preceded the King into the capital. She was carried in a gorgeously decked litter, wearing a black satin gown "all tufted with white and sewn with quantities of pearls and precious stones so lustrous that they outshone the light of the torches".

La Belle Gabrielle

Gabrielle was installed in a house close to the Palace of the Louvre, where once again she charmed herself into the good graces of the courtiers. That winter in Paris was gay. The King insisted that Gabrielle should appear at all the functions and festivities of the court. Always she was beautiful and richly dressed, for Henry, himself short of money and often shabbily clothed, was nevertheless inordinately generous to his mistress. He loved to shower gifts on her and show her off; he took her everywhere and was always laughing with her and caressing her in public.

Unfortunately the son of whom he was so proud was legally the child of Seigneur de Liancourt, so Henry set in train the legal proceedings necessary to secure Gabrielle's freedom. An ecclesiastical tribunal was asked to nullify her marriage on three counts: that she was forced into the marriage against her will by her father; that the marriage had never been consummated due to the husband's impotence; and that it was within the forbidden tables of kindred and affinity since Seigneur de Liancourt's first wife was first cousin of Gabrielle's father. The court rejected the first two counts on the grounds that there was not enough evidence to support them, but declared the marriage null on the third count. (Some time later the ill-used Seigneur de Liancourt bravely married again, but his virility seemed to have been lost for ever, for his third wife also sued successfully for nullity on the grounds of his impotence.)

The King was now able to legitimize his son and reward Gabrielle, and this he promptly proceeded to do, through the Parliament of Paris, in a document notable for its delightful phrases. "Having recognized the many great graces and perfections, as much of mind as of body, that abide in the person of Our very dear and well beloved Gabrielle d'Estrées, We for some years past have sought her to that effect... And whereas the said Lady, after Our long suit and by the exercise of such authority as We brought to bear, did condescend to obey Us and do Our pleasure, and whereas it has pleased God that she should not long since give Us a son... The default in his birth excluding him from all right of succession to the crown and also to that of Our

147

kingdom of Navarre . . . he would remain in very bad state if he was not, by legitimation, made capable of receiving all the gifts and benefits which will be due to him . . ."

With his son's future satisfactorily settled, Henry recognized his debt to his mistress with the title of Marquise de Monceaux. The château and land that went with this title were situated about two leagues from Meaux, close to Paris. Naturally Gabrielle was delighted both with the elegant château and the generous income that went with it. She wasted no time in moving in, and immediately began to arrange her new home in a luxurious and tasteful style.

In the years that followed life became increasingly prosperous both for Henry and Gabrielle. The King's campaigns for the unification and pacification of France proved increasingly successful, and slowly the Spanish interlopers were being evicted. By April 1598 Henry felt that the country was ready for the famous Edict of Nantes which granted full liberty of conscience to the people of France. It has a strangely topical ring today when legislation is being introduced to prevent discrimination against men because of the colour of their skins, but at that time it was those who held Protestant beliefs who needed protection. Under the new edict all schools, colleges and hospitals were open equally to the Protestants as to the Catholics. Protestants were granted all civil rights and became eligible for government office; additionally it was ordained that equal numbers of Protestants and Catholics had to preside in all lawsuits in which Protestants were involved.

This edict was ratified in February 1599 and, as Hesketh Pearson says, it "saved France from unspeakable miseries until Henry's grandson, Louis XIV, revoked it in 1685, letting loose the horrors his grandfather had so wisely and humanely curbed". The King also had a wise, hardworking and above all honest Minister of Finance in Rosny, who later became the Duc de Sully – methodically he put the confused and corrupt finances of the country into order. Step-by-step Henry was achieving his ambitions for his country which he put above all else except, perhaps, his love for his mistress.

La Belle Gabrielle

This love affair between Henry and Gabrielle was one of those very rare personal liaisons in which a king could really be said to love his mistress and she him without the thought of personal gain or other ulterior motivation. Gabrielle was truly devoted to her King, although she did not hesitate to ask for favours for her family, her friends and herself. But at the slightest indication of anger or resentment on the King's part she would retreat. A typical occasion was when the Duc de Sully refused to pay the bills for the trumpeters and other musicians on the occasion of the baptism of her third child. The infant had been baptised with all the pomp and ceremony accorded to a "child of France". The Duc de Sully brusquely pointed out that there was no such thing as a child of France. When Gabrielle protested to the King she was rebuked and put in her place. What the Duc de Sully could do for France was, the King made clear, of first importance. Gabrielle kept sensibly quiet.

Nevertheless, the King loved his "belle Gabrielle" dearly, not only for her physical charms – indeed, she began to grow quite stout – but also for her more durable qualities. He made her Duchesse to Beaufort and he continued to shower her with gifts of land and jewellery, which he could ill afford. He adored his children – two boys and a girl, each of which he described as being more beautiful than the last – and he arranged for them advantageous marriages and positions while they were still only babies. He even began to think of marrying Gabrielle and went so far as to discuss with the Duc de Sully the possibility of divorcing his existing Queen. When he outlined the qualities which he thought a future queen should possess, it was in reality Gabrielle whom he was describing.

He needed someone, he said, of a gentle and compliant nature, of beautiful person, and of such a kind as would give hopes of her bearing children – as well as being wise enough to bring them up in a proper fashion. When Sully, who was perhaps being deliberately dense, continued to suggest one after another of the European princesses, Henry impatiently went so far as to admit that he had Gabrielle in

149

mind. The honest Sully was horrified. Not only was the suggestion a scandalous one, but it was also politically unsound; the claims of the eldest child, born in double adultery (for Gabrielle had then still been married), would be inferior to those of the younger born in single adultery, while both would be less than those of a child born after such a marriage.

The situation would inevitably result in endless wars over the succession, Sully considered, and he was quite sure that the King would appreciate the sense of his reasoning when his ardour cooled. Nevertheless, although Henry's ardour cooled sufficiently for him to indulge in two or three other affairs (one of which produced two children), these were merely *passades*. The truth was that Gabrielle's mind attracted him as much as her body. With her he could be at ease. He could tell her everything and trust her without reservation. His determination to marry her increased in spite of the advice of his courtiers. More and more he treated her as though she were already the Queen, and while his representatives in Rome were entreating the Pope to annul the King's marriage with his wife, Gabrielle was for all practical purposes accepted as the future Queen in that she was present at all State and social functions of the court, and she was attended and waited upon by the highest ladies in the land, all of whom were currying favour but some of whom genuinely liked her as a person.

Certainly foreign ambassadors treated her as though she were the Queen. Robert Cecil, Ambassador of Queen Elizabeth of England, reported that she was "stout but really pleasant and gracious" and said she "expressed herself well and courteously". The consensus of opinion, particularly among those who knew her personally, seemed to be that if the King had to have a mistress, if he had to love somebody so much, and even if he had to marry her, it might as well be Gabrielle – for she never abused her position and she used her great power only for good. Although she was always being sued for favours, she rarely used her influence with the King in this context, and for a woman in her position she had remarkably few enemies in society.

Only among the common people was she unpopular. They called her the *Duchesse d'Ordure,* and they wrote scurrilous verses about her. And, of course, the disapproval which the people always felt towards a mistress of the King inevitably rebounded on the King himself. His public caresses and solicitude met with a somewhat severe disapprobation.

Heedless of criticism, Henry persisted in his avowed intention to marry Gabrielle. She, for her part, was quite prepared to be bought off by a large sum of money, but she was determined to drive a hard bargain. The Pope certainly did not like the way the wind was blowing as Henry's attempts to divorce his wife dragged on and on, and finally His Holiness became impatient and threatening, and accused the King of following the degrading example of Henry VIII of England. But eventually even the Pope surrendered, for the wind was blowing around the Vatican, too. By early 1599 events seemed to be moving towards a satisfactory conclusion.

At any rate, confident of the outcome, the King gave Gabrielle the magnificent ring which he himself had received at his Coronation along with many other gifts. She, equally confident, put in hand the redecoration of the Queen's bedchamber at the Louvre, which she had, in fact, already been occupying for some time. She also ordered a bridal dress of pink velvet embroidered in gold and silver, which the master craftsman who made it insisted on keeping until the great day because the Duchess had not yet paid for it. And then, in March, the King announced that the marriage would be celebrated on the first Sunday after Easter..

To Gabrielle, about to change her status from "favourite" to "queen", it was a dream so dazzling that in spite of all the favourable indications she could not believe that it was really going to come true. She was now pregnant for the fourth time, and although she had carried off her previous pregnancies lightly on this occasion she seemed to be in low spirits. Like all the great ladies of her time she habitually consulted fortune-tellers, and although these "seers" naturally tried to please their clients by foretelling a brilliant future whenever possible, for Gabrielle they had little comfort to offer. She would, they said, be married only once, she would die young, and she would be kept from her great destiny by a child.

Although there had been no difficulties with her previous children, Gabrielle began to be haunted by the fears and anxieties which affect many women in her condition. Henry proved to be as impressionable and superstitious as she, and therefore he was in no state to give her much comfort, being himself desperately worried. Finally, a Florentine soothsayer named Bizacasser went even further than his colleagues. He announced that not only would the Duchess not marry the King of France, but that her eyes would never see the light of the approaching Easter Day.

The court was at Fontainebleau for Lent, and as the Easter festivities approached the King permitted the members of his Council to return to their own homes to undertake their Easter duties. He himself, as was the custom for Catholic kings, prepared to undergo the rigours of Holy Week, and his confessor insisted that he must demonstrate his penitence and give a good example by temporarily parting from his mistress. Gabrielle therefore decided to return to Paris, but Henry insisted on escorting her as far as Savigny where they arrived on 5 April and spent the night together.

The following day King Henry went with her to the Seine, where she was to take a boat along the river to Paris – and at this point Gabrielle wept and clung to him, crying that she was sure she would never see him again. The King was so upset that he almost weakened and took her back to Fontainebleau, but finally, after many fond embraces and "more demonstrations than ever of passionate love and regret for their parting", as an eye-witness described it, the unhappy and despondent Gabrielle was put aboard her boat. It was a sad, tearful and ominous parting. Henry was finally persuaded to return to Fontainebleau while Gabrielle collapsed upon the cushions of the boat and abandoned herself to despair.

That same evening she dined at the house of a man named Sebastien Zamet, a banker of a somewhat raffish reputation who was nevertheless a good friend of the King's – indeed, he often lent money to him, which is always a very good basis for friendship. Gabrielle found that she liked him as a person, and she liked his small but exquisite house. He was amusing company and he served delicious food. On this occasion he had ordered a superlative Florentine menu to be prepared in honour of Gabrielle, but she hardly touched anything, and after dinner she complained that she felt ill. It was surmised that something she had eaten had upset her, though she did not eat very much. Some said it was an orange, others a lemon, and others a salad which had possessed an unusually bitter taste. She retired at once to her bed, where she spent a restless night.

The following morning, although she still felt ill, she insisted on attending a service at the nearby church of St. Antoine. Her sombre and weary appearance attracted some attention, but during the service, as if to reassure herself, she showed to her neighbour, Mademoiselle de Guise, some letters from Rome on the subject of her forthcoming marriage to the King, and two affectionate notes which she had received from Henry earlier that morning.

Before the service was over, however, the heat and atmosphere in the church became too much for her to support, and she was obliged to return hastily to Zamet's house. There she was seized with violent convulsions accompanied by such intolerable pain that she fainted. When she was revived she begged her entourage to take her to the house of her aunt, Madame de Sourdis. So weak was she by this time that she had to be carried out to her litter, and when she arrived at her aunt's home she found that Madame de Sourdis was away. However, a messenger was sent to fetch her, and Gabrielle was duly accommodated and cared for.

After a much more restful night Gabrielle was well enough the next day to visit her own parish church of Saint Germain l'Auxerrois for Mass. But that same afternoon she became ill again, and at four o'clock she began to suffer labour pains, accompanied by repeated uncontrolled convulsions which terrified those who were looking after her. These symptoms ceased after about four hours, leaving her aching and exhausted, but the next day, Good Friday, the pains began again and became even more intense. She was now so worn out that she had not the strength to give birth to her child.

The midwife who had attended Gabrielle's previous childbirths completely lost her head, and the doctors, terrified by their responsibility, decided to deliver the child by force. "They took from her," reports L'Estoile, the historian, "a still-born child of masculine sex in bits and pieces. Then they administered three douches, helped out by four suppositories." Not surprisingly, this treatment produced no discernible improvement, and until six o'clock Gabrielle continued to suffer "frightful pains and convulsions such as had never before been seen by the doctors, apothecaries and surgeons, which caused her to tear herself on her face and other parts of her body".

To add to Gabrielle's misery, all the women of the entourage had abandoned her, alarmed that her mysterious illness might be infectious. Although she called constantly for her lover in the most pitiable tones – and Gabrielle had already written to beg him to come and marry her, for the sake of the children, before she died – he did not appear. The messages had, however, been sent to him. He had in fact set out on the eve of Good Friday as soon as he had heard of her illness, and had sent a messenger ahead of him, to ride as quickly as possible to announce that the King was on his way. When Gabrielle received this news she rallied a little, but by Friday evening she slowly began to lose consciousness. With her features and limbs hideously distorted by her dying agonies, she lay in a coma all night until early on the Saturday morning when death released her.

Henry did not come. Four leagues from Paris he had been intercepted by two dignitaries who informed him that she was dead. Shattered and in tears, he declared that he would go to see her nevertheless, but one of the messengers, the

La Belle Gabrielle

Chancellor Bellievre, persuaded him that a public exhibition of his sorrow at Easter time would offend the people. So, prostrated by grief, Henry allowed himself to be put into a coach and sent back to Fontainebleau. In fact, at the moment that Henry actually received the news, Gabrielle still had several hours to live. The messengers had lied, but perhaps with some justification, for they claimed that they had wished to spare Henry the painful sight of Gabrielle's terrible sufferings.

Gabrielle died on Holy Saturday, so fulfilling the Florentine fortune-teller's prediction. Such a quick, violent and dramatic death naturally gave rise to rumours of poison, but the autopsy showed no signs of foul play whatever and the King himself never suspected it. The Pope, when the news reached him, saw Gabrielle's death before her marriage as the hand of God himself meting out justice.

Henry mourned bitterly and gave Gabrielle the funeral of a Queen. The court was ordered to go into mourning – black for a week and purple for three months. He would have liked to have had Gabrielle buried in the royal vaults, but he did not dare; instead, she and the dismembered body of her child were interred in the Abbey of Notre Dame La Royale, near Monceaux, of which her sister was abbess.

In reply to a sympathetic letter from his sister Catherine, Henry wrote: "I received your letter with much consolation. I have great need of it, for my affliction is as incomparable as was she to whom it is due. Regrets and lamentations will accompany me to the grave. The root of my love is destroyed – it will not sprout again. But that of my friendship will remain ever green for you, my dear sister, whom I kiss a million times. Henry."

And as he told his sister, God had brought him into the world for his country and not for himself. So now he decided to fall in with the wishes of his advisers. He agreed to marry the niece of the Grand Duke of Tuscany, Marie of Medici – and the fact that he owed the Duke the equivalent of £30 million sterling may have had something to do with it. However, his easily triggered passions could not remain dormant for long. His nature was resilient enough for him to imagine himself in love again very soon. Within six months after Gabrielle's death he had acquired another mistress. Indeed, in the ten years of life that remained to him before a religious maniac stabbed him to death, he had many other mistresses. But there is little doubt that Gabrielle was the only true love of his perturbed life.

Chapter 10 Etude in a Minor Key

"Nobody knows better how to love, but nobody more quickly reduces those whom she does love to a state of utter prostration." Those words were written by a young man in his twenties about a woman of forty-six – the celebrated George Sand. Although the young man was never one of her lovers, he had nevertheless accurately summed up the self-destructive quality of her love. Throughout her life George Sand wrote novels and pursued love with equal energy. Before she "retired" from the pursuit of love and lived in the country to write idyllic pastoral novels, her books were strongly influenced by her amatory experiences. The very name by which she was universally known was derived from her first lover, Jules Sandeau.

Her real name was Aurore Dupin. She was born in July 1804, the child of the beloved only son of an aristocratic old lady and a raffish young woman who caused her grandmother much anguish. Aurore was perhaps fortunate in being brought up mainly by the grandmother from whom in due course she inherited a comfortable property and a respectable income. In 1822, at the age of eighteen, she married the presentable young Baron Dudevant and forthwith produced a strapping son. But before long, life in the country began to pall and Aurore suffered from boredom. Whenever a handsome young man appeared whom she found amusing she lost no time in falling in love with him. Her second child was believed to have been the daughter of another old acquaintance whom she had revisited during a trip to Paris.

As time went on she began to spend more and more time in Paris, and it was there that she became involved in a more permanent relationship with Jules Sandeau. After a while she discovered that her husband regarded her as an object of scorn, and she felt that "to go on living with a man who feels for his wife neither respect nor confidence is tantamount to trying to bring the dead to life". Without further ado she decided to leave him – after first informing him that she wanted an allowance from the estate which the marriage had legally made his. Then, with her little daughter, she departed for Paris to live with Jules.

The love affair between Aurore and Jules Sandeau lasted a long time. Their partnership was professional as well as amatory. They collaborated in literary work, and she found herself a job on a new satirical periodical called *Figaro*. She insisted that their writing should be published under the name of "J. Sand". But when she completed her first book her lover generously said that he could not put his name to a book in which he had contributed no part. Nevertheless Aurore was determined to employ the *nom-de-plume* of a man, and as a compromise she settled on the pseudonym George Sand which was to become more famous than she could ever have imagined – and for different reasons.

George Sand, as she preferred to be known, now embarked upon a pattern of life which was to endure for many years. As a rebel, an individualist and a liberal she resented the lack of personal freedom to which women of her day were condemned and she deliberately refused to subscribe to convention. As a gesture of independence she took to wearing men's clothes and smoking cigars. She outraged society with a certain self-assured delight and a complete lack of concern, and she was always surrounded by devoted friends in her literary world who admired and loved her – and she in her turn loved others passionately.

Her dearest friend, Marie Dorval, once asked: "What was it that led her on a hunger of the senses?" She concluded that "it was a craving for something very different, a furious desire to find that true love which ever beckons, ever flies". If that was true, then inevitably that craving finally drove her from Jules who could give her no more. Coolly and without remorse she left him. In the months that followed she suffered one disappointment after another in love, which she described in a book which she wrote at the time – a book in which she poured all of her complex emotional nature into her cold heroine's anguished search for love. Quite apart from men, she deeply loved her great friend Marie Dorval, a successful actress, to whom she wrote long and possessive letters. These so infuriated Marie's lover that he forbade her to answer "this Lesbian who is for ever plaguing her". George Sand was no Lesbian, however, although her kind of love was far from simple and straightforward. For the man she loved she wanted to be not only a mistress but also a housekeeper, a nurse and above all a mother.

Perhaps because of this idiosyncrasy the lovers she chose were many and varied, as if she were in pursuit of some personal emotional holy grail which was always beyond attainment. With Alfred de Musset, the famous poet and playwright, she went to Venice. But their love affair was one of desperation. Their mutual passion reached the heights and depths of exhilaration and despair, and in the end the affair battered itself to extinction on the frenzy of its own excesses. She then abandoned him for a worthy Venetian doctor who barely knew what had hit him but was nevertheless immensely proud of his famous mistress. If she liked him, it was probably because he was soothing and accommodating and allowed her to get on with her work in peace. A few months later she was back in Paris to revive the affair with Alfred de Musset, but this time it ended with so much anguish that the two agreed not to see each other again.

According to Maurois, their affair ended thus: "They were both afflicted by that worst of follies – a craving for the Absolute. From breach to breach, from reconciliation to reconciliation, their dying passion twitched and gibbered in the nervous spasm of approaching dissolution. They were like two men fighting to death, both drenched in blood and sweat, clinging together, raining blows on one another..."

Between elation and despondency George Sand continued her odyssey of love and literature, the former always reflecting itself in the latter. She was now officially separated from her husband who had custody of their son and retained a property in Paris, while she kept the country house which she loved so much and had with her her daughter Solange. She began to take a greater interest in the social and environmental aspects of life and became slowly more absorbed in the political questions of the day.

But all the time she continued to have a succession of lovers. There was Michel de Bourges, a lawyer a few years older than George who was then thirty-one. But he was already bald, and looked a bent old man – quite unlike her masculine ideal which called for youth, frailness and beauty, and of course a dependence on herself as a mother figure. It was not long before his prejudiced and didactic statements and attitudes became intolerably irritating to her, and that was the end of that episode.

More of the type which George Sand worshipped was Franz Liszt, the virtuoso pianist and composer, on whom she had had her eye for a number of years, but Liszt was jealously guarded by his existing mistress, Marie d'Agoult. If Liszt was not available, another equally talented and handsome musical genius was. In 1836, at the age of thirty-two, she met Frédéric Chopin and promptly tried to lure him to her country house in Nohant. But at first Chopin disapproved of her intensely. He was seven years her junior, and sensitive to the point of hating boisterous people, noise,

George Sand (*top left*) broke up her early marriage, showed her independence by wearing men's clothes (*below*), and became Chopin's mistress near middle age (*top right*).

The relationship between Charles
Dickens and the buxom actress
Ellen Ternan (*right*) remains a subject
of speculation. – Madame de Pompadour's future as a royal mistress
was foretold when she was still a
young country girl (*below*). Her
famous portrait by Boucher (*bottom*),
now in the National Gallery of
Scotland, shows an expression of
pretty complacency.

untidiness and gossip. He pined continually for his home-
land of Poland and the refined society that he had known
there. His mind was mainly exercised in attempting to bring
a spiritual rapture to sensitive people like himself through
the medium of his piano.

When he first met "this Sand woman" he considered her
totally antipathetic, and it was only when she came to Paris
in October 1837 that he agreed to meet her again. At that
time he was in the depths of misery over a young Polish
woman whom he had hoped to marry but who was now
gradually withdrawing from him, because her parents disapproved of Chopin's weak physique. George Sand was
only too ready to console this young man who, with his
slender build, fair hair, long delicate hands and melancholy and noble air, appealed so much to her mistress-nurse
instincts.

Inevitably Chopin soon succumbed to her dominant and
vigorous personality. She captured his heart, it is said, by
gazing deep into his eyes while he played sad and reflective
music on the piano. Heinrich Heine, who knew them both
at this time, recorded that "she had beautiful auburn hair
falling to her shoulders; eyes rather lustreless and sleepy,
but calm and gentle; a smile of great good nature; a somewhat dead, somewhat husky voice, difficult to hear, for
George is far from talkative, and takes in a great deal more
than she gives out". Chopin, he observed, was "endowed
with abnormal sensitiveness which the least contact can
wound . . . a man made for intimacies, withdrawn into a
mysterious world of his own from which he sometimes
emerges in a sudden spate of impassioned but charming
speech".

Because of his social and sexual shyness, Chopin needed
more careful handling than George's other lovers. But at
first she hesitated before committing herself, for two main
reasons. First, she was reluctant to damage in any way
Chopin's possible future relations with his Polish fiancée;
second, she herself had no good reason to separate from
her present lover, Mallefille, apart from the fact that she
had been swept off her feet by Chopin. She sought the ad-

F

vice of Chopin's best friend on the first count and was assured that the engagement had been broken off long ago. On the second count she managed to suppress her own feelings of guilt in deceiving a lover – a thing she had never done before in her life. When an affair ended, it ended openly and honestly without deception.

Mallefille found out, however, and created an embarrassing number of jealous scenes. Finally, in November 1838, she and Chopin fled to Majorca, taking her children with them. This was in many ways a wise move. The children would benefit from the warmer climate, she herself could work in greater domestic peace, and Chopin could escape from any distress and recrimination which his scandalous behaviour might cause to his conventional family – quite apart from the fact that he, too, was suffering from a worrying cough and stood to benefit by the change of climate.

Unfortunately, the stay in Palma was far from what they had hoped. At first all went well. The warm evenings spent on the terrace, with the singing and guitar playing, the "delicious existence" was sheer delight, but it did not last for very long. When the rainy season came the house in which they lived proved to be like a sponge. The damp air, and the near-suffocating atmosphere created by the open braziers which they had to use to heat and dry the chimney-less house, made Chopin's cough very much worse. The local people looked at him askance, and doctors insisted that he had consumption, that it was contagious, and that he must be expelled from Palma. The family was forced to move into a deserted and derelict monastery in the mountains, where conditions were even worse.

Although Chopin succeeded in recovering his piano from the grasp of the Customs, and wrote a great deal of music, including some of his best-known masterpieces, his health slowly deteriorated. George for her part was obliged to settle down to a routine of cleaning, cooking, feeding the household and teaching the children as well as striving to continue her own literary work. As a family they were virtually isolated, and the few Majorcan neighbours they had strongly disapproved of them. Before long Chopin, always sensitive, decided that he detested Majorca, and George found him more and more exasperating to live with. In Parisian society he could be tender, charming and even vivacious. but in the intimacy of the isolated sickroom, divorced from society, he could drive her to despair. It was as though his spirit had been flayed.

In the end they had to leave and return to the mainland, but the journey was so arduous that by the time the travellers reached Marseilles Chopin was seriously ill. Any further travelling could be dangerous, and therefore George Sand decided that they would have to remain in Marseilles for a while – at least until Chopin had recovered. They moved to a hotel, and there she found herself responsible for the financial upkeep of the entire "family". Her single-mindedness was admirable; despite the demands of the two children and her devoted nursing of the sick Chopin she still managed to turn out each day some fifteen to twenty pages of manuscript in her large, impeccable handwriting. Slowly Chopin's health improved until he was able once again to delight his "family" with his music, while a crowd of musical and literary fans hung continually outside the entrance of their hotel.

By May of the following year Chopin was fit enough to journey on, and so they set off by slow stages for her country house at Nohant. Although Chopin never really cared much for the bucolic life, they nevertheless settled down happily enough, and it was there that he wrote some of his most famous compositions – his second nocturne, three mazurkas and the sonata in B flat minor which embodies his well-known funeral march. He loved playing to George Sand, for she seemed to understand what he was trying to say with his piano, and she always listened attentively. In October of that year he wrote: "Aurore's eyes misted – they shine only when I play, and then the world is full of light and beauty."

In due course the household returned to Paris, for although George much preferred to live in the country she found the mansion at Nohant, with its constant stream of visitors, twice as expensive to maintain as life in Paris. In the city she and her children at first lived apart from Chopin, but then for reasons of economy they moved together into a flat in Rue Pigalle and later to two apartments in Place d'Orleans. They were now installed in a self-contained block, in a pleasant setting in which a number of sympathetic friends also lived. They met in the evenings for music, reading aloud and conversation, and frequently arranged to eat together, and in the summers they would all leave Paris and go to Nohant.

Life was sociable and pleasant and, for George Sand, more placid than it had been for many years. Around this time she came to the conclusion that Chopin was not made for the ecstasies of love and that his physique was too weak to endure the violence of passion. In spite of his protests she remained adamant in her attitude, and as a result of her new solicitous policy the occasions of love-making became fewer and fewer until eventually they ceased completely. Nevertheless, he continued to love her in a spiritual sense, while for him she felt a tender maternal affection – and, of course, all the time they respected each other's genius and talent.

Their tastes were very different. George Sand, for instance, was amused and diverted by the boisterous company which frequented their Paris home; Chopin abhorred it. In matters of politics they were at total variance, and they frequently disagreed when it came to a question of interpreting or tolerating the actions and attitudes of friends. Chopin seemed quite incapable of putting himself in other people's shoes or of understanding their point of view, and this often irritated George immensely, but she continued to watch over his delicate health with undiminished care, always striving to avert the melancholy moods, the silences and the mental suffering to which he was prone. But their psychological differences did not disturb their deep and close friendship; he was always the faithful adorer, ready to be stirred and inspired by her personality and her gift for words.

During these more leisurely years with Chopin, George Sand's passionate nature softened and mellowed. She produced some of her greatest works – *Spiridion* (of which many friends said that they could not understand a word), *Consuelo, La Comtesse de Rudolstadt,* and *Les Sept Cordes de la Lyre* which was essentially the product of her philosophy and politics and her exchanges with the great minds of her day. She also had time to engage in spirited personal and literary tiffs with a number of friends, including Liszt's mistress who under the mask of friendship had always borne spite against her.

Worst of all, however, were the family rows which went on at Nohant. Her daughter Solange, as she grew up, turned into a good-looking but hard-boiled young woman without a jot of consideration for her mother or anyone else but herself. She was highly class-conscious, and as she continually flattered Chopin and was one of the few people who did not treat him as a spoilt child, he tended to side with her. Maurice, George Sand's son, remained devoted to his mother. When George adopted a young girl, a distant relation, with the long-term view of promoting a marriage between her and Maurice, the peace of the household was torn apart by fearful rows and disputes.

Solange then exacerbated the situation by insisting on marrying a wildly exuberant sculptor (who, it must be admitted, won over the mother as well by his handsome virility), but he turned out to be as hostile and ruthless as his young wife and waged an even more vindictive war with her against the members of her family. On one occasion George Sand had to resort to violence herself to separate her son and her son-in-law, while Solange merely spurred on the combatants. It was after this incident that George turned out Solange and her husband and declared that she never wished to see them again.

All this took place at Nohant, and during these scenes of domestic unrest Chopin was in Paris. When Solange and her truculent husband arrived in the capital they went to see him and set out to poison his mind against George. Solange alleged that George had been the cause of the hostile scenes, and that she had turned them out of the mansion so that they should not discover that she had a new lover – a young man named Victor Borie, a companion of one of George's literary associates, who was a frequent guest at Nohant. Moreover, she claimed that son Maurice was engaged in an affair with his cousin and encouraging Borie's presence as a cover for his own amorous activities.

Chopin, to his discredit, believed every word of this denunciation. He wrote an injured and pontificating letter to George – "for all the world," she cynically pointed out, "like a good father and family man". She was naturally very angry at his credulity and ingratitude. There she had been at Nohant, she pointed out, awaiting daily his arrival from Paris and worrying about his non-appearance, and she would herself have gone to Paris to see if he was well if she had not been afraid of missing him on the way. In a firm, cool letter she said that she was hurt and disappointed, but that if he wished to take the part of her daughter he could do so – she herself was filled with horror by this sort of squabble. Since he had so frankly confessed what was in his mind she would not reproach him. Although she was astonished by his change of face, if he felt freer and more at ease in this way, she would not allow herself to be hurt by it. He could send news of himself from time to time, but it was pointless to imagine that things could ever be the same between them.

The stronger the attachment, the more surely disappointment turns into a kind of hatred. While George Sand was not so small-minded as to be carried away by hate, she was emotionally exhausted, and from that point on she wanted to hear only the most trivial things about Chopin. In truth, she was not entirely sorry that things had turned out this way; she felt that he and his friends had been taking advantage of her, and she had been aware that he was becoming more and more soured in attitude, making scenes in front of her children and friends and generally acting as though he owned her in every way.

Even so, she experienced no great resentment against the people who were to blame, and she made no further moves in the situation, perhaps because she suspected that Chopin's own friends would take the view that she, in spite of her forty-three years, had rid herself of him in order to take another lover. Certainly she was more hurt than she made out in her letters to her friends. Some three months after their separation there arose the question of a piano which Chopin had left at Nohant, and which George believed he had hired. But through a message via Solange, Chopin told her that she could keep it and he would attend to the financial transactions involved. Nevertheless she sent it back to him. "I feel perfectly calm now," she wrote to a mutual acquaintance, "and the past is explained. I want no more than that he *should not do me a service...*"

In another letter she admitted that "my heart and body have been bruised and broken by grief. The pain is, I think, incurable. For an hour or two I can banish it from my mind, but it always returns to tear at my feelings and darken my sky."

Their last meeting was by chance, and it was almost tragic in its banality. George Sand went to visit a friend, and accidentally met Chopin coming out of the house. His manner was polite and formal; he asked how she was and whether she had had any recent news from Solange. George said she had heard nothing. He then told her that Solange had given birth to a daughter. George "with every show of interest" asked about Solange's condition and then enquired after Chopin's own health. He said he was well, bowed and left.

In her *Histoire de ma Vie*, George Sand gave an account of this meeting. She had hoped, she admitted, that a few months spent apart might have healed the wound and make possible a tranquil friendship – but when she met him on that March day and took his hand she found that it was icy cold and trembling. She wrote: "I should have liked to talk with him, but he took to his heels. It was my turn to say that he no longer loved me, but I spared him that pain, and I left everything in the lap of the Gods and the future. I never saw him again."

Chopin, however, did not possess George's generosity of spirit. He persisted in making spiteful remarks about her and when she became involved in political troubles took a delight in throwing mud. But it is said that when he died, on 17 October, 1849, he murmured: "She said that I should died in no arms but hers."

When the news of Chopin's death reached George Sand she put a lock of his hair, which he had given to her, in an envelope on which she wrote "Poor Chopin! 17 October, 1849." Two years later Alexandre Dumas the younger came across all the letters which George had written to Chopin. But, she said, "for me there is more of pride than embarrassment in having tended and consoled that noble heart, which nothing could cure, as though it had belonged to my own child . . ."

During the remainder of her life – she died at the age of seventy-two – George Sand had many "sons", young men who stayed with her for longer or shorter periods at Nohant, but Chopin was her last lover. Some of the young men were devoted to her, and one, Manceau, lived at Nohant as her secretary and aide for many years, but it is unlikely that their relationship was ever more intimate than that. George Sand had, in fact, at last settled down.

She turned her attention to politics and spent her last years in the countryside she loved so much, writing a series of pastoral novels. Her love of men became transmuted into love of people, of nature and of God. Despite the masculine attire which she insisted on wearing as a symbol of her personal autonomy, she was entirely feminine and she fought always for woman's emancipation – not in politics, but in law and in love. She believed that the only sin for which there can be no forgiveness is the sullying, by lies and reticencies, of the love which should be complete and absolute communion.

Perhaps she herself did not always manage to remain true to her ideals, but she believed that a woman was entitled to the freedom of refusing to give herself to someone she did not love, even if he were her husband. Such was her philosophy of life, but she was the kind of woman who would always attract strong emotions in others.

She was, they said, "the Prudhomme of immortality — a complicated creature — charming and wanton, she breathes love — boredom incarnate, dreamer, idiot, nun — led on by passion she has done many foolish things — very proud in love and very good-hearted in friendship — she is a gentle queen and looks down on everything from a great height".

Chapter 11 The Maybe Mistress

There is a widely accepted theory that each man or woman has his or her true and unique counterpart – a "soul mate" – either in this life or some other. To many emotional and sentimental people this concept is perfectly valid, and they may go through life searching for the ideal mate. Invariably, and usually inevitably, they are doomed to disappointment, not so much because of some deficiency in their partner but more likely through their own selfish and inconsiderate demand for an impossible ideal.

Charles Dickens was such an individual. His frustrated search for his "other half" lasted all his life. "Often," he said, "I feel a vague unhappy loss or want of something." He pursued his single-minded search with vigour, juvenile folly and complete lack of concern for the havoc he created round him.

His pursuit of women was even more remarkable for the cloak of respectability in which it was shrouded. It was part of the Victorian hypocritique. The time was the mid-

170

19th century; Queen Victoria and her Albert were displaying an admirable example of domestic bliss to their subjects, and the court which only too recently had been the centre of scandalous incidents was busily presenting a new image of pious decency and sobriety. Smug rectitude was the order of the day, fortified by the self-satisfaction engendered by the booming economic prosperity of the country in terms of trade and industrial development.

Charles Dickens married Kate Hogarth in 1835 when he was 24 years old, and they produced no less than ten children. But Kate soon palled. Dickens felt that she had failed him, and yet he had given her little opportunity or encouragement to do otherwise. From the very beginning of their marriage one of Kate's sisters lived with them, and Dickens promptly fell in love with her. When she died another sister, Georgina, arrived to take over the running of the household from the inefficient Kate who in any case was kept fully occupied with child-bearing and bringing up children. Dickens fell in love with Georgina, too, although there is no evidence to show that the adultery was physical rather than mental and spiritual. Even so, it was no less culpable and gave rise to a great deal of gossip among their friends and acquaintances.

Dickens was furious, of course, and denied it all in the most positive terms. By now he was a widely read author and a well-known public figure, and any breath of scandal must be avoided at all costs. But along with these semi-permanent liaisons Dickens had a number of other love affairs, more or less serious, which greatly upset his wife and sister-in-law. They were carried on in an ebullient and often childish fashion. Indeed, his eager advances were not always welcomed by the young women who took his fancy. Even his many children, remarking on his vagaries, would say resignedly: "Papa is in love again." They were simultaneously intrigued by him and afraid of him, and they dared not openly sympathize with their mother.

Dickens was a fascinating and complex character. He was possessed of incredible energy of mind and body. He could be so entertaining, lively and full of fun that life in his presence could never be dull, and yet on the other hand he was always resentful of the proofs of his continuing physical relationship with his wife which she kept demonstrating in the form of children. While he loved them as babies, as they grew up he lost interest. He sent his seven sons out into the world to fend for themselves. In the conventional manner of the Victorian father he often terrorized his family.

As time went on he resented his wife, Kate, more and more, and she was undoubtedly afraid of him. The girl who had once been his "dearest mouse" turned into "the skeleton in my domestic closet". He told everyone that she was impossible as a companion to himself, and impossible with the children who, he said, actively disliked her. As a housekeeper she tended to be careless and clumsy, which infuriated the fastidiously tidy Dickens.

While he conceded that his wife was "amiable and compliant" he alleged that there was no bond between them and that they were a strangely ill-assorted pair. Nevertheless, for twenty-two years Dickens lived and slept with his wife, and the many letters he wrote to her hardly prove that there was no sympathy or interest between them. For no clear reason Dickens grew more and more restless and dissatisfied with his domestic environment. Even so, there seems little doubt that he would have endured the faulty relationship with his wife for the sake of his reputation, his books and possibly his children had it not been for the arrival on the scene of Charles Dickens's last love, Ellen Ternan.

Dickens had known Ellen's family slightly for many years. They were a theatrical family, and all were on the stage, but the father had committed suicide when Ellen was only a child. Ellen's mother, Francis, was one of the most popular actresses of her day, and her three daughters all showed some promise of talent, although Ellen's gifts as an actress were no more than mediocre.

Dickens was 45 years old when in 1857 he met Ellen Ternan during a performance of *Atlanta* at the Haymarket Theatre in London. She was then eighteen years old, and her demure manner, her pretty face with fair hair and blue eyes, and her well endowed figure were sufficient to attract the middle-aged child that was Dickens – for in matters of love he never grew up.

Two months went by uneventfully, and then a journalist friend of Dickens named Douglas Jerrold died. Believing that his widow and children needed financial help, Dickens organized an amateur theatrical performance to raise money for them. Two private performances before a most distinguished audience were presented, with a cast consisting of Dickens's family and friends. The success of this enterprise was such that he decided to arrange a much more ambitious public performance in the huge Free Trade Hall in Manchester, but this obviously called for professional actresses. His choice fell upon Mrs. Ternan and two of her daughters, Maria and Ellen. So he brought them to his fine house in Tavistock Square in London to rehearse. And there his own daughters watched jealously as little "Nelly" went in and out of their father's study with impunity – an intrusion which, on any pretext, was forbidden to the family.

Further domestic trouble arose when a valuable bracelet which Dickens had ordered for Ellen (he often gave gifts to actresses who worked in his plays) was delivered to Mrs. Dickens in error. For her this was the final humiliation. But when she protested in tears Dickens was furiously indignant. He insisted that there was nothing improper in his relationship with Ellen Ternan, and demanded that his wife must accept proof of his denial by calling upon Ellen and challenging her. Kate's daughter and her parents begged her not to comply, but she was afraid of her husband and in the end she went.

This episode, though inconclusive, marked the end of the unhappy and insecure marriage. Dickens's attachment to Ellen developed into a wild passion. Once more he was convinced that he had found his ideal "soul mate". Katey, his second daughter, recorded that in the following weeks her father behaved "like a madman". This new affair brought out all that was worst in him, and all that was weakest – "he did not care a damn what happened to any of us". Their mother wept in her room, and their father seemed in the intolerant vehemence of his obsession "like a frightening stranger". Nothing, Katey added, could surpass the misery and unhappiness of their home.

In the end Dickens and his wife agreed to separate. She was to move to a house of her own near Regent's Park and she would receive an allowance of £600 a year. Charley, the eldest son who was then twenty-one, would go with her, since it was regarded as his duty to do so. All the other children were to remain with their father and their efficient Aunt Georgina in a new home at Gad's Hill House, near Cobham in Surrey. Only Katey dared to protest and sympathize with her mother. In her unhappiness, after her mother had left, she herself escaped into a loveless marriage.

The first dramatic result of the separation was a tremendous scandal. It was hinted in the press and elsewhere that the cause of the separation was an incestuous relationship between Dickens and Georgina. This faded, and soon the rumour was circulating that Dickens was involved with some actress. Regardless of the valid reasons and matrimonial undercurrents it was inevitable that Dickens's separation from his wife would cause great disapprobation among the tight-laced Victorian society of the day. Dickens himself went to great lengths to deny everything and to justify his own actions, and he kept Ellen Ternan discreetly in the obscure background. In the event he succeeded admirably (and well he might as an accomplished and plausible scribe), for the fact remains that his public image remained untarnished for many years and conjecture as to whether Ellen was really his mistress lasted for almost as long. It was never generally realized, in spite of his suspected record, that his marriage had in fact broken up because of another woman.

There is evidence to suggest that Dickens installed Ellen in a cottage in Slough and later in a house in Peckham. From time to time he took her with him to a villa in France. Still determined to preserve the Victorian proprieties, he acquired these houses for Ellen under a false name and frequently visited her under the same pseudonym. Such was his determination to keep the affair discreet that no letters between the couple survive. Passages concerning Ellen in certain letters to his secretary and in his diary were heavily inked out and were only discovered when they were subjected to modern infra-red photography. So much subterfuge hardly added to the happiness of the relationship. It was, moreover, inevitable that Ellen, too, should turn out not to be the ideal love that Dickens believed he had found at last.

In the early days of the romance, while he was courting her and trying to please her, he achieved a great but transient happiness. The trouble was that, as usual, he expected more from her than she or any other woman could possibly give. Ellen, though intelligent and considerate, could not compensate for all the things which Dickens lacked in his own nature, and this seems to have been what he was basically seeking all his life. When it became apparent that she failed to embody his impossible ideal he became disappointed and irritable with her, although the liaison nevertheless lasted for nine years. During this period there is little doubt that Dickens, who died at the age of fifty-eight, was in declining health; as the years went by his energy and sexual drive diminished until in the end he was simply too tired to bestir himself into pursuing further the fruitless search for his unattainable ideal mate.

As love affairs go, therefore, this one was a disappointment, although it aroused a storm of controversy which has lasted nearly a hundred years. To Dickens, at the beginning, Ellen embodied the fresh innocence of his own daughters – she was certainly about their age. She was his "dear girl" and his "darling" and he was madly in love with her, but he went to extreme lengths to cover up the affair. The erased passages in his diary, the telegram he had sent to her by hand which was carefully phrased so as to have "a special meaning for her", the destroyed letters, the false names under which he arranged visits – all have confused the pattern of truth and have given Dickensian scholars immense excitement and no little mental exercise.

Unforeseen incidents helped to shed some light on the relationship of the lovers. For example, a woman acquaintance met Charles Dickens and Ellen Ternan on the Boulogne cross-channel packet; Dickens, she said, "strutted about the deck with the air of a man bristling with self-importance". And in 1865 Ellen was with Dickens on a train which met with a serious accident at Staplehurst in Kent. (The carriage in which they sat was suspended by its coupling over the side of a bridge.) Although Dickens behaved in a heroic manner, he never recovered from the shock of the near-disaster, and remained terrified of trains for the rest of his life.

If it were not for such rarely reported events, there would be nothing concrete to suggest that Dickens and his mistress ever went about together. But was she in fact his mistress? Students of Dickens have never ceased to speculate, and a mass of verbiage has been published on the subject of whether Ellen Ternan was, in any carnal sense, his mistress at all.

On the other hand, his daughter later told an intimate friend that Ellen Ternan was not only her father's mistress, but that there had also been a child of the relationship which had died in infancy. This statement has, however, been largely discounted, because there has never been any evidence to support it. The truth is that the facts are few and far between and the written records slender.

Perhaps a point of some significance is that when Dickens lay dying Ellen was sent for, but not his wife. It seems unlikely, in view of Dickens's highly emotional, passionate and demanding nature, that his relationship with Ellen remained purely platonic. The controversy still rages and the arguments are still deployed, but to little purpose. Nobody will ever know for certain unless some hitherto undiscovered letters or diaries are eventually discovered, and this seems somewhat improbable. Today the mystery of the rather colourless young woman who was Dickens's last love has become more famous than the mistress herself ever was.

Chapter 12 The Indefatigable Pompadour

When the Duchesse de Châteauroux, the third of three sisters who one after another had been mistresses of Louis XV, died, the more ambitious ladies of Versailles instantly began to prink themselves in the hope of gaining the coveted and now-vacant status of *maîtresse-en-titre* to the King. But one young woman already had a toe on the threshold of the royal bedchamber and pursued her advantage to the uttermost. She was Jeanne Antoinette d'Etoiles who, before her marriage to an amiable and wealthy young member of the lesser nobility, had been common-or-garden Toinette Poisson.

Her background was far from auspicious for a woman with ambitions in the royal echelons. Her father was the son of a peasant; he had managed to work his way up to a respectable job with a firm of army contractors and bankers, but when they were accused of fraudulent dealings Monsieur Poisson, threatened with arrest, was forced to flee the country. He stayed away for eight years until he was cleared of the charges.

Meanwhile, his attractive wife survived and indeed flourished, by a series of liaisons which culminated in her settling down with a rich farmer, Monsieur de Tournehem. It was to his generosity that Toinette owed her excellent education which included all the arts and graces required in a society lady of the period. At her father's wish she was sent to a convent for a year, but her mother, when she was told by a clairvoyant that little Toinette was destined to be a *morceau de roi*, proceeded systematically to groom her for just such a future and even gave her the pet name *Reinette*, which meant "little queen". And so, in this slightly disreputable bourgeois background grew up the girl who was to become one of the most famous mistresses of all time.

By the time she was nineteen, Toinette had more or less perfected her feminine mystique. She took care to frequent the salons of such ladies as Madame Geoffrin, where she not only observed the manners of society but also met such leading intellectuals of the day as Voltaire and Montesquieu. But while her manners were generally regarded as perfectly acceptable, her rather vulgar mother proved an embarrassment to hostesses who would have preferred to receive the daughter alone. The problem was soon solved, however, when Madame Poisson became seriously ill with cancer. Shortly afterwards, Monsieur de Tournehem provided a husband for Toinette in the shape of one of his relations, and gave her a handsome dowry.

While presumably she settled down happily to married life with her devoted husband, she never forgot the destiny which the fortune teller had promised her. The young couple lived in Paris with de Tournehem, and occasionally in the country at the Château d'Etoiles, near Choisy, which was one of the King's favourite hunting boxes.

Toinette was delighted to find that in her new position as a well-to-do married woman she could entertain a great deal. With her lively interest in literature, music and the arts, she made a point of inviting as guests the intellectuals of the time, and she herself was frequently a guest at the elegant supper parties given by Hénault, President of the

First Chamber of the Paris *Parlement*. (This was a kind of Supreme Court of Justice, and the only legislative authority outside the King which existed in France.) She also acted with vivacious enthusiasm in amateur theatricals in a small theatre specially built for her at d'Etoiles. Gossip about this clever and pretty little bourgeoise inevitably filtered through to Versailles, and King Louis XV cocked a ready ear, for he had often said that he thought a bourgeoise would make a good mistress and would not be so demanding as an aristocrat.

In due course Toinette decided that the time had come for her to bring herself to the notice of the King. Unfortunately she was not received in noble circles, and even the impoverished aristocrats who were her nearest neighbours at d'Etoiles declined to call on her. It occurred to her that she was unlikely to fulfil the clairvoyant's prophecy unless she gave fate a helping hand.

On learning that the court was installed at Choisy and that King Louis was to hunt there, she arrayed herself in her most fetching gown, climbed into the small phaeton which her doting husband had bought for her and, with her black servant perched behind her, drove off into the forest. In a woodland glade she located the court engaged in a picnic. She hesitated for an instant to identify the King, and then drove her phaeton smartly along the ride and past the courtiers.

Louis looked up to behold an unexpected vision in pink and blue. In an azure horse-drawn carriage, painted with pink flowers and fitted with pink reins, sat a beautiful and charming young woman who bowed and smiled at him as she passed. Her figure was slim and supple, and her oval face was framed in light chestnut hair. He noted her large eyes arched by pretty brows and her perfectly formed nose. Her elegant gown of coral pink taffeta was trimmed with blue, and above her head her coloured servant held a coral parasol.

The King, immediately entranced, demanded to know who she was. The answers he received from the Duchesse de Châteauroux and her friends were far from flattering, but Louis nevertheless ordered his chief huntsman to send the lady some game. Suitably encouraged by this gesture Toinette decided to drive in the forest again, but this time she ran into opposition. The Duchesse de Châteauroux had ordered one of her own lackeys to frighten Toinette away if she should approach too close to the King, and this he did most effectively. Toinette took the hint and was afraid to persist with her plan, despite the encouraging gifts of game that poured into her home while the court remained at Choisy.

That autumn Toinette became pregnant for the second time – her first child had died at birth – and she was forced for a while to withdraw from the royal pursuit. The following summer, in 1744, she gave birth to a baby girl who, following the custom of the time, was sent away to be reared by a wet nurse and was rarely visited by the mother. Toinette's recovery from her confinement received a traumatic setback when she fell into a fever on hearing that the King, who was away with his troops, had become seriously ill. But he quickly regained his health, and her spirits were greatly improved when in the December of that year the Duchesse de Châteauroux died.

Now was her chance, she realized. When she heard, two months later, that there was to be a masked ball at Versailles to celebrate the marriage of the Dauphin, she made up her mind to attend at all costs. It was not difficult for the middle classes, if they had money, to obtain admission to such public functions, and indeed many of Toinette's acquaintances took advantage of this facility, to her chagrin. The King, among a group of gentlemen all disguised as yew trees and covered in leaves, was not difficult to identify, and Toinette took good care to place herself in his way. The manoeuvre was successful. The King seemed to be thoroughly enjoying himself and did not hesitate to respond to her advances. He arranged to meet her again at a masked ball to be held at the Hôtel de Ville a few days later – he also made assignations with a number of other personable ladies. But, in fact, it was Madame d'Etoiles with whom the King supped and danced at the ball, and it was she whom he drove home afterwards.

During the following weeks the King was all too frequently in Toinette's company. Monsieur de Tournehem, aware of what was brewing, tactfully spirited Toinette's husband away. And in no time at all Toinette had achieved her ambition. She was installed at Versailles and granted the title of Marquise de Pompadour. When her husband returned and discovered what had happened he begged her to come back to him, but he received short shrift; the Pompadour had no intention of being thwarted in her plans by a mere husband. In due course the *Parlement* dutifully granted a deed of legal separation between the d'Etoiles.

During that summer the King was away with his troops. When he returned in September, the official presentation of the new favourite took place in the royal palace. The courtiers were agog and the galleries were crowded with curious onlookers. The Marquise de Pompadour was officially presented by the Princesse de Conti, and first she was escorted to his Majesty to be formally received. Beautifully dressed and outwardly calm and poised she followed her sponsor towards the throne on which the King, looking extremely uncomfortable, was seated. And then she was led to the Queen, while the courtiers strained their ears to hear what that long-suffering woman would have to say.

They were probably disappointed, but the Pompadour was certainly pleased and disarmed when, instead of the scorn she had expected, she was received by the Queen with courteous and graceful resignation. The Queen merely asked after some mutual acquaintance who was related to Toinette's husband, and no doubt she in turn was relieved by the Pompadour's assurances of her total respect for and desire to serve the Queen. After the humiliations she had suffered at the hands of the King's previous mistresses, it probably made a pleasant change for the Queen to meet one who was at least well-intentioned. The Dauphin, however, was not so polite. It is said that after a brief exchange with the new favourite he stuck his tongue out at her!

The Pompadour was lodged in a suite of six rooms of

modest size above the King's private rooms in the north wing of Versailles. From these private rooms – they, in turn, were located above the King's official rooms where all state business was conducted according to a strict protocol – a private staircase led up to the Pompadour's suite. The King could come and go as he pleased. There was no danger that he and his mistress would be disturbed, for the footmen would admit nobody to these suites except by invitation. On the roof were delightful retreats adorned with flowers, shrubs and aviaries.

To these rooms would come the King in the mornings after his official *lever*; then he would leave her to go to Mass, return for a light luncheon, and stay with her until the time came for his evening engagements. After a late supper with her he would go to his official apartment two floors below for his official *coucher* and then return to her for the rest of the night.

The Pompadour was continually at the King's beck and call. She had to be forever changing her dress, renewing her make-up, and thinking of ways in which to be gay and amusing. Louis tended to be listless and bored, and perhaps jaded. He had little imagination and even less conversation, so that to the Pompadour who was accustomed to the sparkling conversation of intellectual friends her royal lover proved to be rather heavy going. She tried to bring changes in her entertainments – a new song, a recitation from some comedy, a tune on the harpsichord – which was trying enough. It did not help matters that she was often ill, for she suffered from a chronic weakness of the chest. But even so she was allowed no rest and was required to drag herself from her sick-bed to keep the King diverted and amused. She had her reward, for slowly the King came to rely on her completely, and in a sense she was privileged in that her presence was required wherever he went. He also became better humoured and more expansive. Even so, it was an exhausting life for the Pompadour who had imagined that most of a mistress's activities occurred in bed.

She also had to put up with the jibes and mockery of the courtiers who, having discovered all they could about the

Pompadour's dubious origins, did not hesitate to spread the facts in a much embroidered form. They were constantly on the alert for the slightest giveaway sign of her bourgeois background in her manner of speech, in the tiniest breach of etiquette, or in a small gesture of effrontery. The common people of Paris, tired of the excesses of kings and their mistresses, made up slanderous songs about the Pompadour which became known as *poissonades* – the courtiers repeated them with glee. The Pompadour was, of course, well aware of all this malicious and contemptuous talk and *bavardage*, and behind her smiling face she nurtured thoughts of revenge, only biding her time until she was properly established. Nevertheless, she began to tread more warily and make fewer gaffes.

She had many friends as well as enemies. Some were friendly for her own sake, for she was intelligent, good-natured and generous; others cultivated her friendship for what they could get out of her. It gave her great pleasure, now that it was within her power, to use her influence to oblige and promote her friends. Voltaire was one of her earliest beneficiaries for whom she obtained lucrative posts. And although she now had attained high estate, she did not forget her low-born relations. Her brother was made Marquis de Marigny and Superintendent of Buildings, and he turned out to be both popular and very good at his job. She was also planning to arrange an advantageous marriage for her daughter, but the little girl died at the age of ten.

Perhaps her most implacable enemy was Maurepas, the King's Minister for Paris. Louis liked Maurepas, for he was an able and witty man, and he would amuse the King with his little satirical songs and mimicry, his gossip and his entertaining but hurtful mastery of the art of ridicule. The Pompadour was Maurepas's chief target. He mimicked her bourgeois manners and accent, spread slanderous rumours about her and invented scurrilous verses which he had circulated among the delighted courtiers. Maurepas had always been the sworn enemy of all the King's mistresses, probably because he was jealous of their influence over his master. The Pompadour acknowledged him as an enemy and constantly urged Louis to dismiss him, but he would not take her seriously.

So she battled on to consolidate her position as a leading lady of the court as well as the King's mistress. She fought, often with lack of taste and finesse, for small privileges of status such as a seat in the Queen's coach, or a place at the dinner table. Once, in the autumn of 1745, when the King was ill at Choisy, the Queen asked if she might visit him – and to her surprise the suggestion was cordially accepted. But when she sat down to dine with the King, she was infuriated to find Madame de Pompadour among those present at the table.

The Queen avenged this humiliating trick, and others, by subjecting the favourite to snubs and slights which her position enabled, and indeed entitled, her to dispense. But as time went by the Pompadour's consistent demeanour of respect, consideration and loyalty towards the Queen and the royal family finally won them over. In due course the Queen came to accept the situation to the extent that when, after a typical evening of playing cards with the Pompadour and her own ladies-in-waiting, the time came for the favourite to join the King, she would quite good-naturedly grant leave for her to depart.

The Marquise de Pompadour enhanced her popularity at court by introducing her old love – amateur theatricals. Among the many hundreds of bored but well-educated courtiers there was adequate talent, and on the whole the performances were a great success. At least they were well received, but they were also very expensive; all the costumes and properties had to be of the very best, and structural alterations were required to create a suitable stage and auditorium. As productions became more ambitious, these facilities proved inadequate. When the common people of France learned that, because the existing stage in the long gallery at Versailles was too small, a new large theatre was to be built, they began to grumble and complain. Poverty was on the increase throughout France, the national debt was expanding day by day, and yet money could always be

found for the King's buildings, and even worse – new buildings for his mistress's amateur theatricals.

The tumult of the resentful muttering of the people grew
so loud that the King tactfully decided to close the new
theatre, and the Pompadour, not to be deprived of her
hobby, arranged to erect a miniature theatre at her new
château at Bellevue. This château, built on a hillside of
Meudon, commanded a beautiful view over the Seine, the
hills of Saint Cloud and the distant plain of Paris. Lovingly
planned by the Pompadour, the château though not large
was a work of art, for her taste in design and décor was
impeccable and she was passionately interested in the arts.
To the planning of Bellevue – incidentally, it was destined
to be totally destroyed by revolutionary mobs – she gave a
great deal of thought, for she hoped it would serve to distract
and amuse the King.

Louis, always possessed of a macabre and gloomy turn
of mind, seemed to have relapsed recently and had renewed
his obsessive interest in subjects such as death, graveyards,
gloomy sermons and morbid anecdotes. She worked inde-
fatigably to lend his thoughts a happier turn, and she was
hopeful that the carefully planned delights of Bellevue
would divert him. But on the winter evening in 1750 when
he first visited the château everything went wrong. It was
bitterly cold and all the fires smoked abominably, and these
discomforts made Louis so peevish that the evening was a
fiasco despite the elaborate entertainments that had been
arranged. After such an initiation Louis never took to Bellevue, and it was doubtless for this reason that the Pompadour soon tired of her masterpiece. Seven years later she
sold it to Louis in order to pay her mounting debts, and
after her death he gave it to his spinster daughters who
promptly changed everything that could be changed.

The Pompadour's debts were a constant worry to her. In
the early years of her "reign" the King had provided her
with a large if somewhat erratic allowance, and had loaded
her with gifts. But after about five years the gifts eased to
a trickle and then ceased altogether, and the allowance crystallized into a regular though not over-generous sum. By

that time the Pompadour had acquired houses and land which demanded large staffs (who stole all they could from their mistress) and she fell more and more deeply into debt.

However, on the internal political front, she did eventually succeed in getting rid of her dearest enemy, Maurepas, after he had written the famous "hyacinth" couplet about her, a particularly offensive lampoon. The Pompadour had one evening been wearing a corsage of white hyacinths which had fallen and scattered under her feet, and this incident inspired the following verse with its oblique reference to a feminine disorder, the truth of which Maurepas could only have discovered by bribing the lowest of the chambermaids.

> *Par vos façons nobles et franches,*
> *Iris, vous enchantez nos coeurs;*
> *Sur nos pas vous semez des fleurs*
> *Mais ce ne sont que des fleurs blanches.*

This barb was too much for the Pompadour who promptly revived her campaign to have Maurepas dismissed. When Louis continued to refuse, she deployed her histrionic ability to such good effect that she finally wore him down. She pretended that she had reason to believe that Maurepas intended to poison her, and insisted that relatives should supervise the preparation of her food and that there should always be physicians close at hand. She became chronically impatient and bad-tempered. She arranged for someone to inform Louis that Maurepas had admitted to having poisoned the Duchesse de Châteauroux. And in the end the King, whether he believed it or not, got fed up with the whole business and despatched a brief note, at one o'clock one morning, ordering Maurepas to be dismissed. It was probably a case of "anything for a quiet life".

Maurepas never returned to court while Louis lived, but in his place he left another dangerous enemy for Madame de Pompadour – his colleague d'Argenson. The King liked d'Argenson for the very good reason that this Minister relieved him of virtually all responsibility and trouble and showered him with flattery. In many ways he was a more subtle intriguer than Maurepas, for he pretended to be on the best of terms with the Pompadour while maintaining good relations with the royal family by telling them that in fact he despised her.

Naturally the Pompadour hated and distrusted him, and with good reason, for d'Argenson managed to turn the Comtesse d'Estrades, her most intimate friend, against her, even though the Comtesse was related to her and owed everything to her. It seems likely, however, that she was also spitefully jealous of her benefactor; for the Comtesse, from her privileged position as the Pompadour's closest friend, spied on her and reported everything to d'Argenson – including the important disclosure that the Pompadour, a woman of naturally cold temperament, regularly took aphrodisiacs. Only when the conspirators, in an effort to displace her, plotted to introduce a niece of the Comtesse into the King's bed, the scheme was discovered and betrayed to the favourite.

The Marquise de Pompadour was now learning how to handle vicious court intrigue. With reciprocated cunning she bided her time until she could lay a suitable trap for the Comtesse – then she left a letter from Louis lying carelessly about for the other woman to steal. The ruse was successful. The Pompadour immediately rushed to the King and with a brilliantly acted display of tears and coquetry finally persuaded him to dismiss the Comtesse d'Estrades. The plotters were foiled and furious, but they nevertheless persisted in spreading damaging rumours about the Pompadour and the court – little realizing what they were contributing to the eventual revolution and the Terror.

However, despite hostilities and intrigues, the Pompadour's position became more and more secure as the years passed. She became a power to be reckoned with, and at her formal *lever* and morning toilet her rooms were crowded with courtiers, tradesmen and others anxious to curry favour with her. She established herself as a sympathetic patron of the arts: Voltaire, Rousseau and Crébillon among writers, Nattier, Boucher, Greuze and La Tour among artists, all owed her a great deal. She had difficulty in persuading La Tour to paint her, although he finally agreed; his famous portrait, now in the Louvre, was first exhibited in 1755. The Pompadour is depicted holding a sheet of music – her own suggestion, for she liked to be associated with culture – and her features wear an expression of pretty complacency. Fortunately she did not see the study that La Tour had made of her when preparing this official portrait, for it shows, with the truthful realism for which La Tour was famous, the common cast of a bourgeois face ravaged with ill health.

By now the delicate constitution and weak chest from which the Pompadour had suffered all her life, exacerbated by the strenuous, restless life she led at court, were beginning to show their effects. She had to be carried upstairs in a wicker chair, for her heart beat so fast at the effort that she would often faint. She suffered from migraine, colic and occasional miscarriages, and the universal medical treatments of the day – bleeding and emetics – did not help at all. What she really needed was rest and relaxation in the fresh country air, well away from the tight corsets, rich foods, overheated or icy rooms and almost total lack of exercise which made up her daily routine life at Versailles. The very cosmetics with which she plastered her face to disguise the shrunken sallowness of her failing health contained poisons such as red lead and mercury, and these chemicals ruined her complexion further and produced other minor complaints as they were absorbed into her system. The whole disquieting syndrome was aggravated by the diet of spicy foods and aphrodisiacs which she habitually consumed in an attempt to conquer her increasing sexual frigidity.

Finally her devoted maid and her doctor persuaded her that she must give it all up. She realized the sanity of their advice. For a considerable time the King had been making jibes about her coldness and she recognized the even colder fact that her days in his bed were numbered. In compensation she began, with the patience and cunning which she had by now learnt only too well, to make herself indispensable to the King as a friend. She redoubled her efforts to amuse him, to take a lively interest in the affairs of state and to give him sensible advice. He was well accustomed now to the Pompadour, indeed she was part of his life and he knew he could rely on her loyal support and sympathy. So, although in 1750 the King and his mistress separated physically, she nevertheless retained all her power and position.

The King, however, still had his physical needs, and in order to satisfy them his valet procured for him pretty young girls from Paris – preferably virgins. At first a couple of rooms in the palace were set aside for this purpose, but later a small house was acquired in the nearby town of Versailles where the King would keep one or two girls at a time, in the charge of a chaperone. He would sneak out at night to visit the little house incognito, and every few weeks the girls were changed to provide novelty. If they became pregnant they were whisked off to another house in Paris for the accouchement, and the children were sent for adoption.

Madame de Pompadour knew all about this clandestine diversion of the King's, but as they were invariably simple girls of little intelligence they generally presented no threat to her security and status. Only one girl, of rather superior status to the others, was presented with a house of her own, but when she started proudly telling everybody that her child was fathered by the King himself, Louis became annoyed and married her off to an innocuous country gentleman.

Meanwhile, the King was so gratified by the Pompadour's complete acquiescence in his new pastime that he made her a Duchess. At last she had achieved all her ambitions; she was allowed her own tabouret (the stool upon which only persons of a certain high rank were allowed to sit on in the presence of royalty), she could attend all public receptions and audiences of the King and Queen, and she was entitled to sit at official dinners with the royal family. And there were many other small privileges which were considered to be of enviable importance in the court of Versailles.

While the Pompadour was relieved of the unwelcome need to take the King into her bed, she continued to spend many hours in his company. Their love had been transmuted into friendship. She now had time to take an active interest in other matters, supervising her many houses and gardens, building up a large and catholic library, encouraging artists and writers, and, more specifically, starting a school for the sons of soldiers killed or impoverished in the service of the King.

But she remained unpopular with the common people of Paris. As her beauty faded the *poissonades* turned to describing her "drooping bosom", her "thin and skinny arms" and her "stomach in flounces". On one occasion, when she was rash enough to drive into Paris stones were thrown at her coach and she was almost kidnapped by the mob.

Her small daughter to whom she was devoted died in 1754, and only a few days later old Monsieur Poisson followed her to the grave. "Fishy", as he was known to the mocking courtiers, had remained unashamedly bourgeois despite the title of Marquis de Marigny granted to him by the King, and to his credit, perhaps, blithely unconcerned by the sneers and jibes directed towards him. His daughter mourned him sincerely. The only one of her own family now left to her was her brother, a simple man of integrity and self-effacing modesty.

By 1755 the Pompadour fully realized that the power she had held through her beauty had virtually faded, so she turned to politics. Flattered and encouraged by Maria-Theresa, the Empress of Austria, who saw in her a pliant tool for her own ends, she succeeded in persuading King Louis to enter into an alliance with Austria against the northern alliance of Germany, England and Russia. The treaty was signed in 1756, and a first military subsidy of 24,000 armed Frenchmen was promised to Austria. The war had barely started when a half-witted lackey named Damiens attempted to stab the King as he was coming from the palace. Louis suffered a minor scratch (the wretched

Damiens was racked and torn from limb to limb), but he was greatly shocked and hastily began to repent his sins while he lay on what he was convinced was his death bed.

At this point the royal family, d'Argenson, and Machault as head of the army, saw their chance to get rid of the Pompadour. She herself was naturally in an agony of apprehension. Machault went so far as to tell her that the King no longer wanted her. Later, however, when her friend, the Maréchal de Mirepoix, came to find her weeping and surrounded by packed trunks, he reassured her and advised her to stay. It was only Machault who wished to get rid of her, he insisted, and if she left the field now she would lose the game. So she stayed, and the Maréchal de Mirepoix was proved right.

When Louis recovered his stamina and his nerve he turned again to her staircase, as was his old habit. The Pompadour greeted him with her usual gentle sweetness and not a word of reproach – but she strove, with implacable resentment and hatred, to discredit and dispose of both Machault and d'Argenson, and in the end succeeded. Thus, the heads of both the army and the navy were removed at the start of the war in alliance with Austria, and within a year that war had reached the point of disaster.

De Bernis, an old friend of the Pompadour's and an able politician who had originally favoured the Austrian alliance, now begged her to persuade the King to bring the war to an end. The Pompadour was outraged at such political interference. When de Bernis then tried to arrange peace negotiations on his own account, she unhesitatingly betrayed her old friend to the King by deliberately misrepresenting his words and actions. De Bernis was sent into exile and the Duc de Choiseul – frivolous, incompetent and self-seeking, but popular – took his place in court.

The Seven Years War was finally brought to a close by the humiliating Peace of Paris in 1762. Under the terms of the treaty France lost Canada, Cape Breton and Nova Scotia, and the country itself had been brought to the very verge of bankruptcy and ruin. The loathing of the people for both King Louis XV and the Duchesse de Pompadour had grown more intense and bitter than ever before.

In 1757 the Pompadour had been so seriously ill that she had considered it advisable to make her will. After the defeat of the treaty of Paris she fell into a persistent melancholic decline which slowly undermined her health, and some two years later, worried by her mounting debts, her illness became much worse. For some months she had been complaining that she suffered palpitations of the heart every time she passed the Queen's apartments; then, in April 1764, at the age of 42, she contracted an inflammation of the lungs which aggravated her already weak heart condition. She was taken ill at Choisy, but after a while she had recovered sufficiently to be moved to Versailles. There she was attended by a new doctor who, not so familiar with her delicate constitution as the devoted physician who had looked after her for so many years previously, forced her to take such strenuous exercise that she inevitably suffered a relapse which brought her a step nearer death.

The King continued to visit her with unfailing devotion, but the once beautiful Pompadour was now only a travesty of her former self. Even heavy make-up could not hide her raddled cheeks and sunken hollow eyes. Perhaps mercifully her fatigue and lassitude were so overwhelming that she contemplated the approach of death with indifference and was unmoved when Louis urged that she should send for a priest. Towards the end she asked to see her husband, d'Etoile, but he refused to come. On the night of 14 April, the priest arrived to hear her last confession and administer the sacrament, and at that point she realized that once this was done Louis would not come to see her again – she would die alone.

Nevertheless she submitted to the ministrations of the priest, after having turned her back on the church for nineteen years, but still she lingered on. In the morning her maid powdered and made up the now cadaverous face for the last time, and dressed the faded hair of the dying woman who had once driven gaily through the forests of Choisy, bedecked in silks and ribbons of pink and blue, as a bait

The Dark Lady of Shakespeare's
Sonnets was the black-eyed, black-
haired Mary Fitton (*left*), a Maid of
Honour to Queen Elizabeth I.
Though she rejected the great poet,
she inspired some of his finest works.
– Barbara Villiers (*below*) would not
rest satisfied until she had become
mistress of Charles II. It was
rumoured at the time that she used
black magic and aphrodisiacs to
hold her royal lover in thrall.

The charming young Jane Shore (*right*), daughter of a leading mercer of the City of London, was unhappily married. Then King Edward IV's attention was drawn to her and she became his mistress for ten years. After his death, his successor, Richard III, persecuted her and accused her of harlotry. She was sentenced to do public penance at St Paul's, walking through the crowds barefoot, with her hair unbraided, wrapped only in a sheet, and carrying a heavy candle (*below*).

for a royal lover. Now in the room above hers that same royal lover paced up and down, waiting for the death of the woman who had so often saved him from boredom and apathy.

During the day the Pompadour sent for three old friends to sit with her, but towards evening she sent them away, saying, "*That thing* draws near ..." The priest stayed behind to exchange a few words with her. Then, as he prepared to leave, the Duchesse de Pompadour detained him. "One moment, Monsieur le Curé," she said, "we will go together." When the priest turned back to the bed she was already dead.

Louis, when he heard the news, cancelled the public dinner which was about to take place that evening. Some months after her death he spoke of his late mistress to an inquisitive court lady. No, he told her, he had never loved Madame de Pompadour, but he had allowed her to stay for as long as she wished because he knew that to have her sent away would have killed her.

Chapter 13 The Dark Lady of the Sonnets

Mistress Moll, or Mall Fitton, is famous not because she became the mistress of the man who immortalized her, but because she refused him and became another man's mistress instead. The man who immortalized her was William Shakespeare, and the name under which her actual identity has been hidden is "The Dark Lady of the Sonnets". She was the black-eyed, black-haired beauty of whom Shakespeare wrote in as many as twenty-six of his sonnets, expressing his most impassioned love, anger, jealousy, lust and despair.

Mary Fitton was born in June 1578. She was the second daughter of Sir Edward Fitton of Gawsworth in Cheshire. Her family was of ancient lineage and enjoyed a respected status in the country – Mary was to become its black sheep. Her elder sister Anne, who had been married at the tender age of twelve to the eldest son of a Warwickshire land-owner, finally left her father's house in 1595 to join her young husband. At the same time Mary was successful in obtaining an appointment as Maid of Honour to Queen Elizabeth, and so came to court in London.

She was, as her portraits show, a proud-looking young woman with a mass of black hair, a pale oval face and dark eyes. Shakespeare describes her with a bitter truthfulness and a clarity of sight engendered by her cool treatment of him:

> *My mistress' eyes are nothing like the sun;*
> *Coral is far more red than her lips' red:*
> *If snow be white why then her breasts are dun;*
> *If hairs be wires, black wires grow on her head.*
> *I have seen roses damasked, red and white,*
> *But no such roses see I in her cheeks . . .*

And the heroines of many of his plays written after he had met the fascinating Mall reflect her physical characteristics – for example, Rosaline, a lady-in-waiting to the Queen in his play *Love's Labour Lost* is

> *A whiteley wanton with a velvet brow,*
> *With two pitch-balls stuck in her face for eyes.*

When this beautiful, raven-haired and sprightly young woman arrived at court, her father asked his old friend, Sir William Knollys – who was then Comptroller of the Queen's Household and therefore an important and influential person – to keep a watchful eye on Mary. This Sir William proceeded to do with such dramatic effect that, although he was over fifty and had a rich wife, he promptly fell in love with his ward and cherished ardent if impractical hopes of marrying her.

Mary, however, far from being a naive and vulnerable young thing in need of someone to protect her and help her find her feet in her new and demanding appointment, turned out to be a practised coquette. She kept eager Sir William well and truly dangling and alternately blowing hot and cold, so that he was constrained to write miserably to her sister Anne, who seemed to have approved of this unsuitable romance: "Let me entreate your ffayre selffe to perce the heavens with your earnest and best prayers to the effecter and worker of all things for my de-liverye, and that once I maye be so happye as to ffeele the pleasyng comffort off a delightful summer which I doubt not will yield me the deserved fruite off my constant desyres which as yet no sooner budd by the heat off the morning sonne but they are blasted by an untymelye ffrost, so as in the midst off my best comfforts I see nothing but dark despayre."

Poor Sir William Knollys never did taste the "deserved frute" of his "constant desyres" – indeed, he had to put up with a great deal not only from Mall but also from the other Maids of Honour. His lodging at court, it is related, was next door to that of the Maids of Honour, where the spirited young women "us'd to friske and hey about" to his "extreame disquiete at nights though he often warned them of it".

Sir William, however, managed to get his own back on them. One evening, having arranged for someone to bolt the door of their room so that they could not escape, he stripped down to his underclothes and, with a pair of spect-acles balanced on his nose and a book in his hand, marched in through the door adjoining his own room and marched up and down, reading gravely for an hour or more. The Maids, it was said, endured a "sadd spectacle and pitiful fright" – it seems more likely that they fell about with laughter. Sir William, it has been suggested, probably pro-vided the pattern for Shakespeare's Malvolio, the ridiculous and pompous steward in *Twelfth Night*, and it has been ingeniously supposed that the name Malvolio was made up from *Mall voglio*, meaning *I want Mall*, by the jealous Shakespeare.

By this time Shakespeare had been moving around in court circles for a few years, and he was on very good terms with a number of noblemen of the day who were interested in encouraging the art of drama. A particular friend was William Herbert, the eldest son of the Earl of Pembroke, and he was almost certainly the "Mr. W. H." to whom Shakespeare addressed the passionate affection expressed in his first 126 sonnets. From the consistent tenor of these it is apparent that Shakespeare loved a youth of high rank and great personal beauty. Throughout his life Shakespeare rated the friendship between men as more valuable than that between men and women – perhaps he also had hopes that William Herbert might become a powerful patron and advance him in his career. Whatever the motive, he certainly addressed to him, in the extravagantly affectionate language which was quite common in those days, a large number of what were probably no more than sycophantic poems.

Whatever Shakespeare's precise relationship with William Herbert might have been, when he met Mall Fitton in 1547 it was his handsome and aristocratic young friend whom he sent to her as a kind of emissary to plead his cause. Shakespeare was then thirty-four years old, but already balding and putting on weight. He probably imagined that a beautiful and flightly young lady would rather listen to an attractive and charming aristocrat than a middle-aged playwright. His judgment was correct, but the plan rebounded cruelly on him, for no sooner had the coquettish Mall set eyes on the handsome young man of noble birth than she promptly seduced him – and Shakespeare found himself without either mistress *or* friend.

The behaviour of Mistress Fitton soon began to cause a great deal of gossip at court, even among her livelier and more irresponsible companions. It is related how, while she was mistress of the Earl of Pembroke (William Herbert had succeeded to his father's title), she would "put off her head tire and tucke upp her clothes and take a large white cloak and marche as though she had been a man to meete the said Earle out of the Courte". Sir William Knollys, who was still forlornly hopeful, was considerably distressed by these goings on and counted himself an "unfortunate man alyke to ffynd that which I had layed upp in my hart to be my comffort should become my greatest discomffort".

But Mall did not care. She continued in her wild ways, sneaking out of the Palace at night in the guise of a man to meet her lover – with the inevitable, predictable result. In a letter he wrote in 1601, Sir Robert Cecil recorded that "there is a misfortune befallen Mistress Fytton, for she is proved with child, and the Earl of Pembroke being examined confesseth a fact but utterly renounceth all marriage".

To be thus betrayed by her lover was indeed a misfortune, for the Queen was so annoyed that she threatened to send both of them to prison. In the event, however, she relented in Mall's case and ordered her to the house of Lady Hawkyns for her confinement, while Lord Pembroke languished for a while in Fleet prison.

The baby died. As Lord Pembroke steadfastly refused to marry his mistress, she was eventually taken home in disgrace by her father. Sir William Knollys, with equal steadfastness, continued to write hopefully to her, but she never bothered to reply. By the time his wife died three years later he had finally given up, and he married someone else. Mistress Fitton had still not learnt her lesson, for she produced at least one more illegitimate child before she made an unsatisfactory marriage, and even then she continued her promiscuous behaviour.

As for Shakespeare – before he met Mall Fitton he must have been a reasonably happy and cheerful person. In the previous three or four years he had written *A Midsummer Night's Dream, Romeo and Juliet, Richard II, King John, The Merchant of Venice,* and the two parts of *Henry IV.* At the age of thirty-three he had already achieved success, and his gentle-gay and kindly character brought him popularity as well as acclaim. The Queen had been exceedingly kind to him; he had money, status and was received at court.

He was also a sensual man to an ungovernable extent, and it was this idiosyncrasy which had led him into his unfortunate early marriage at the age of eighteen to Anne Hathaway, who was to survive him by seven years. But he was involved with a number of other women and eventually found himself at the feet of unconcerned Mary Fitton. She had the type of proud dark beauty that Shakespeare admired, and to a large extent her attraction for him was that of opposite poles; she was strong, resolute and bold, whereas Shakespeare was weak, vacillating and timid. The impact she made on him was intense, and when she turned him down his despair, his jealousy and his wounded vanity were as impassioned as his admiration, desire and worship had been.

But he did not remain faithful to her – "love and her soft hours" were irresistible to him, and famous as he was there is no doubt that he enjoyed a number of minor liaisons in the years that followed. But there is reason to believe that he never really loved any other woman, and it has been agreed by students of Shakespeare that his "dark lady" influences virtually everything he wrote after he loved and lost her.

Quite apart from the eloquent sonnets in which he poured out in exquisite words his love-hate syndrome, the "dark lady" turns up again and again in his plays. She is Rosaline, Cressida, and Cleopatra, as well as the Queen in *Hamlet*, and Portia, Beatrice, Rosalind and Lady Macbeth are facets of the same character. All of these women present a composite portrait of the appearance and character of one woman, and she is passionate, aristocratic, faithless, proud, charming, strong, resolute and high-spirited. And into the mouths of Othello, Lear, Hamlet and Brutus does Shakespeare put his own tortured reactions and his own troubled thoughts as he tries to work out of his system the consuming obsessive passion which is destined to colour his life for years to come.

For Shakespeare, once he had been rejected, it was a destructive – indeed, vindictive – passion, for he was quite unable to perceive any of the nobler side of his mistress's character. In an agony of wounded vanity, for there is no doubt that he was a vain man and only too conscious of his age and physical inferiority, he turned to jealous denigration of the object of his love. She had, he said, "the soul of a strumpet, the tongue of a fishwife and the proud heart of a queen," but nevertheless he was fascinated by this superb gipsy who so casually disdained him.

Yet she inspired some of his greatest works, and he remained obsessed by his insane desire for her for many years. Throughout the sonnets he never ceased to accuse and indict her. She is "tyrannous", "faithless", "the bay where all men ride... the wide world's commonplace", "false", "coquettish", and "proud". She "cheated, betrayed and lied" and he thought her "as black as hell and as dark as night". Although this consuming obsession undermined his health and spirits and probably contributed to his early death, this woman whom he described as his "female evil" stimulated Shakespeare to produce the fantastically rich harvest of genius which has made him perhaps the greatest writer the world has ever known.

Chapter 14 Firebrand of the Nation

"I never heard any commend her but for her beauty," wrote Bishop Burnet of the Duchess of Cleveland in the year 1683. "She was a woman of pleasure and stuck at nothing that would either serve her appetites or her passions; she was vastly expensive, and by consequence very covetous; she was weak and so was easily managed." Apart from the last comment – for her career shows little sign of her being easily managed – this would seem to be a very fair summing-up of the character of Barbara Villiers, the famous mistress of Charles II.

From an early age Barbara exhibited the tendencies which were destined to bring her to the King's bed. By the time she was fifteen she was already embarked upon an affair with Philip Stanmore, the Earl of Chesterfield. He, although only twenty one years old, had the reputation of being a notorious womanizer, and Barbara eagerly added herself to his list of available mistresses. But even with such a promiscuous individual as Philip it was Barbara who made the running with him, sneaking off to his lodgings, writing him passionate letters and making assignations in which he could come to her secretly.

Her mother – she had married for the second time in 1646, when Barbara was five years old – and her step-father, the Earl of Anglesea, apparently took little interest in her; they were no doubt greatly relieved when at the age of seventeen their flighty daughter decided to get married.

For reasons best known to herself she chose an unlikely man. Roger Palmer was a quiet and studious individual, not very strong and no match for the vivacious and tempestuous Barbara. Indeed, within a year of her marriage she had resumed her relationship with Lord Chesterfield. When Palmer learned of it he was extremely resentful, and he attempted to put an end to the affair by carrying her off to the country. There she fell ill from smallpox which, fortunately, did not mar her beauty.

It has been suggested that it was in her husband's company in 1659 that Barbara first met King Charles II. Roger Palmer was a devoted royalist who was very active in the King's cause. At that time Charles, whose prospects of being restored to the throne were growing brighter every day, was living in Holland, and it is possible that Palmer and his wife visited the King there on some royal errand. What is certain, however, is that Charles was introduced to Barbara some time before his triumphal return to London in May 1660. Two contemporary writers record that she was with the King at the palace of Whitehall on the night of his return, while another states that he left the palace to join Barbara at the house of a friend. But perhaps the most concrete evidence of their previous acquaintanceship lies in the fact that Charles accepted as his own the daughter to whom Barbara gave birth nine months later.

During the year that followed Barbara reigned supreme in the King's affections. No doubt he found in her a welcome relief from the crowds of courtiers all jealously manoeuvring to secure places in the establishment. The King, in fact, became so fed up with the disaffection, disputes and resentments among his own circle of people that he tended to withdraw more and more from his apparently insoluble problems in search of other diversions. His Chancellor, Lord Clarendon, relates that he "indulged to his youth and appetite that licence and satisfaction that it desired". Indeed, the Chancellor was shocked by the amoral frivolity of the court and its courtiers who, encouraged by the King, appeared to be concerned only with pleasure. The young people of both sexes were, Clarendon remarks, "educated in all the liberty of vice, without reprehension or restraint".

In this free and easy atmosphere Barbara no doubt flourished. But there were storms ahead. In May 1661 Charles announced to Parliament his intention of marrying Princess Catherine of Braganza, of Portugal – a marriage which had first been recommended sixteen years earlier. As a consolation prize for his mistress he granted to her husband, Roger Palmer, the title of Baron of Limerick and Earl of Castlemaine, but the title was to descend by inheritance to the "heirs of his body gotten on Barbara Palmer, his now wife". The title did not in the least please Palmer for, although he presented a complacent face to society, he was well aware of his wife's liaison with the King and very much disliked it. Nor was it much consolation to Barbara who, with the advent of the new Queen, was afraid of losing her position and influence.

A year went by before the new queen arrived in England. Charles, who was fundamentally an eager and friendly creature, had been looking forward very much to meeting his new wife, but he was sadly disappointed. Princess Catherine, although only twenty-five years of age, looked a great deal older, and her short legs and long body made her appear almost deformed, particularly in the ugly farthingales which were still in fashion at the Portuguese court. Moreover, the fastidious King, who had an obsessive mania for personal cleanliness in that unhygienic age, was revolted by the offensive breath and body odours of his bride.

He was a kind man, however, and he appreciated that this foreign princess was desperately anxious to please him. Therefore he treated her gently and with utmost consideration. She was at first installed at Hampton Court so that she might find her feet among her new and strange country-men. Fortuitously the need for any confrontation with Barbara, about whom the new Queen had been forewarned, was temporarily avoided, for Barbara was heavily pregnant. The child was born within a few weeks and was openly accepted by the King as his own son.

A slight fracas followed. Roger Palmer who had recently been converted to the Roman Catholic faith carried the baby off and had it baptised in a Catholic church. Barbara was naturally furious; as soon as she was fit she recovered the child and went off with it to St. Margaret's Church, Westminster, where with the King, the Lord of Oxford and her aunt, the Countess of Suffolk as witnesses, she had the child baptised and christened Charles.

The incident was more than Palmer could tolerate. A bitter quarrel ensued between him and his wife with the result that she left his house and moved to a house in Richmond. She took with her so many of her possessions that her unfortunate husband was left with not even a dish to eat off.

There was so much gossip and scandal concerning Barbara and the King that he felt constrained to make some reparation to his mistress for the difficult situation in which she was now placed. He therefore summoned her to court and presented her to his new Queen. Catherine, it is recorded, was so overcome by emotion that "her colour changed, the tears gushed out of her eyes and her nose bled, and she fainted"! This display of traumatic emotional reaction was observed by the King with "wonderful indignation, and as an earnest of defiance", and his determination that Barbara should be properly received at court strengthened into a resolve that the Queen, whether she should like it or not, must accept her as one of the Ladies of the Bedchamber. It was a delicate challenge – or, perhaps indelicate might be the better word – which was to have important ramifications.

For her part Catherine was stubbornly determined not to accept her husband's mistress, and her resolve was strengthened by the stiff, pious and proud Portuguese women she had brought with her to England. She answered the King's anger with tears and reproaches. Both were adamant – the one in his determination that the reputation of his mistress should be refurbished "to the utmost of his power", and the other in her resolution to reject the insult which the King was trying to foist upon her.

The King was determined to be master in his own house, and he enlisted the aid of his Chancellor in persuading the Queen to accept submission. Lord Clarendon disliked this chore intensely, for he himself disapproved of Charles's behaviour in this affair. Nevertheless, he did his best to prevail upon the Queen to surrender, but in vain. The royal couple continued their hostile cold war. Charles alleged that Catherine was stubborn and lacking in a sense of duty, while Catherine accused him of tyranny and lack of affection for her. He threatened to bring Barbara to court anyway, and to send Catherine's servants home. Catherine countered by threatening that she herself would return to Portugal.

The relationship between the King and the Queen became unbearably strained. Charles carried out his threat to send her retinue back to Portugal, and thereafter he bothered no more with his wife. When a few weeks later they moved to Whitehall he gave Barbara a place at court, after which she was seen everywhere in court circles and even rode in the royal coach with the King and Queen.

In June 1663 Barbara was officially appointed a Lady of the Bedchamber, and Catherine's defeat was complete. The King congratulated himself on his "ill-natured perseverance by which he had discovered how he was to behave himself hereafter". He now openly despised his unlucky Queen, and she, who had been pious and modest, began to take refuge in flightiness and became avaricious and pleasure-seeking.

For Barbara life was now secure and sweet. She became, reports Bishop Burnet, "very insolent" and "would not rest satisfied unless she were publicly owned". She went everywhere with the King who dined at her house four or five times a week. He was often seen returning to the palace at dawn, but was rarely seen in the presence of the Queen.

Barbara's jewellery was far more magnificent than Catherine's, and one Christmas the King gave to her all the seasonal gifts that had been sent to him by the peers. And while Catherine failed to show any signs of producing the heir which Charles and the country so greatly desired, Barbara again became pregnant. In September 1663 she produced yet another son for the King. Before long he moved her into the palace and gave her a room next to his own.

But Barbara's smug self-satisfaction and sense of un-shakeable security began to go to her head. She flirted with other men, and stories that she was sharing her favours with lovers other than the King began to be whispered round the court. She behaved in an undeniably indiscreet fashion, and further aroused the hostility of the people by her coarse language and immodest behaviour. It was rumoured that she made use of black magic and aphrodisiacs to hold the King in thrall. But the truth of the matter was probably that Charles physically found himself unable to resist her. He himself admitted that she knew "all the Aretino that are to be practised to give pleasure".

Gradually, however, Barbara's charms lost their fascination for the King, and he began to look elsewhere for stimulus and satiation. There were many beautiful women at court – the series of paintings of them which Charles commissioned Lely to execute can be seen today at Hampton Court – and one who particularly aroused his desires was the beautiful Frances Stewart. She cleverly contrived to hold him at arm's length and thus heightened his desire for her. Lord Sandwich referred to her as a "cunning slut" for the steadfast way in which she resisted the King's importunate courtship, although she was only seventeen years old.

Barbara was, of course, intensely jealous, but Charles would not tolerate any interference, and he forced her to be pleasant and friendly to Frances, even if only superficially, and to make sure that she included her rival in all her social and official activities. The courtiers who as onlookers could see most of the game laid wagers as to whether Frances would succumb to the King's increasingly urgent demands or not. When Queen Catherine became dangerously ill they realized only too clearly that Frances Stewart might well be their next queen, even though Charles in his considerate way spent hours beside his wife's bed praying for her recovery.

Throughout this period of intense rivalry Barbara stormed and swore and made frightful scenes. Her relief when the Queen recovered from her illness knew no bounds, for at least the throne had receded from the hated Frances. Yet relations between herself and the Queen continued to be as bad as ever. Indeed, the Queen tended to favour Frances whose persistent refusal of her husband pleased her enormously. Barbara's next move was to change her religion and become a Roman Catholic, but if her motive in doing this was to curry favour with the Queen then she failed dismally. Catherine remained antagonistic.

If Barbara was less in royal favour than she had been formerly, at least Charles turned a blind eye to the trifling amours she was said to carry on with various courtiers. He was as accommodating as ever when, in 1664, she gave birth to a second daughter, christened Charlotte. Despite rumours of her other lovers the King accepted the baby as his own child. The news was carefully concealed from the general public, for Barbara's husband had been abroad for a long time.

Even so, the news of the birth soon spread abroad. A little later, when Barbara was returning home after an evening spent with the Duke and Duchess of York at St. James's Palace, she was set upon by three masked men who abused her in harsh language and reminded her of Jane Shore, mistress of Edward IV, who died scorned and abandoned on a dunghill. As soon as he heard of the incident Charles ordered the gates of the park to be closed and all the people therein to be arrested, but the three men were never identified. Then, in 1665, when the court had moved to Oxford to escape the Black Death (bubonic plague) which was then devastating the population of London, Barbara gave birth to her third son (and fifth child). This time neither Charles nor anyone else doubted that he was the father. She redoubled her avaricious attempts to extract from Charles as much as she could in the way of revenues, titles and gifts both for herself and for her children. Her position and security were immensely strengthened when Frances Stewart, to the King's great annoyance, eloped with the Duke of Richmond, and when the Lord Treasurer who had always disapproved of Barbara and her financial demands died. Once more she reigned supreme. Under her influence the frivolity of the court increased and she was able to apply greater pressure to her demands on the King. In fact, he gave her nearly everything she asked for. Even so, she did not hesitate to upbraid him angrily when he refused any request, however small. Charles himself was earning the anger and criticism of the people for spending more time on the affairs of his court and his mistress than over the affairs of the nation.

At that period England was involved in war with the French and the Dutch, and was in constant strife with the Roman Catholic faction. Barbara herself began to dabble in politics, to the extent of allying herself with the Catholic movement. She enjoyed the personal satisfaction of being largely instrumental in persuading the King to dismiss her great enemy Lord Clarendon, the Chancellor; he was relieved of his post and ordered to live in exile. Meanwhile, the treaty of Breda had been signed, and from the commemorative medal which Charles ordered to be struck is drawn the model for our copper pennies of today. The woman who posed for the figure of Britannia was Frances Stewart!

The King started to take a lively interest in the theatre, and particularly in its ladies, much to Barbara's annoyance. Malicious gossips were delighted, and lampoons about the King's favourite became more and more numerous and outrageous. It was partly to soften the blow of a particularly vitriolic barb, in which the whores of London addressed a petition to their illustrious sisters that the King gave Barbara the magnificent Berkshire house which stood on the other side of the park from Whitehall, near St. James's Palace.

But it was also a subtle form of banishment from court, for Charles made it quite plain that he expected Barbara to live there. Although she was in receipt of a handsome annual income from the King, she was invariably in debt, for in addition to her passion for fine jewels she gambled heavily and usually lost. From time to time rumours circulated that the King had offered her a generous pension on condition that she would retire to France – but nothing ever came of this.

Barbara may have been out of favour, but she continued to wield substantial influence over the good-natured King who could not be bothered to argue with her and found it easier to surrender to her whims. But he also observed with cynical amusement her contest with him in the matter of their lovers. She had in her single-minded way sworn to get her own back on him, and while he dallied with the ladies of the theatre she picked first on the actor Charles Hart, and then even descended to the rope dancer Jacob Hall, for her romantic diversions.

But even the King's good-humoured patience had its limits. He drily pointed out that even he could not be expected to father every baby that was born at court, and he resented her constant mercenary demands. As a gesture, perhaps of dismissal, he gave her the title of Duchess of Cleveland, probably in the hope that she might regard this as a farewell gift. He was, however, destined for disappointment, for her demands continued unabated. Nevertheless, he remained on friendly terms with her – no doubt very largely at her own insistence – and visited her periodically even after she had been supplanted by Louise de Keroualles, a pretty French girl who had become a maid of honour to the Queen.

Although his good nature would not allow him to abandon her completely, he became more and more insensitive and immune to her tantrums and hysteria. Even Barbara herself had to recognize that her day was over. After a reign

H

of eleven years she had reluctantly to admit defeat. This was the woman of whom the Earl of Rochester wrote:

Imperious, bloody, so made of Passion,
She is the very Firebrand of the Nation.
Contentious, wicked, and not fit to trust,
And covetous to spend it on her lust;
Her Passions are more fierce than Storms of Wind.

Barbara continued her amorous and avaricious career as best she could, but after six years she finally retired to Paris with the handsome pension which Charles had promised her – plus his injunction that she should live "so as to make the least noise she could". She disregarded this admonition, for in 1678 she became involved in a scandalous intrigue with the English Ambassador and the Marquis de Chatillon. This considerably annoyed Charles and ruined the Ambassador.

Charles, as usual, forgave her, and when she returned to England he received her amiably and allowed her to come to court. She was there shortly before his death in February 1685. She was so hated by so many people that the Earl of Dorset wrote of her:

O Barbara, thy execrable name.
Is sure embalmed with everlasting shame.

Yet her fascination for Charles must have been enormous and deeply rooted for him to have remained on such intimate and friendly terms with her throughout his reign. Also, of course, he was undoubtedly dominated by her stronger and less compromising personality.

After his death she continued to live a life of pleasure, frustrated occasionally only by lack of money. She died, respectable at last but still unrepentant, in Chiswick at the age of sixty-nine.

Chapter 15 Domina Rosa of the Vatican

The second half of the fifteenth century witnessed the rise in Rome of one of the most remarkable and controversial families in all history – the famous and infamous Borgias. Biographers galore have written about them, tending always to concentrate on the notorious brother and sister, Lucrezia and Cesare, to whom innumerable ruthless and cold-blooded crimes (generally involving the use of a mysterious and deadly poison) have been attributed. The evidence for the crimes of mayhem and murder ascribed to this somewhat sinister family has always been inconclusive and sometimes slender, but contemporary chroniclers were convinced of their guilt. Behind the smoke, however, there must in many instances have been some fire.

The founder of the family fortunes was Alfonso Borgia, a Spanish Cardinal who was elevated to the Papacy in 1455. Like all the Borgias he was devoted to his family, and he used his power and influence to shower gifts and honours upon them. Among his relations was his nephew, Rodrigo, whom he created a Cardinal at the age of twenty-five. The fact that Rodrigo who was later destined to become Pope had no particular vocation or even liking for the church was neither here nor there; in the fifteenth century a sense of dedicated calling was not a prerequisite for the recipient of ecclesiastical honours.

Rodrigo, as an individual, was very far from possessing either the character or the taste for his high position in the hierarchy of the church. He was a lover of luxury and beauty, and had a passion for women. In later years he strongly displayed the Borgia trait of egocentric love for his own family. As a man he was tall and handsome enough, with adequate strength and vitality, although from time to time he was subject to fainting fits which, it was suggested, were due either to a form of *petit mal* or to syphilis. He had an insinuating voice, penetrating eyes and a sensuous mouth. His bearing was graceful but dignified. He was persuasive, eloquent and good-humoured; even at the age of seventy he was described as growing "younger every day – troubles never last over night with him. He is naturally cheerful . . . and his one thought is the advancement of his children".

These qualities apparently made Rodrigo irresistible to women. He was the father of no fewer than eight children born during his period as Cardinal, and a ninth was born five years after he became Pope. Although facts such as these may seem startling today, standards of conduct within the church of that period was very different. It was a corrupt age in every aspect of society, including the church, and a Cardinal of that time behaved very much in the same fashion as did a nobleman. Rodrigo proved to be no exception to the general rule; he hunted and attended lively and often libidinous parties, and he loved dancing. Altogether he lived in a sumptuous and self-indulgent manner with a great display of wealth. At carnival time he joined actively in the riotous fun. He himself entertained lavishly, and gambled, and in general allowed himself the "utmost licence".

Although this kind of conduct was accepted without protest by the laity of the day, there was nevertheless a limit to what even a Cardinal could get away with, and he was expected at the very least to show some regard for decorum and convention. Rodrigo had been a Cardinal for only four years when his uncle the Pope – himself a diligent sower of wild oats in his early days – felt obliged to write him a letter reprimanding him for disgraceful conduct during a party at the house of a friend. Rodrigo, it seemed, had danced "with complete absence of restraint", had flirted and made love with a number of ladies, and had behaved so indecorously, the Pope charged, that "decency forbids me to repeat in detail all that is said to have occurred there". Rodrigo had a number of mistresses. It is therefore somewhat surprising that such a man should eventually choose to enter into a more permanent relationship with a woman, one that lasted some thirty years. The woman who held his regard for so long was Vanozza de Cataneis, and to hold the attention of an ecclesiastical profligate like Rodrigo must have called for a great deal of character as well as charm.

Vanozza was born – nobody knows quite where – in 1442. It has been argued that she was a Mantuan and that it was at the Church Council of 1461 in Mantua that Rodrigo Borgia met her. Only one portrait of her exists, and there is some doubt as to whether even this is authentic. However, it does reveal a remarkable resemblance to portraits of her son, Cesare. It is no masterpiece, but it does depict an almost sinister quality in the strength of character delineated in her face, with its deep eyes, straight and prominent nose, and firm mouth. Her hair was light while Rodrigo's was dark, so that it was presumably from Vanozza that daughter Lucrezia inherited her fair hair, while her sons acquired the reddish tinge in their own hair.

She is described on her tomb as the mother of four children, but it is possible that she was also the mother of Rodrigo's first three children who were born between 1458 and 1473 and who died early in life. After that, Cesare was born in 1475, Giovanni in 1476, Lucrezia in 1480 and Gioffredo in 1482. Of the two further children of Rodrigo, one was by the mistress who succeeded Vanozza and the other by an unknown woman.

Even in the permissive and promiscuous climate of the age Vanozza could not be openly installed as the mistress of a Cardinal, and so she lived in a house of her own near the palace and remained discreetly in the background. She is only occasionally mentioned by contemporary chroniclers, and they always referred to her as "Domina Rosa".

In 1474 Rodrigo found an elderly husband for her who was prepared to act as a cover for her association with the Cardinal, and who survived long enough for his son Cesare to be born in wedlock. Unfortunately, Rodrigo was unable to recruit another husband in time to legitimize his next child, Giovanni, who was therefore legally a bastard. But in 1480 Rodrigo contrived to marry off Vanozza once again, to a certain Dirogio da Croce of Milan, just in time for Lucrezia's birth – but he too did not last long. Rodrigo's fourth child was also born without the legal protection of a father's name.

As soon as the children were old enough Rodrigo arranged to have them removed from their mother's care and proceeded to bring them up under his own doting eyes. Daughter Lucrezia was allowed to stay with her mother longer than the boys, but in the end even she was taken away from Vanozza. Perhaps his mistress's middle-class background was not good enough for the proud and arrogant Cardinal. Lucrezia was sent to live with and be educated by Adriana Orsini, Rodrigo's cousin. It was Adriana's daughter-in-law, the beautiful nineteen-year-old Giulia Farnese (whom the Romans cynically christened the Bride of Christ) who eventually became Vanozza's successor as mistress to Rodrigo.

Italian women tend to age early. In 1486, when Vanozza was turned forty, she ceased to be Rodrigo's mistress. It was only to be expected that a man of his temperament would be looking around for another mistress. Nevertheless, there remained a strong bond of sentiment and affection between Rodrigo and herself, and he treated her with kindness and generosity. Then, in 1486, she was married again, for the last time, to Carlo Canale, a Mantuan. Canale was something of a scholar, and he seemed to take a curious pride in his new status as husband of the Cardinal's one-time mistress. He often referred to Giovanni as his step-son and did not hesitate to make the most of what small influence he had (mainly through Vanozza) at the Vatican. He even quartered the Borgia coat of arms – appropriately a bull on a field of gold – on to his own.

Vanozza led a very much retired life. She was rarely seen in the Cardinal's palace and the Vatican, but the children who had been taken from her at an early age remained genuinely fond of her. But all was not peaceful in that turbulent era. Trouble arose with King Charles VIII of France over his titular claim to the Kingdom of Naples. The Pope put up a strong opposition, for Naples was a fief of the Holy Roman church, and the resultant dispute ended in the arrival in Rome of King Charles himself with a large force of men, thirty-six big guns and, he insisted, peaceable intentions.

The French King settled himself and his guns in the Palazzo San Marco, while his troops were quartered all over the city, with licence to plunder, rape and murder. Among those they robbed was Vanozza who lost 800 ducats worth of property. Her son, Cesare, never forgot this crime, and later, after Charles VIII had withdrawn most of his troops from Rome, Cesare organized an attack on some of the Switzer mercenaries who were in the service of the French. The men were assaulted in Saint Peter's Square. Many, including a woman, were killed or wounded, while others were taken to the Vatican to be stripped and robbed. In such a way did Cesare avenge his mother, and it was to set a pattern for further violence in his later life.

Vanozza watched, powerless to intervene, as the headstrong, greedy and ruthless characters of her former lover and her children drove them to extremes of tragedy and made them objects of loathing and terror among their contemporaries. While Cardinal Rodrigo heaped honours upon his children – Cesare became Bishop, Cardinal and Duke, Giovanni a Duke, Gioffre a Prince, and Lucrezia was advantageously married – he did not hesitate to use them for his own devious ends, or to arrange their advancements with little concern for their own preferences. In the cloak-and-dagger atmosphere of the age, violence lurked round every corner in such a family, and jealousy was rife.

Cesare's wilful nature brought tragedy to the family and misery to his devoted mother. In 1497 both he and his brother dined with their mother at the property she had inherited from her second husband – a vineyard near San Pietro. A number of other friends were present on the occasion. Vanozza, now fifty-three and with the too-full figure of the ageing Mediterranean woman, presided over the festivities. The atmosphere was genial and convivial. She was proud of her sons, and especially proud of the young Cardinal who so closely resembled his strong-minded mother. There was little love lost between the two brothers, for Cesare was jealous of Giovanni's being the Pope's favourite. Vanozza was determined, however, that on this evening, when Giovanni was about to receive the investiture of his new duchy which could eventually lead him to the crown of Naples, that there should be an atmosphere of happy family unity.

The party finally broke up. The two brothers left together and later parted. The next morning Giovanni was nowhere to be found. Twenty-four hours went by before the first clue was received: a woodman aboard a boat moored along the Tiber said he had seen a group of men throwing a body into the river the night before. The river was duly dragged and Giovanni's body, with its throat cut and eight stab wounds, was lifted out of the water. The Pope and his former mistress were both prostrate with grief.

The murderer was never discovered, but it was generally believed that Cesare was responsible. Three years later Lucrezia's husband was also murdered, and few had any doubt that Cesare's hand was behind the killing, either from motives of jealousy or perhaps because he felt that Lucrezia could be remarried more advantageously.

Lucrezia was heartbroken, and her mother could do little to comfort her. It is more than likely that her children owed their tempestuous natures as much to herself as to their father who was elected Pope in 1492. When he died in 1503 she ran into a number of problems from which there was now no powerful protector to extricate her.

For example, she arranged for Cesare's soldiers to carry off 160 sheep belonging to a member of the Orsini family, and was condemned to pay for them. Knowing the tendency of the Roman courts to sequester the property of anyone in debt or unable to pay fines, she transferred ownership of her property (of which she owned a considerable amount, including three popular drinking houses right in the middle of Rome) to other people until circumstances improved. A number of lawsuits followed. One of the litigants in court called her a "devilish woman" with whom nobody could live.

Her letters show her determined character. She was insistent that others must do as she ordained, and she was always hard and practical. As the years passed, however, she became respectable and developed a religious fervour. She gave generous donations to the Hospital of San Salvatore with a request that Mass should be said on the anniversary of her death for all time to come. This was, in fact, carried out for about two hundred years, so she would have little cause for complaint.

She died in November 1518, aged seventy-six. She was buried with great splendour – "almost like a Cardinal". The Pope's Chamberlains were at her funeral – an unheard of honour for a lay person – and she left nearly all her fortune to St. John Lateran. The Pope who had succeeded Vanozza's lover Rodrigo treated her in death almost as if she had been the widow of his predecessor. Her long life and years of piety and dedication had finally brought her to an honoured position.

Chapter 16 The Rose of London

The tragic and romantic story of Jane Shore, loved by one king and persecuted by his successor, has inspired the work of poets and dramatists throughout the centuries since her death around 1530. Much that has been written about her is fictitious since for the ten years in which she was mistress to a king there is little documentary evidence. The best known periods of her life are the manner in which she became a royal mistress and the tragedy of her later fate and death, and they are dramatic enough in themselves.

There is no authentic portrait of her, for at that time portraiture as an art was hardly known in England. The earliest pictures of her which exist date from about the middle of the sixteenth century when she was a popular figure of romance; they are obviously imaginary and they differ greatly from descriptions of her given by contemporary writers. Perhaps her most famous biographer was Sir Thomas More who saw her before she died and recorded: "Those who knew her in her youth say she was both proper and fair; there was nothing in her body that you would have changed unless you would have wished her a little higher, yet this beauty so near perfection was not the thing which charmed men so powerfully as her admirable and never-failing wit, which made her conversation incomparably delightful . . . A proper wit she had and could both read well and write, merry in company, ready and quick in answer, sometimes taunting without displeasure and not without disport."

Drayton, the Elizabethan poet, wrote that she was of "moderate height. Her hair a dark yellow; her face full and oval. Her eyes grey but quick and piercing. Her complexion of a due mixture, neither inclined to pale nor too florid . . . Her body inclined to be fat for she was full bosomed, and her skin smooth and white."

The man who won the love and loyalty of this pretty girl well deserved the constancy and affection which she reserved for him over a decade. Edward IV, who succeeded to the throne in 1471 after the House of York had defeated the House of Lancaster at the end of the War of the Roses, was a strong and virile king. When he was crowned at the age of twenty-two he was tall, handsome, resolute and ardent. He possessed an enormous attraction to women, and in character he was not unlike the King who was to reign two hundred years after him, Charles II.

In typical fashion Edward had made a secret marriage with Lady Elizabeth Grey, a young widow with two children who had rejected the King's advances. Having discovered that Elizabeth was not prepared to become his mistress the King impulsively decided to marry her. Naturally this idea was eagerly encouraged by Elizabeth's mother, the Duchess of Bedford. This secret marriage was destined to cause much trouble at a later date when the legitimacy of Edward's children was challenged by his brother Richard. The disappointed Councillors, however, who had been hoping for an advantageous foreign alliance for their King were obliged to accept it as legal and Elizabeth was duly crowned Queen.

The marriage did not cramp Edward's amatory style. His

royal status allied with his personal charm facilitated his conquests of the fair sex. He was also a popular king. He had intelligence, wit and wisdom, and if fierce and resolute he was also just and merciful. He encouraged the advancement of the sciences, and Caxton, the first English printer, enjoyed his unstinted patronage. By the time he met Jane Shore he had had three children by his wife who had already become resigned to his having mistresses.

Jane herself was the daughter of a bourgeois, and the idea that she might ever adorn the court in any capacity whatever had never entered her mind. Her father was, however, the leading mercer of the City of London and a much respected man. He was wealthy enough, and was much patronized by the ladies of the court who came to him for their silks and laces. Jane's parents gave her an unusually good education for the women of her day, and by the time she had reached the age of fifteen she could play several instruments, read and write with great fluency and speak the Norman French which was still in use in polite circles. She spent a great deal of time in her father's shop busying herself with embroidery in a quiet corner, and it was perhaps from the court ladies who visited the shop that she learned her manners and acquired her air of good breeding.

This educational experience, coupled with her growing beauty, charm and good humour, gave her a reputation which very quickly spread abroad. She became known as the Rose of London. Her admirers among the apprentice boys – she kept them at a disdainful distance – were legion, but her "image" spread beyond the boundaries of the city to the court itself. The court gallants began to visit her father's shop to take a look at her and pay her amorous attentions.

Foremost among Jane's courtly admirers was young Lord Hastings, a trusted friend of the King. He was rich and powerful, "a gentleman of great authority with his prince," wrote Sir Thomas More, but "in living he was somewhat dissolute". As Lord Chamberlain he had a fine house at Westminster which was luxuriously furnished, and he was a "loving man and passing well beloved". That he certainly loved Jane Shore is beyond doubt, but despite all he had to offer and despite his amiable and devoted character she did not respond to him. She steadfastly declined his offers of "protection". And all the time her doting father watched suspiciously as the court gallants tried to turn the head of his beautiful daughter.

This was an age when to seduce and abduct a desirable girl was considered a feather in the cap of a young buck, and tradition has it that Lord Hastings, provoked by Jane's continued refusal, plotted to carry her off. He bribed her maid to persuade Jane to walk alone by the river one evening after dusk, but the maid, concerned that her young mistress might come to some harm, informed Jane's father. He took his daughter's place at the tryst and felt his suspicions justified when a barge loomed out of the darkness and hastily made off again at the sight of a man waiting on the towpath.

Jane's father quickly came to the conclusion that the best way to protect his daughter from the wolves who constantly pursued her would be to marry her off, so he began to look around for a suitable husband. He finally picked on a certain William Shore – a man of considerable wealth and position in the city. Jane was far from pleased. Shore was a reserved, dour man, physically unattractive, and twice the age of Jane who was then fifteen. For a long time she held out against parental pressure to marry this relatively old and staid creature, but Shore was a gentle, amiable and persistent lover and showered her with rich gifts, and finally Jane surrendered to the siege. The wedding was celebrated with lavish splendour; the bride was laden with jewellery and gold and the festivities went on for several days.

All of this, however, did not add up to a happy marriage. She had no children to occupy her time, and now she tended her husband's jewellery shop, and again found herself the object of affection by the court gallants who used the excuse of patronizing Shore's establishment to visit her. She possessed fine clothes and much valuable jewellery, but had little opportunity to wear them as her introverted husband seldom, if ever, took her out.

Lord Hastings was among the clients who took the trouble

to renew their acquaintance with Mistress Shore; indeed, he became such a regular visitor that the delighted jeweller would often invite his distinguished customer into the parlour to take a glass of wine with his wife. But after a while Shore began to be suspicious and jealous of these frequent calls, and he warned his wife against Hastings. She merely laughed at her husband, but on one occasion, when Shore had been called away, Hastings took the opportunity to make passionate advances to the somewhat anxious and reluctant Jane. Shore returned to interrupt this tender episode and in great fury turned the nobleman from his shop, ordering him never to come back again.

Needless to say, Lord Hastings was highly chagrined by this dismissal in such a summary manner by a mere city merchant, and he plotted a subtle revenge. He had more than once procured a pretty girl for his royal master, the King, and he now proceeded to extol the virtues and charms of the jeweller's pretty wife. Edward, always impressionable in matters of romantic interest, was interested. Disguised as an ordinary gentleman who wished to buy from Shore he visited the merchant's house in Lombard Street and contrived to see for himself the beauty which Lord Hastings had so enthusiastically eulogized. He was not disappointed – the enchanting vision was one, he decided instantly, which must grace his court.

The King who was fond of pleasurable diversions often held masques in the gardens of his palace at Westminster, and his guests would include leading citizens of London and their wives. He promptly decided to arrange such a masque and instructed Hastings that Jane and her husband were to be invited. The festivities lasted from noon until sunset and were lively and informal; all the guests, including the King (who tradition demanded should not be recognized), were masked or disguised in bizarre costumes.

Shore, in his typically antisocial fashion, refused to attend the masque, but he grudgingly allowed his wife to go in the company of a respectable city matron. On the lawn the guests danced to the music of a group of minstrels. Jane stood watching. Then a tall, elegantly dressed gentleman appeared at her side and asked her to dance. She acquiesced, and together they performed the "courante" – fashionable in that period – which was danced on tiptoe with skipping steps and many bows and courtesies.

After the dance came the revelation the tall handsome man whom she had seen before in the Lombard Street shop was none other than the King. This disclosure was rapidly followed by a royal protestation of love, and an urgent request that she should leave her husband and go to live in the palace. Jane hesitated for only a brief moment. She had little to lose, and she did not really spare her husband a thought. When she had finally made up her mind she sent a message to the palace accepting the King's invitation. Then, telling her husband that she was going to visit her father, she walked out of the house to meet the men who were to escort her to the King.

When his wife failed to return from her "visit", William Shore searched high and low for her. Her father, he soon discovered, knew nothing – he had not even seen her. He went from house to house seeking news of her, and eventually heard that she had been seen at the palace. Neither Jane nor her royal lover had thought it necessary to inform the abandoned husband of her whereabouts. Shore was powerless to act; he could do nothing in the face of the important and influential people who had stolen his wife. So, without a struggle, he surrendered her to the King.

After a brief period alone together at Hampton where the King had a hunting box, Edward took Jane back to court where she was installed in a magnificent suite of apartments. It soon became apparent that the King was devoted to her. He gave her expensive gifts and spent every spare moment in her company. He took particular delight in her merry conversation. As his affection for her grew, so the courtiers realized the power which she wielded at court and they waited, warily, to see how she would use this power.

Jane, however, turned out to be a very unusual royal mistress. Although she herself was well aware of the power at her disposal she used it only when she was urged to intervene in some worthy cause. She never used her influence with the King to commit an unkind or revengeful act and she never accepted bribes. When she did intercede with the King on someone's behalf it was always for a just purpose, and Edward soon grew to recognize this trait and to trust her judgment. Even the nobles sought her help, and very quickly she became loved and popular among the people. She had her enemies, of course, as did all influential people in those days (and today), but with her gentle manner she succeeded in deflecting their barbed shafts of jealousy and spite.

Attracted by her beauty, many men sought to seduce her from the King, but Jane was always faithful. The King's younger brother Richard, Duke of Gloucester, may well have been one of those who made advances to her, only to be repulsed. With all the bitterness of a man lacking physical attraction, Richard's resentment of her rejection of him might well explain the ruthlessness with which in later years he pursued her to the depths of poverty and degradation.

Lord Hastings waited and watched. He still loved the beautiful Jane and had expected that very soon his fickle master would tire of her and that his turn would come. But to his surprise the King's fondness for his mistress seemed to grow stronger, while she – who to her sorrow remained childless – occupied her time in studying his moods, soothing his cares and beguiling his leisure. For ten years she managed to maintain her difficult status. A chronicler of the times, discussing the King's other mistresses, said of her: "but the merriest of them all was Jane Shore in whom he took special pleasure. For many he had, but her he loved."

The history of Jane's ten years with the King, incomplete though it is, relates nothing but good of her. She was apparently sensible, kind, loyal and loving, and in turn Edward treated her with sympathy and generosity. Their life together was harmonious, but it was not to last. In 1483 Edward fell ill. At first his physicians thought he had plague, but his intermittent fever was more probably the result of years of self-indulgence. Although he was only forty-two, his much abused body did not possess the stamina to resist infection.

In the fashion of the time he was bled by his doctors. The fever abated, but soon dropsy set in and his legs swelled enormously. The doctors of the day were helpless; the King's condition became more serious and his family were sent for to take leave of him. Jane, one of those who had cared lovingly for him, was now weeping for her dying King. Before he died Edward seriously charged Lord Stanley and his friend Lord Hastings with the care of his Queen and his two young sons. To Hastings alone he confided Jane's future.

Some days later the King's body was buried with great pomp and ceremony in the Chapel of Saint George at Windsor. Jane retired in mourning to her own luxurious home which had been given to her by Edward. And Richard, the Duke of Gloucester, at once ordered that Edward's eldest son who was only twelve years old should be proclaimed King Edward V.

At that time Richard was in the north of England, but at the first Council of State over which the Queen presided he was proclaimed Protector during the minority of the young King. The boy was then living in Ludlow Castle with his uncle, Earl Rivers, and another relation of the Queen, Lord Richard Grey. They set out to London, but Richard and his henchman, the Duke of Buckingham, intercepted the party, imprisoned Rivers and Grey, and seized the young king.

The Queen, thoroughly alarmed, took refuge in the sanctuary at the "Abbot's Place" which adjoined the Palace of Westminster, taking her children with her. Meanwhile Richard brought the boy King to London and lodged him in the Tower on the grounds that it would be a convenient place to await his Coronation which was all ready to take place. But the Protector's motives were giving rise to serious concern and doubts among the nobles, and when Richard called a meeting of the Star Chamber to demand the custody of the Queen's other children there was strong opposition. Although the lords spiritual and temporal in the end reluctantly agreed that the children could not legally claim sanctuary, their opinion was so divided that the Archbishop of Canterbury offered to persuade the Queen to give up her son. Needless to say, the Queen refused obdurately until finally she accepted the emotional argument that the young King, alone in the Tower of London, was very much in need of company. So, weeping, the Queen bade farewell to her second child who was led triumphantly by his uncle Richard to the Tower from which neither he nor his brother were ever to emerge.

The Queen was terrified by the trend of Richard's activities, and she looked for allies among the nobles. She knew that Lord Hastings hated Richard the Protector, but she had never been on good terms with him because she also knew that it was he who had encouraged her husband in his profligacy. On the other hand, she had been on good terms with Jane Shore, her husband's mistress, who had never failed to show courtesy and due respect towards the Queen, and who had already taken great pleasure in playing with the royal children.

Jane was now living with Lord Hastings, and it was through her, therefore, that the Queen approached Hastings to enlist his help in thwarting Richard. But Hastings only laughed; he was positive that Richard would content himself with the all-powerful position of Protector. He blithely brushed aside the idea that Richard regarded him as an enemy, and he ignored the possibility that Richard might also hate him for having taken Jane Shore as his mistress.

This insouciant attitude was to cost him dear. On Friday, 13 June, 1483, a remarkable meeting of the Council of State was convened in the great council chamber that occupied the upper floor of the White Tower. Richard's unusually affable mood merely made the Councillors aware that it masked some evil plot. After a while he excused himself, and while the Council continued its business he gave orders for the gates of the Tower to be locked and guarded. Then he returned to the Council Chamber and this time his mood was black and threatening.

Treachery, he shouted, was being planned against his person by the Queen and Jane Shore – they were trying to kill him by witchcraft! To prove it he waved the withered arm which every Councillor knew perfectly well he had had from birth, but which he now swore was due to the sorcery of Jane Shore and the Queen. The astonished Councillors said nothing as Richard, his voice rising to a scream, continued his vicious denunciation. One noble made a mild interpolation and Richard immediately turned on him with the accusation "Traitor!". This was the signal for armed men to rush into the Council Chamber, and the nobleman was felled with a blow from an axe. Suddenly the Protector turned upon Hastings and ordered his arrest, swearing that he would not touch food or drink until he had Hastings's head separated from his shoulders.

This incredible scene has been interpreted by historians in many ways, some insisting that Hastings and other nobles were, in fact, plotting to assassinate Richard at that very Council meeting. Whatever the truth, Hastings's trial was a hasty procedure which took place more or less on the spot. No record of it remains, since hundreds of documents from the royal archives were subsequently destroyed at the command of King Henry VII.

Lord Hastings was, of course, found guilty and less than a week later was dragged from his prison into the Tower and on to the green, where he was forced to put his neck across a log while one of Richard's men hacked off his head. Sir Thomas More commented: "Hastings was very faithfull and trusty enough, but trusting too much was his destruction."

As Lord Hastings had been a very popular man, Richard and Buckingham sent for the leading citizens of London and told them of the terrible and treasonable plot which they had uncovered – Hastings, at the instigation of Jane Shore and the Queen, had tried to trap his cousin Buckingham and himself. Next he issued a proclamation which had obviously been prepared before Hastings's execution. This again denounced Hastings for having been involved in a subversive plot with Jane Shore, and it stressed that he had deliberately encouraged the late King in his life of debauchery by "procuring lewd and ungracious persons to gratify his lusts and particularly Shore's wife who was one of his secret council in the treason."

All this, Richard said, had not only shortened the King's life but had also caused him to oppress his people with heavy taxes in order to pay for the satisfaction of his indecent desires. And as for Lord Hastings, the proclamation pointed out that he had lived in "continual incontinency" with Shore's wife since the death of the King, and "lay nightly with her and particularly the very night before his death, so it was no marvel his ungracious life brought him to so unhappy a death".

Having, as he hoped, allayed the doubts of the people, Richard now turned his attention to Jane herself. His first action was to obtain a legal order for her arrest and the sequestration of all her property. Although Jane knew of Hastings's death she had not fled – where could she go, anyway? Her father had cast her off, and nobody who knew of Richard's proclamation would dare to harbour her, for life was held very cheaply in those days. She was arrested almost immediately and imprisoned in the Tower of London where she remained alone, penniless and friendless. She fully realized that nobody would dare to help her and that she herself, bereft of her powerful protectors, was completely helpless and vulnerable.

The Council was hastily summoned, and Jane was brought before it as a wretched prisoner to face a charge of witchcraft which in that day was one of the most serious of crimes, and carrying the penalty of a most unpleasant death at the stake. Richard was determined that Jane should be found guilty – indeed, her conviction was essential to justify his action in having Lord Hastings murdered. But in the event the evidence against Jane was non-existent, her trial was a farce. and the Council knew perfectly well that the charges were false. Her defence against the charge proved to be flawless and she was properly adjudged innocent. To Richard's fury she was set free – but not for long. She was very quickly arrested again which at least gave her a roof over her head.

Meanwhile Richard was pushing ahead with his plans

and intrigue. Doctor Shaw, a famous preacher of the time, had been persuaded by Lord Buckingham to join the King's faction, and he gave a sermon at Saint Paul's Cross in which he suggested that King Edward IV had never been legally married to Elizabeth and that in consequence his children were illegitimate bastards. Richard turned up expecting the acclamation of the crowd for their rightful King, but he was sorely disappointed. The sermon fell flat and the crowd drifted silently away.

Two days later Buckingham tried to retrieve the situation by a similar speech; this time he strengthened his arguments by deliberately blackening the dead King's name, emphasizing his lust and quoting as an example of his corruption the manner in which the King had lavished his favours on Jane Shore who, he claimed, was his chief minister. He also insinuated that the mother of Richard and Edward had committed adultery of which Edward had been the illegitimate fruit.

On this occasion Buckingham made sure that his speech would be well received by the crowd. Among them he infiltrated a large number of supporters of Richard who cheered and cried "God save King Richard", and so influenced the crowd to follow their lead. In this way Richard could modestly pretend that he had only accepted the crown through popular demand. But he made sure of his position when in the second week of August the two young sons of Edward mysteriously disappeared from their beds in the Tower. The princes were smothered, it is said, by their jailer.

Meanwhile, Richard had not overlooked Jane Shore. Having so far failed to achieve her death or imprisonment he proceeded to humiliate her to the utmost, and much further than her beggared state had done already. He had her arrested and committed to Lud Gate prison, which for many years had been used as a jail for debtors. Most of the inmates were merchants and tradesmen who had been financially ruined by losses at sea, and the prison came under the jurisdiction of the Sheriffs of London who on the whole were humane. Although it was a stinking miserable place and life within its stark stone walls was hard, the debtors were not on the whole badly treated and for many it was a refuge rather than a prison. The inmates were allowed to send certain of their number out into the streets to beg for food or money, and any receipts were shared among all.

But Richard had not yet finished his campaign of persecution. His next move was to charge Jane with harlotry. Technically this charge could not be denied for her relationships with the late King and Lord Hastings were common knowledge and well substantiated. The usual penalty for such a conviction was a public penance to be performed at specific places in the city. The object of this further humiliation of Jane was to demolish what little residual influence she might possess and to alienate her few remaining friends.

She was duly taken into custody and handed over to the ecclesiastical courts which dealt with charges of harlotry, and finally she was brought before the Bishop of London. This minion of King Richard III very quickly found her guilty and sentenced her to do public penance at Saint Paul's. The form of the penance varied slightly; sometimes the wrong-doer was required to make more than one journey through the streets for the enjoyment of the crowd which jeered and threw mud and stones. But Jane was fortunate for she was only sentenced to do it once.

There is some argument as to the precise distance which Jane walked to her final destination by Saint Paul's, and also as to her exact route. Certainly the circumstances of the penance became known for a great crowd gathered in the streets and around Saint Paul's to watch the mistress of a dead King being thus humbled. With her hair unbraided, barefoot and wrapped only in a sheet, Jane set off through the streets. In her hands she was obliged to carry a heavy candle while before her walked a servitor of the Cathedral and two priests.

Richard III had hoped that Jane would suffer the full mockery and hostility of the crowd and looked forward to seeing her pelted with stones and dirt, but once again he was disappointed. The citizens of London apparently had a soft spot in their hearts for the lovely Jane, and when she appeared with her eyes downcast and her golden hair flowing over her shoulders, the onlookers were moved to sympathy and pity. She walked slowly with bowed head through the rough streets, and the sharp stones and cobbles quickly bruised and tore her feet until they began to bleed. No mud, garbage or stones were thrown, and after circling the cross which stood before the cathedral, she entered the building itself and was escorted to the altar where she offered her candle.

Then she was taken before the pulpit in which stood the pontifical Bishop of London. In the prescribed form for such an occasion the man who had received many favours from her in the past now admonished her for her sins and the evil end to which she had brought the men with whom she had associated in wickedness. In a quiet voice Jane then confessed her sins and promised to repent. Her penance was at last over and she could now be cast back, penniless, into the streets.

But again Richard's scheme had misfired. Far from ruining Jane he had merely excited sympathy for her. Sir Thomas More described the scene: "She went in countenance and pace demure . . . while the wondering of the people cast a comely red in her cheeks . . . And many good folks that also hated her living and glad were to see her sin corrected, yet pitied they more her penance than rejoiced thereat . . . In all this action she behaved herself with so much modesty and decency that such as respected her beauty more than her fault never were in greater admiration than of now."

For a time after her penance she found another protector in Lord Dorset, who was the eldest son of the Queen by her first husband. They were around the same age and had known each other well when Jane was mistress to the King. Dorset, however, was involved in intrigue against the throne; he tried to raise a party against the King and planned a revolt in the north of England. When Richard learned of the plot he promptly issued a proclamation offering a large reward for the capture of Dorset who, he accused, had not only plotted against him but had also lived a life of debauchery with "sundry maids, widows and wives whom he had devoured, deflowered and defouled, holding the unshameful and mischievous woman called Shore's wife to adultery".

It is more than probable that Jane's association with Dorset inflamed the King's antagonism towards the Earl, but Dorset remained undaunted. He joined an insurrection organized by the Duke of Buckingham who had quarrelled with the King. When it failed, in 1484, Dorset fled to France, leaving Jane once more friendless and poverty-stricken.

There have been many tales told of Jane's hardships during this period. It is said that she had to beg for bread and that she slept in fields in the neighbourhood of the city. A story which was current in the seventeenth century relates how one day Jane was passing the shop of a baker whose life she had saved during her influential reign as King Edward's mistress. The baker saw her and, touched by her air of exhaustion and hunger, took one of his loaves and rolled it along the street after her. She thanked him with sincere gratitude, but neighbours, it is said, informed against him, and he was arrested and executed for helping her.

This story is no doubt a romantic exaggeration, as is the tale that she continued to live for many years in dreary poverty, wandering through the garbage-strewn streets of the city until she finally died on a dungheap in the street that afterwards became known as Shore Ditch. This fate became a legend calculated to throw any later royal mistresses who were reminded of it into a tantrum.

But it is probably true that for a while Jane remained homeless, hungry and destitute – until, on Richard's orders, she was once again arrested and sent to Lud Gate prison. In the impoverished state to which she had fallen she must have regarded this as a welcome refuge, despite the severity of jail life. And it was there that she discovered that she was not entirely friendless after all. Her new friend was Thomas Lynom, a lawyer who had had a nebulous contact with the court in the reign of Edward IV and had since been appointed King's Solicitor by Richard III. It is likely that he had perhaps helped Jane in her trial on a charge of witchcraft. He certainly visited her in prison and after a while made an offer of marriage. Jane was then still in her early thirties and despite her privations had no doubt retained much of her beauty. She certainly welcomed such an opportunity to escape from the miseries of her life – yet she reckoned without Richard.

Somehow the King learned of his solicitor's intentions. As he was out of London at the time he despatched a letter by messenger to the Bishop of Lincoln who was Chancellor at that time. In view of the fact that Lynom, "marvellously blinded and abused with the late wife of William Shore, now being in Lud Gate by our commandment," had contracted to marry her, the King asked the Bishop to send for Lynom and "exhort and stir him" to change his mind. If, however, Lynom insisted, and the marriage could properly take place within the laws of the church, then he would be content. But in any event the marriage must be put off until he, the King, returned to London, at which point, if surety could be found for her good behaviour, Jane could then be discharged from Lud Gate and handed over to the care of her father or any other person whom the Bishop considered suitable.

From this letter it would appear that Jane's husband had either died or divorced her and that her father was still alive, although up to that time he had made no attempt to help his errant and wretched daughter. Once again, however, Richard's evil genius blighted Jane's life, for there is no record that she ever did marry Lynom. The lawyer doubtless put discretion before valour and decided that it would not be in his best interests to defy the King by going ahead with what Richard clearly regarded as an undesirable marriage.

What became of Jane thereafter nobody knows, but she did not obtain a swift release from her unhappy life, for Sir Thomas More actually saw her in about 1527 when she must have been approaching seventy. "Some that see her now," he wrote, "would not believe that she had ever been beautiful . . . for now she is old, lean, withered and dried up, nothing left but wrinkled skin and hard bone." And after philosophizing on the theme that "the evil that men do lives after them, the good is oft interred in their bones," More goes on to say that "at this day she beggeth of many at this day living that at this day had begged if she had not been".

It seems astonishing that at a time when her arch-enemy Richard III had long been dead she should still be living in dire poverty, and that all her old friends who no longer needed to fear Richard's wrath and ruthlessness, still turned away from her. The closing years of her life are obscure. She was known as Mistress Shore until the end of her days. She died shortly after Sir Thomas More had noticed her passing through the city streets, but her grave has been lost.

Select Bibliography

H. L. Young, *Eliza Lynch, Regent of Paraguay.* Anthony Blond, 1966

W. E. Barrett, *Woman on Horseback.* Peter Davis, 1938

B. Field, *Miledi.* Constable, 1942

H. Tours, *Life and Letters of Emma Hamilton.* Gollancz, 1963

Selected by L. Norton, *Saint Simon at Versailles.* Hamish Hamilton, 1958

Noel Williams, *Mme de Montespan.* Harper & Bros., 1903

Nancy Mitford, *The Sun King.* Hamish Hamilton, 1966

G. P. Good, *Louis XV.* Longmans, 1962

Margaret Trouncer, *The Pompadour.* Hutchinson, 1937

Lesley Blanch, *The Wilder Shores of Love.* Murray, 1955

John S. Glennie, *Women of Turkey.* Nutt, 1891

F. Markham, *Napoleon.* Weidenfeld, 1963

J. M. Thompson, *Napoleon Bonaparte.* Blackwell, 1958

Charlotte Haldane, *The Last Great Empress of China.* Constable, 1965

Du Cann, *The Love-Lives of Charles Dickens.* Muller, 1961

Christopher Hibbert, *The Making of Charles Dickens.* Longmans, 1967

Otto Dietrich, *The Hitler I knew.* Methuen, 1957

Alan Bullock, *Hitler, A Study in Tyranny* (rev. ed.). Odhams Books, 1964

Heinrich Hoffmann, *Hitler was my Friend.* Burke, 1955

P. W. Sergeant, *Cleopatra of Egypt.* Hutchinson, 1909

Plutarch, *Parallel Lives.* Bell & Sons, 1903

Henri Carré, *Gabrielle d'Estrées—Presque Reine.* Librairie Hachette, 1935

Hesketh Pearson, *Henry of Navarre*. Heinemann, 1963

G. P. R. James, *The Life of Henry IV* (3 vols.). 1847

André Maurois, *Lelia ou La Vie de George Sand*. Librairie Hachette, 1952

Jaques Vivent, *La Vie Privée de George Sand*. Librairie Hachette, 1949

Lady Newdigate-Newdegate, *Gossip from a Muniment Room*. David Nutt, 1897

Frank Harris, *The Man Shakespeare*. Frank Palmer, 1909

Ivor Brown, *The Women in Shakespeare's Life*. Bodley Head, 1968

Philip Sergeant, *My Lady Castlemaine*. Hutchinson, 1912

Barbara Cartland, *The Private Life of Charles II*. Muller, 1958

Doris Leslie, *The Sceptre and the Rose*. Heinemann, 1967

C. J. S. Thompson, *The Witchery of Jane Shore*. Grayson and Grayson, 1933

Guy Paget, *The Rose of London*. Paternoster Library, 1934

Nicholas Rowe, *The Tragedy of Jane Shore*. 1714

Sir Thomas More, *The History of Richard III*. Rastell, 1557

Mario Buggelli, *Lucrezia Borgia*. (Milano) 1929

P. Gregorovius, *Lucrezia Borgia* (ed. Ludwig Goldschneider). Phaidon, 1949

Index

Abdul Hamid I, Sultan,
112–19
Abramowicz, Elizbieta, 91,
93–7, 99, 100

Borie, Victor, 165–6
Borgia, Cesare, 213–16
Borgia, Giovanni, 213–16
Borgia, Lucrezia, 213–16
Borgia, Rodrigo, 211–17
Bormann, Martin, 80, 83, 84,
87
Braun, Eva, early life, 78;
early meetings with Hitler,
78; suicide attempt, 78–9;
moves into Hitler's house,
79; life with Hitler, 79–89;
influences choice of films for
Hitler, 81–2; last years,
84–8; marriage, 87; death,
88–9
Buckingham, Lord, 225, 227,
229, 232

Catherine of Braganza, 203–7
Charles II, 202–10
Chopin, Frédéric, 160–8
Cleopatra, legends about,
125–6; character, 126, 137;
early years, 126; early
meeting with Mark Anthony,
128; as ruler, 128;
relationship with Caesar,

134–8; the *thalamegos*, 135;
birth of son to, 135; visits
Rome, 136–7; and death of
Caesar, 137–8
Cleveland, Barbara Villiers,
Duchess of, early life, 201–2;
marriage, 202; first meeting
with Charles II, 202;
Charles's children born to,
204, 206, 207, 208; leaves
Palmer, 204; appointed Lady
of Bedchamber, 205;
indiscretions of, 206;
Charles starts to look
elsewhere, 206; takes other
lovers, 207; retires to Paris,
210; last years and death,
210

De Bellegarde, Roger, 141, 143,
144
De Brinvilliers, Madame, 60–1
De Cataneis, Vanozza
(Domina Rosa), birth, 213;
physical appearance, 213;
relationship with Rodrigo
Borgia, 213–17; children of,
213–14; husband found for,
214; ceases to be Rodrigo's
mistress, 214; family
violence, 215–17; last years
and death, 217
De Châteauroux, Duchesse de,
177, 179–80

Index

Index

Index